# Get A F*cking Divorce Already

*Laurie Frazier*

Copyright © 2022
Laurie Frazier
Get a F*cking Divorce Already
All rights reserved.

No part of this publication may be reproduced, distributed, or transmitted in any form or by any means, including photocopying, recording, or other electronic or mechanical methods, without the prior written permission of the publisher, except in the case of brief quotations embodied in critical reviews and certain other non-commercial uses permitted by copyright law.

Laurie Frazier

Printed in the United States of America
First Printing 2022
First Edition 2022

10 9 8 7 6 5 4 3 2 1

This book is for entertainment purposes only. This publication is meant as a source of valuable information for the reader; however, it is not meant as a substitute for direct expert assistance. If such level of assistance is required, the services of a competent professional should be sought. This book is not a legal text and the information contained within does not constitute legal advice or assistance in any respect. No responsibility is assumed for legal actions or problems related to domestic disputes. The author is not a lawyer and does not claim to be a lawyer. The author is not a therapist and does not claim to be a therapist. The words in this book constitute an expression of freedom of the press based on the author's own personal opinions. The author is not responsible for the actions, results or events that may incur in the lives and cases of any readers of this book. Under no circumstances should you undertake any activities in reliance on this book. Consult an attorney specializing in matrimonial law to address legal questions or a therapist for therapeutic advice. The purpose of this book is to entertain and impart the personal opinion of the author to those who it might interest. To those who benefit from it to those who disagree with it, and to those that get a good laugh from it, your letters and responses are welcomed. Unless otherwise indicated, all the names, characters, places, events, and incidents in this book are either the product of the author's imagination or used in a fictitious manner. Any resemblance to actual persons, living or dead, or actual events, is purely coincidental.

You can contact the author at:

shefreedom@protonmail.com or www.lauriefrazier.com

# Get A F*cking Divorce Already

*It's a luxury to pursue what makes you happy;*

*it's a moral obligation to pursue what you find meaningful.*

~Jordan B. Peterson

# Table of Contents

Introduction .................................................................................... 1

Disclaimer ...................................................................................... 6

Part One ......................................................................................... 8

   *The Ground Work*

      Chapter 1 ................................................................................. 9
         *It's Not What You Think*

      Chapter 2 ............................................................................... 16
         *The Four Tenets*

      Chapter 3 ............................................................................... 25
         *"Fine" is a Four-Letter Word*

      Chapter 4 ............................................................................... 33
         *Transcending the Muggle Slumber*

      Chapter 5 ............................................................................... 39
         *Going Beyond Shame*

      Chapter 6 ............................................................................... 44
         *Trust Your Heart, Not Your Stories*

Part Two ...................................................................................... 52

   *Everybody Changes*

      Chapter 7 ............................................................................... 53
         *You're Not the Person I Married*

      Chapter 8 ............................................................................... 61
         *Somebody Got Fat*

      Chapter 9 ............................................................................... 66
         *Somebody's Libido Changed*

      Chapter 10 ............................................................................. 76
         *Somebody's Core Beliefs Changed*

      Chapter 11 ............................................................................. 81
         *The Spark is Gone*

Part Three ................................................................................... 86

   *The Seven Deadly Archetypes*

      Chapter 12 ............................................................................. 87
         *When the Dynamic Changes*

Chapter 13 .................................................................................... 90
    *The Rescuer*
Chapter 14 ....................................................................................94
    *The Dream Thieves*
Chapter 15 .................................................................................. 100
    *The Punishers*
Chapter 16 .................................................................................. 105
    *The Tolerators*
Chapter 17 ....................................................................................111
    *The Bullies & Abusers*
Chapter 18 .................................................................................. 116
    *The Control Freaks*
Chapter 19 .................................................................................. 121
    *The Caretaker & The Chronically Ill / Addicted*
Chapter 20 .................................................................................. 131
    *A Little Self-inquiry Before You GAFDA*

Part Four........................................................................................ 135
*Self-Betrayal & The Real Infidelity*
    Chapter 21 .............................................................................. 136
        *Self-Betrayal: The OG Sin*
    Chapter 22.............................................................................. 144
        *To Thine Own Self Be True*
    Chapter 23.............................................................................. 148
        *Infidelity & Accountability*
    Chapter 24.............................................................................. 157
        *So Your Man Cheated: Why It's All Your Fault*
    Chapter 25.............................................................................. 166
        *Three Questions: Radical Honesty Required*
    Chapter 26.............................................................................. 170
        *So Your Girl Checked Out: You're Probably A Pussy. Time To Daddy Up!!*
    Chapter 27 .............................................................................. 187
        *I Need Your Trust: Is That True?*
    Chapter 28............................................................................... 193
        *Betrayal Trauma: The Ultimate in Victim Mentality*

Part Five .................................................................................................. 201
  *Illegit Reasons to Stay*
    Chapter 29 ........................................................................................ 202
      But I'm Comfortable: Are You Really?
    Chapter 30 ....................................................................................... 210
      The Timing is Off: When You Know But You Delay...and Delay ........................................................................................... 210
    Chapter 31 ....................................................................................... 220
      Staying for the Children: The Holy and Noble Grail
    Chapter 32 ....................................................................................... 223
      But Marriage is Sacred, Right?
    Chapter 33 ....................................................................................... 232
      If It Isn't a "Hell Yes," it's a "Fuck No!"
Part Six .................................................................................................. 238
  *Kids Are People Too*
    Chapter 34 ....................................................................................... 239
      Consciously Consider the Children In Your Choice
    Chapter 35 ....................................................................................... 246
      Best Way to Help Your Kiddos? Don't Be an Asshole
    Chapter 36 ....................................................................................... 253
      Why Divorce Really Hurts Kids: YOU!
    Chapter 37 ....................................................................................... 258
      Conscious Co-Parenting with a New Partner
    Chapter 38 ....................................................................................... 265
      Custody: Beyond Money and Misery
Part Seven ........................................................................................... 273
  *Your Heart-Felt Decision*
    Chapter 39 ....................................................................................... 274
      When Hope Arises from the Ashes
Epilogue ............................................................................................... 281
Appendix A ......................................................................................... 285
Acknowledgments ............................................................................. 286
About The Author .............................................................................. 288
Resources ........................................................................................... 291

# Introduction

Maybe you've found yourself asking:

"Is this all there is?"

"How'd I get here?"

"Who is this person I married?"

"Who the fuck am I, anyway?!"

This doesn't always look like a mid-life crisis. Maybe you're only 25 or 30 but you've been married since you were 19 or 20. You've changed, your partner's changed, and you're just not feeling it anymore. Maybe you've been re-evaluating your life for some time now and determining what is important to you and what isn't.

It can feel like waking up from a bad dream, asking "What have I been doing in this sham of a marriage? Why have I been allowing myself to be treated this way? Why have I been such a dick/bitch? Have I really been *this* asleep at the wheel? How have I not noticed any of this? This is not my beautiful world!"

And yet, here you are…still. You've asked the questions, and maybe some of you even have the answers—this relationship is *not* working. But you do nothing. Why? You keep living this life. Why? You don't choose yourself and your happiness first. Why?

You may experience tremendous guilt because you feel everyone in your space is expecting you to do everything you've been doing, being the same person they thought you were…but it's just not you anymore, and maybe it never was.

So here you are, wondering what to do next. You couldn't possibly follow your heart when so many voices are telling you to do things the "right" way, which is really just "their way."

So you acquiesce. You give in to the other voices.

We've learned, especially since 2020, how very easy it is to allow some "voice of authority" to tell us what is best for us, what we should or shouldn't say, what we can and can't put into our own bodies, and where we can and can't go. Hiding who we really are, how we feel, and what we really think, will never be for the betterment of humanity, our families or ourselves.

Here's a truth that can be hard to hear: You don't really know who you are and what you stand for anymore. You may not know the voice of your own Higher Self, or have a relationship with your Divinity. Do you understand your own sovereignty—that you and *only* you are the boss of you, that your feelings matter, that you can make a difference, and that you deserve to have a life of purpose and meaning? If you did, you wouldn't allow yourself to be pushed around, told what to do or blindly obey things that insult your soul.

So…is it any wonder that you are afraid to speak your truth to those other voices in your life when you are still afraid to speak your truth in your own fucking home? You can't tell your husband you're pissed that he's always working late, or that you'd like more intimacy. You can't tell your wife you don't like what she's teaching the kids, or that you wish she dressed a little sexier sometimes. Some of you parents can't even reprimand your kids because you're afraid they'll have a tantrum and won't like you. You certainly can't tell your boss to go fuck herself because you don't think you have any other options.

We've become a complicit bunch of scaredy cats. Stuffing our emotions at every turn, living in fear of so many things, biting our tongue continually, and sucking it up on the daily. We willingly allow ourselves and our feelings to be dismissed—a.k.a. cancelled—without so much as a whimper.

We continually bow to the "voice of authority" and give our power away. We give our power away when we tell somebody that we agree with them when we really don't. We give it away when we tell somebody it's OK when it really isn't. When we take a doctor's diagnosis at face value and don't get a second opinion. When we go along with our church of choice's dogma without question, even when it doesn't feel right or make sense. When we distrust and ignore our mother's intuition and we don't do our own research, but instead follow blindly.

Perhaps you've lost faith, begun to doubt yourself, or your purpose and your choices in these challenging times. If you've found yourself biting your tongue, burying your feelings, and being easily triggered, there may be something to see here. If you've been thinking about divorce for years, maybe even decades, and just don't have the words to say so, you may find them here, along with a good dose of courage.

My hope is that by the end of this book, you will have much more clarity about who you are, what's of value to you, and what you want to do about it. My intention is that you will be able to make an honest assessment of your marriage, perhaps seeing the truth of your relationship for the first time. Take a look at where you've allowed yourself to be mistreated, or have been the one doing the mistreating, and make a stand to do something different.

Perhaps you will read parts of this book with your partner—instead of pointing fingers, try taking accountability whenever you see one of *your* behaviors popping up. For example, "I do that sometimes, babe. I don't want to be that way anymore. I'm sorry." My heart hopes that you will be the bigger person in your union and be 100% accountable for the state your relationship. If you can do that…then you may just be able to fix it. It really only takes one. The misconception is that marriage and relationships are a 50/50 thing—I say otherwise. They're a 100/100 thing. Just one side can make all the difference. We really are that powerful.

As you read, please allow yourself to let go of all of your "should's," "ought to's," and shame. Let go of "I should have done this sooner," and give yourself a clean slate. Let go of any guilt you may have if you're just not into somebody anymore. Take a listen to that cute little heart of yours that always knows the way. Let go of what you *think* everybody will think, and do what's best for you for a change. If divorce is the truth of your heart, it will be the best thing for everyone involved. If you are miserably coupled and shackled by the judgment of others (including your own), you do no one any favors by remaining enslaved.

Break free of your own chains and the weight of living an inauthentic life, and get access to your unlimited power, energy, vitality, and creativity. The world needs you to show up in all your magnificence—whether that means remaining in your marriage or getting out. This book is about taking a deep dive within to answer the questions about what is most meaningful to you and what, oh what, is the truth of your beautiful heart? Time to check in with your own North Star and intrinsic truth. Looking outside of yourself will only increase your confusion—too many voices that are not your own.

When your eyes are open and you are fully accountable, *all* things are possible. Areas you thought were hopeless will now be seen through a different lens. Multiple ideas and new ways to do—or undo—your partnership will now be available. Sometimes it looks like nothing has changed. You stay in the same home, with the same partner, doing the same job as before, but inside everything has changed. You notice how the light peaks through the curtains in the morning, you start hearing everything your children are saying as if they already knew the magic you just discovered. Maybe your spouse takes on a new beauty or a new appeal because you've somehow let go of every insult and injury that you've been holding on to, and you now see that *you* were the one in the way of creating the intimacy you so desperately desired.

If it is time to go, let's do it with some gentleness, grace, and radical accountability. Leave with your integrity intact. It's really all you've got. The most authentic thing you can do is to let somebody know how you really feel. The worst thing you can do is to pretend that you still want to be with somebody when you don't. That energy will be felt. You will be miserable, it will feel heavy, and your partner will feel like a charity case because that's exactly what they are and what you've turned them into. The best thing you can do is to be honest about it and stop living a lie.

Make a stand for your own truth and just do the thing already.

Your life has been on hold long enough. Whether you want to rectify and recreate something new together, or if you're just ready to get a fucking divorce already (GAFDA), either way, you'll have access to more authentic answers as you go through this book.

Oh…one last thing. I use a few acronyms in this book, most of them contain the "F-word" (#sorrynotsorry). Here they are in case you're not quite familiar with such vulgarities:

GAFDA: Get A Fucking Divorce Already

GTFO: Get The Fuck Out

AF: As Fuck

FFS: One of my favorite sayings…For Fuck's Sake

# Disclaimer

In parts of this book you may find me to be quite snarky, mean or perhaps even somewhat rude in the way I write and deliver some concepts. Rest assured, I could write the same thing in ten different ways—more polite, sweet or tender. However, on occasion, I write that way for effect, for entertainment, or for a metaphorical slap to the face to simply get a particular point across. It's really not directed to you individually (unless the shoe fits), but rather to a particular attitude, energy or way of being.

If you picked up a book with the word "fuck" in the title, I'm going to assume that you can put on your big girl/boy pants while you read it, and if and when the shoe fits…well, I'll leave that for you to decide. Ultimately, it's only done to rattle your cage a tad into waking up and seeing what there is to see sans blinders. I believe we are all Be-ings of Light, that we are all equal, and that none of us is greater than another. I honor your courage to pick up a book like this in the first place.

Oh…and another thing. I use the word "Muggle" in a derogatory way to mean someone who wants to remain stuck in their unconscious behavior, that points the finger of blame at everyone but himself, and that is incapable of being accountable for the shit show of his own life. A Muggle is what I'd call a status quo-er, who never questions what he's been programmed to believe, needs a rule book to regulate his behavior, and has no clue that he is enslaved. When I'm being a shit-talker and calling names, it's usually about "Muggle behavior," which I'm clear I am demonstrating by the above noted behavior myself. ;)

Please take it in the spirit it is delivered. It's not personal, so please, no whining. I envision sisters, girlfriends, and groups of men reading it to and with each other while laughing and crying at their own—or another's—

ridiculous behavior. I hope to lighten the issue a tad with humor so one may more easily see themselves. Or, perhaps, it will trigger others so deeply that their own denial of what I'm sharing will come out in a predictable, shaming projection onto this cute lil writer—*moi*. In which case, well…that will tell us all we need to know—about them. ;)

Also, if you detect another bias that feels out of touch from your experience, know that I live in a state where the predominant religion is extremely patriarchal, where many women stay home to raise children, and traditional roles are still very entrenched in the society. This is also typical of many fundamentalist groups. So if my approach feels a little bit out of touch—because the stats are that two-thirds of married women actually do work outside of the home—then you'll know why. I teach and coach to this bias every day.

And one last thing…I'm not a therapist! The only research I've done is my own life, two divorces, and the experiences of my family, friends, and numerous clients. I won't be quoting any studies either, because in my brief foray into divorce research I've found many conflicting reports that could support either side of an argument. Whether you are in favor of divorce or not, there is research to prove whatever point you'd like to make. I've consciously chosen to leave out the research because this isn't a book about statistics, dogma, or any dusty, old rule book. This book is about following your heart and learning how to do that without stats, without relying on how everything appears on the surface, and without all of the usual programmed voices in your head that tell you what you should do in every instance of your life…including WWJD. You're not Jesus…or your mother!!

# Part One
## *The Ground Work*

## Chapter 1

# It's Not What You Think

I know. I know. What am I thinking writing a book like this? I understand that the things I'm going to say here may create more haters than fans. Luckily for me, I have thick skin—and having fans isn't the point. I really do care if people are happy and are living meaningful lives. And sometimes that means divorce. A world full of free, happy people living their passions and purpose is truly my ultimate goal for the betterment of humanity. For many people this doesn't even feel like a possibility with their current partner in tow. So please, read this with that understanding, even when it gets hard…or I sound a lil snarky. My intention is your true, authentic joy.

If you've picked up this book, I'm sure by now you've had all the therapy and unsolicited advice that you can stand. You've listened to all the podcasts and YouTube videos and read all the books about how to save your marriage, rekindle the flame or endure til the end. You could rattle off all of the reasons people divorce and what you are "supposed to do" to fix it and stay married. You already know what your parents think about divorce, what your friends think, what your priest, minister, rabbi, or shaman think, and how your hair stylist and bartender feel about it. So there is zero need to repeat what everyone else has already said, agreed?

I'm here to tell you no amount of therapy is going to make you fall back in love with somebody you don't even like, let alone respect. No amount of prayer or wishing will have you be magically attracted to someone that you were never attracted to in the first place—having married them for all the wrong reasons.

If your needs and desires are diametrically opposed to the authentic desires of your partner, no amount of talking to each other about those needs, until you're blue in the face, will have those needs being met, at least not long-term. Are there exceptions? Sure. But if one of you now claims that you suddenly do have the same needs and desires as your partner (that you never had previously), I'd venture to guess that you're probably faking it—or you're just doing your best to talk/pray/convince yourself of it—before I'd believe that you'd had a genuine, organic, and *sustainable* turnaround.

I'm sure that you're aware that the divorce rate in America is now a whopping 50%—and is even higher in subsequent marriages. What we don't know is that of the 50% that stays married, how many are actually happy? I mean really happy. Like excited to be there, still in love, have common goals and at least a *decent* sex life? How many happily married people do you actually know, personally? You can count them on one hand, right? And is it possible that of the couples that appear to you to be happily married, that it's a façade? Ever think you knew the perfect couple, only to be shocked to hear they divorced? It's devastating, huh?

How many people in those marriages are, as Thoreau would say, "leading lives of quiet desperation?" *Quiet* desperation—has a nice ring to it. Meaning you aren't broadcasting your misery, you're just sucking it up, putting on a happy face and trying to get by. You're going through the motions, wishing you were anywhere but where you are. Asking yourself, "Is this all there is?" Resigning yourself to a passionless life for your big reward in Heaven for keeping your marriage "intact."

And how about all the fearful legions of folks keeping it together because they are so concerned with how it will look, how their image may be tarnished, how their mother might feel, and how their ecclesiastical leaders and neighbors may judge them. They're worrying about whether or not it will harm their position at work, their chance at that promotion, an election, etc.

Then there's the Holy Grailers, upholding the self-righteous banner of "staying for the children," biding their time for yet another decade til their youngest leaves the nest. Nobody dares argue with that one. All of these contribute to an unspoken life of "quiet desperation." We'll take an in-depth look at all of these lame reasons that people stay married and several more in later chapters.

Now, if you really do want to *stay* in the marriage and are committed to healing your relationship, there will be plenty of new concepts here for you as well—beyond just having better communication—that may just do the trick. These concepts, if put into daily practice, will undoubtedly assist you with *all* of your relationships, including the possibility of creating a happy and meaningful marriage where one does not currently exist. And if you choose to just "Get a Fucking Divorce Already," then the ideas shared here may assist you in exiting gracefully, and may be useful on your next go-around.

This isn't the dark ages anymore, where the powerful got married to merge their dynasties. It's not the 50's when people stayed in the same neighborhood they grew up in, attended the church they were raised in, worked in the same chosen career, often with the same company, for 40 years until they retired—all the while living in the same house! That's just not who we are anymore. It's not how we roll. The times have drastically changed.

With unlimited access to infinite knowledge and wisdom via the internet, we have more ways to grow and a plethora of paths available to us. As we shift and evolve at a more rapid pace than ever before in our history—

mentally, emotionally, spiritually, and intellectually—there is equally as much potential for us to grow apart. In this information age, we cannot be expected to remain the same person we were in our 20's, when many of us got married.

As we mature, we hone our preferences along the way. After a time, those preferences may no longer match or even resonate with our partner's proclivities, which have most likely also evolved—and not necessarily in league with our own. If that chasm becomes too wide to be bridged—not unlike a career that no longer feels like "you" anymore—a healthy divorce may be just what the doctor ordered.

We seem to think that we need a reason, like infidelity or abuse, to walk away. That we somehow need to make the other person the "bad guy" so we can legitimize our departure. What if it were just OK and understandable that you grew apart? What if it were just OK that no one was the "bad one," but that you both just wanted something different because you've changed? What if there were just no shame in divorce? Like there is no shame in changing careers?

And what about affairs and cheating? Is the one who strays *always* the selfish one or the narcissist? Is the unfaithful one always the perpetrator, and the one who was cheated on always the victim? Is the cheated upon *always* the injured party? Is it always about damage caused, or could a betrayal potentially inject a new vitality into your relationship? Is there ever anything good about it? And how is the cheated upon every bit a co-creator with the cheater? Ideas we will discuss at length.

For the aggrieved victims, bent on "finding fault," this book will show you it's never just one person's fault. No matter if you feel like you are the innocent one and your partner is a lying, cheating s.o.b., I'll be happy to show you how you created exactly what you are experiencing yourself, and that there's never anyone else to blame. We will also be looking at transcending "blame," as it doesn't exist as truth in the world. Yeah…we're going to hit some revolutionary stuff here. Put your seat belt on. Spoiler alert: it doesn't bode well for the victims, blamers, and shamers.

Also, I'd like to add that if you are a Muggle[1], or a non-spiritual person, or a person who does not believe that there is "something" that is bigger than yourself, and you are more interested in money, positions, possessions, and being right, this book is *not* for you. You will stay married for all the wrong reasons. But perhaps you'll get to keep your cars, property, titles, trips to the plastic surgeon, and annual vacations to the Caribbean. You'll join all of your other materialistic friends who are also hiding their internal misery by quenching their insatiable desires—and filling the gaping black holes in their souls—with new toys, drugs, property, and affairs with younger playmates. You deserve to be miserable. When that gets old, revisit this book or schedule an appointment with me.

If you are a Muggle, just as you may stay married for the wrong reasons, you will also get divorced for all the wrong reasons. Your divorce will turn into a war, you'll use your kids as pawns, and duke it out for the last dime. If that's your plan, I repeat, this book is not for you. I won't be giving tips and tricks on deception, how to exit with the most toys or how to stick it to your soon-to-be-ex. You may want to put this book down and just hope to catch your partner cheating, then blame them for everything so you can feel justified in taking everything. That way you can just get the fuck out without ever having to take a look at YOU. #Chickenshit

---

[1] The word "Muggle" has been around since the 13th century. It has been used to mean everything from someone who lacks a particular skill, to your common, everyday type of person, to a type of fish, a wife, and a marijuana joint! Of course, J.K. Rowling popularized the word by using it to define a non-magical person. My adaptation of Muggle is someone who has no interest in developing their consciousness or awareness, and who has no vision of the soul's eternal nature or journey. Think of your typical Joe Citizen sitting on the couch after their 9-5 job, eating Doritos and drinking beer and expecting nothing to change for the next 40 years. More on this later.

Lastly, this is *not* a pro-divorce book. It's not a "find a reason to blame your spouse and GTFO" book. This a *pro-follow your heart* book. It's an "open invitation to discover who you are and what's important to you" book. It's an "examine yourself before casting the first stone" book.

This book is for the sincere seeker who's brave enough to take a long, hard look in the mirror and make their own course corrections. And it's permission to get a divorce when your marriage is no longer your truth, after you've done everything in your power to clean up your side of the street.

Time to give your heart the first vote—or at least an equal vote with your mind. You deserve to move forward, follow your dreams, and find the love of your life (if that is your desire). You deserve to create a passionate, healthy, and fascinating relationship that totally lights you up, instead of one that has you wanting to slit your wrists!

So…

If you find yourself on a new path and are just learning how to follow your heart, acknowledge your feelings, and speak your own authentic truth…

If you actually have love for your partner and don't want to hurt them…

If you are wondering if this is all there is and are seeking more meaning in life…

If you believe you'd be happier with a life filled with purpose, passion, and peace…

If you need permission to live your life—to have someone tell you it's not selfish to want to go through life with someone that you're crazy about and who shares those same dreams and ideals…

If you want to end your marriage consciously, without the typical divorce war…

If you have been treated poorly for years (pretending not to notice) and think you're just supposed to suck it up because you made a commitment…

If you have been cheating for years, are miserable AF, and are completely disinterested in your partner…

If you are afraid of how it may be perceived if you leave, and you don't want to hurt anyone's feelings…

If you want to learn how to renegotiate your commitments and move on in harmony, without resentment, rage or make-wrong…

If you want to cause the least stress and heartache for your children when you separate…

If you want to know how to move on in your next relationship…

If you want to know how to best blend a future family and how to be a conscious co-parent and/or step-parent…

If you'd like to create the healthiest divorce possible…

…then this may just be the book for you.

And if you are on a more enlightened/conscious path and understand that you are 100% accountable for your life and that you are creating your own reality, this book is definitely for you. If you have no clue what I just said, I'll break it down in the following chapters.

## Chapter 2

# The Four Tenets

Now, before we get to the "juicier" stuff, I want to lay the ground work of where I'm coming from, why I've written this book, and for whom I've written it.

Since the time I was 15, there has not been a day that I have not been earnestly seeking, pondering, teaching or writing about the mysteries of the Universe, God, why we're here, and personal evolution. I received a degree in Theology and World Religions at the age of 22, and consciously left 3 major religions after joining two of them and being born into another. I've been a Chopra Certified Instructor for over a decade and have been studying ancient and new age philosophies and spiritual traditions since I was 12 and praying for wisdom. I've taught and coached thousands of people that have put the principles I share into practice, resulting in more peace, passion, purpose, and emotional freedom in their own lives and my own.

I share this only to establish that I'm not just some new-age hippie here to tell you that the Universe has your back… though that may also be true. Or perhaps more true, the universe is neutral and simply delivers course corrections in the direction of our highest awareness and acceptance of "what is?"

This book is for people that are either on a spiritual path, just beginning one, and/or looking for more meaning in life. Regardless of the title, this isn't a get-out-of-jail-free-card type of book. I'm not going to tell you to kick your spouse to the curb or that your desires are all that matter and fuck anyone else in your life that tells you otherwise. If that's what you were thinking, I apologize for the false advertising. It's more about getting clarity as to who you are, what you want going forward, and taking an honest assessment of your marriage while doing everything you can to clean your side of the street. And only then making the determination as to whether your marriage is viable—is it a help or a hinderance to your overall purpose, your spiritual evolution or simply a life of meaning.

My plan is to assist you in discovering the truth of your soul, why we are here, and the current energetic blueprint that is coming forth to advance the evolution of humanity and why it's time you align with your life's passion and purpose. This book will also cover the contrast between what you may be experiencing currently and what it might look like to consciously co-create a more authentic relationship. If put into practice in your current relationship, these ideas and principles may actually assist you in *staying* married or, at the very least, show you how to exit without creating World War III.

Let's start from the beginning.

## Tenet Number 1:

*We are eternal beings on an evolutionary journey to grow and evolve our souls.*

We all have a vibrational essence/frequency we will call our soul, it's the part of us that is eternal. We chose to come to the Earth School (and other places as well) to experience life for the purpose of the evolution and expansion of our souls. We are not merely a meat suit, put here on Earth just once, to be buried in the ground and eaten by worms. Nor are we here to grovel our entire life at the altar of any number of religions, essentially placing our bets on their version of what is "right" to assure ourselves of the best afterlife for all of our good behavior. Time to expand that old paradigm.

We are energetic beings, and what we know about energy is that it can neither be created nor destroyed—it simply transforms. Our soul or particular vibrational frequency is what remains and is eternal.

We are here to experience the fullness of the human experience, which is simply not possible with the limited thinking that says, "we only get one life." We come here repeatedly over lifetimes, playing out different roles and themes, experiencing dualities like: masculine and feminine energies, poverty and abundance, grief and joy, sickness and health, faith and despair, drama and peace, career vs. relationship and everything in between— ultimately to arrive at the conclusion (spoiler alert!) that there is no duality, that separation is an illusion, and that we are indeed all one…even if sometimes I call you a Muggle.

## Tenet Number 2:

*We are co-creators, never victims, of every experience that comes into our orbit.*

I don't want to spend a lot of time on this here, but rest assured, before you came here you had a plan with other souls. There were lessons you wanted to learn, experiences you desired to have, and feelings you wanted to feel, all in order to advance the evolution of your soul. We tend to travel in soul groups or pods, playing different roles for each other over lifetimes. We make sacred contracts, soul agreements and plans, pre-incarnation, to provide experiences for each other's growth as souls.

From this 30,000-foot view, it may be easier to see that life is always happening *for you* and not to you, even when it's really hard. In fact, especially then. There is no way to grow with only joyful experiences—it would be like creating the mosaic of all of your lifetimes with one color. Boring! We cannot know joy without the experience of pain. It is often the very thing that at once brought us joy that is now, in the case of marriage or divorce, bringing us pain. #Duality

Every experience that has ever come into your space, your soul has drawn to you. Your results/consequences are a direct result of your soul's desire for expansion. Whether you know it or not, it is the nature of your soul to grow, evolve, and expand. Although your lessons may seem harsh at times, make no mistake about it, they are custom designed *by you* and *for you* with love. I understand this concept may be hard to accept for some, especially in the case of such a disruptive change as divorce. To fully comprehend this truth, you would have to ascend to a higher level of consciousness where it becomes much clearer. More on this later...

Here's a tip: if you are hating/blaming/shaming your ex or soon-to-be-ex for anything–like your life sucks, or isn't the way you want it to be– you don't quite get it. That's OK, keep reading. Just pretend for a moment that you do, or just try it on as a possibility that some people, somewhere, actually break up amicably, both taking 100% accountability like grown-ass adults. Feel the peace that would be available to you when you're there. It's the world we are creating. We will never achieve peace in the world if we cannot create a peaceful divorce. Time to be the change, already!

## Tenet Number 3:

*The world is speeding up and transforming in a variety of unexpected ways.*

Initially, when I first started writing this in 2019, I said that technology was the catalyst for this transformation, as it has provided virtually unlimited access to wisdom and information. I then stated that, "We don't live in the same world anymore."

Then the 2020 pandemic happened, showing us just how fast things can change right before our eyes.

One day you're traveling about the globe visiting family and friends, breathing fresh air, attending concerts and sporting events, saying exactly what you mean to say, and very clear that your body is your business. A few short months later your wings have been clipped.

Life as we know it has changed alright.

Now back to my pre-pandemic musings. This big change is right on par and in perfect alignment with the evolution of our souls. It's time we learn how to let go of and rid ourselves of past toxic emotions, traumas, karma, and ancestral patterns from this life and previous lifetimes. By doing so, we are able to unburden ourSelves, shed some layers and "masks" that have not been serving us, and access the truthfulness of who we are on a soul-deep level. Only then can we tap into our own raw power and purpose in this new age.

What is this new age, you may be asking? Surely you've felt it. Things are no longer business as usual! We are moving away from an age of looking outside of ourSelves to be led, fed, guided, and programmed by religious institutions, governments, patriarchal societies/philosophies, antiquated healthcare, and a Newtonian educational system. We are moving towards a more Self-empowered way of being. In this new era of quantum physics, we understand that all things are energy and that we are more powerful than we ever imagined. We are learning to look within, to trust ourSelves as individuals, and tap into our own inner knowing and resources.

We are moving away from the passive acceptance of being told by others what to do and what is right for us by others. We are moving towards taking our power back and empowering ourSelves with our own intuitive wisdom as to what is right for us as individuals and honoring that same process in others. What is right for one, may not be for another—whether it's food, exercise, religion, sexuality, politics, healing, areas of study, or spirituality. No longer is there a one-size-fits-all in ANY area. It's becoming ridiculous to believe there is only one true religion on the planet, or one way to eat that is best for everyone, or one way to treat disease, or one way to learn. This is simply *not* truth.

For those who have a third eye to see and a sixth sense to hear, there are a plethora of "new ways" to do EVERTHING—from generating free power to healing incurable diseases. Why wouldn't the institution of marriage also be due for an upgrade/transformation?

Just as the Earth continues its evolution at a staggering pace, so too our souls are changing, growing, and ascending quicker than we ever have in our history. In each lifetime we are evolving exponentially more than in each previous life. Different than the 1950's, where most things stayed the same, currently it seems as if we live several lifetimes in one—often with the demarcation of monumental happenings like divorce, second marriages, career changes, belief changes, lifestyle changes, living in foreign lands, etc. It makes sense that we may not be able to get everything we need for our soul's growth from being with one partner our whole life. As we learn to follow our own soul's trajectory, we create a space to receive new energies, people, and tribes that are more in alignment and resonant with where we are headed. Nothing wrong here. Just evolution.

## Tenet Number 4:

*You have a mission here and you deserve to figure out what that is.*

It requires courage to tap into your inner power and truth. Your purpose is to be who you were created capable of being—that person your soul longs to be. What is it that you do in your spare moments when you lose all track of time? What are the topics that keep you up at night buried in research? What is it that you rarely run out of steam doing or creating? There is something you do, a passion that you have, that is uniquely yours that the world desperately needs.

It's time to show up. It can no longer wait. The time is now. In all areas of life, in all professions, conscious people are needed like never before to usher in a new world.

You may have no clue at the moment what that is, but you have felt the pull. The pull that says there is more, the pull that says you are meant to make a bigger contribution on this planet. For some it's felt like a gentle nudge, for others it may feel like a ton of bricks to the head, and for others an inner knowing/nagging that something is happening and you are supposed to get ready for it.

To become who we truly are requires a journey into our own shadows. A dark night of the soul most often accompanies this venture. It can feel a little ominous, so many prefer to never take that journey. They settle instead for the status quo and do nothing, while the blood slowly drains from their wrists. It is through this shadow process that we transcend our deepest fears and have the courage to act and get on the road to a more authentic way of living and align with our life's purpose. (See my upcoming book, *Beautiful Darkness* for in-depth details on this life-altering process.)

The person you share your daily life and your sacred sexuality with must needs be on par and in harmony with your soul's mission. If that is not the case, it would be better to go it alone. It will not serve you to be attached to those that do not share your vision, that are not 100% supportive, or worse, want nothing to do with this new direction you seem to be heading.

Whether you're the one who stepped off the path in a new direction initially, or you both did, it's perfectly OK...nothing wrong here. Your previously shared path has just been diverging, like Frost's less-traveled path in the woods. There may be a huge chasm between you already—time to acknowledge the elephant in the room. It doesn't have to be miserable. It's just a time of acknowledgement and restructuring.

When one person in a pod (a family, marriage, tribe, church, group of friends, etc.) has the courage to break free and follow their heart and their truth (different than the desires of the ego) it will *always* be best for the group at large, whether they understand it in the moment or not. It can be no other way. For some this may simply look like a need for more authenticity—an overdue desire to say how we feel, express who we are, and do what we've lacked the courage to do previously. In other cases, it may mean making choices that will either lead you away from the pod or the pod choosing to leave you if your truth is no longer in alignment with theirs. Or maybe it will be somewhere in between. But ultimately, the courage to follow your heart into the unknown, even and especially into the shadow, is what leads us to our real purpose and ultimate freedom—getting in touch with and speaking our truth.

The beginning of this transition can be challenging as you are learning to redefine yourself, and it may likely be a departure from your traditional ways of being. As you become more honest with yourSelf, you may feel that you cannot continue with the unhealthy family/societal patterns you may have inherited and that to do so is no longer acceptable to your soul. As a result, you may find that connecting with people with whom you feel more aligned will be a healthier way to live. Your relationships will change dramatically because you have changed. Relationships that are no longer authentic, will no longer be sustainable. This is simply forward movement, not devastation.

When you are clear what is best for you on a Soul Level and you choose to ignore it, due to various fears and programming, you are holding up everybody in your particular pod's evolution. When you choose what is best for you, it will inevitably be best for everyone touched by the ripple of your choices. Those remaining in their unconsciousness may beg you not to change, while others will be inspired by your clarity and courage. All will benefit, whether they know it in the moment or discover it as they reflect years down the road.

~ ~ ~

In summary, going forward, unless stated otherwise, we will be operating under the assumption that we are all eternal beings on an evolutionary journey, living on this big-blue marble where time is speeding up, life is unfolding perfectly, and it's time to figure out our purpose, passion, and raison d'etre.

Let's explore the most optimum ways to do this, and those that cause the most harm.

## Chapter 3

# "Fine" is a Four-Letter Word

*I always imagined I would have a life very different from the one that was imagined for me, but I understood from a very early time that I would have to revolt in order to make that life. Now I am convinced that in any creativity there exists this element of revolt. -Leonor Fini*

I never dreamed of having a "fine" life. Have you? Have you ever heard a kid in a super hero cape say, "When I grow up, my life is going to be fine!?" When you got on one knee to propose or when you said, "Yes!", did you say yes to "fine"? Do you ever even go to a movie hoping for it to be "fine"? NO, no and nooooooo!! Yet as we grow older, we seem to settle into it. We justify our unsatisfactory feelings of fine with thoughts like, "Well, at least it's not horrible. Susie's husband is abusive." "Joe's wife gained 100 pounds." "You can't expect things to stay amazing, forever—you just need to lower your expectations." "It could be a lot worse." "It's good enough." Or worse, "I don't deserve better."

What this sounds like to me is resignation. Surrendering to a life of mediocrity. It wreaks of what Henry David Thoreau astutely described in

Walden as "the mass of men (who) lead lives of quiet desperation." Is that the way you want to go?

Because lurking under the surface of "quiet desperation" is often anger, resentment, frustration, hopelessness, apathy, passivity, and a whopping dose of dissatisfaction. All of which lead to a lack of vitality, energy, life force, passion, and excitement. Not only that, but because you are most likely stuffing all the other negative emotions under the surface, that repression leads to stress, anger, and being reactive. Years of repression lead to chronic pain and illness and eventually an untimely death because you really have nothing to live for, in your opinion.

A life that is just fine is only fine for someone that believes that's all they deserve. A life that is just fine is only fine for someone that is drowning in shame, guilt, grief, fear, and apathy. A life that is just fine sucks if you truly want more out of life. A life that is just fine is for someone that has given up on their dreams, their passion, their vision, and their purpose. Do you want to settle for fine, or might there be something within you that wants more, that craves anything but mediocre?

At the ripe old age of thirty I was married to a good man, had two amazing daughters ages six and three, and happened to have been crowned Mrs. Utah. I was in great shape and had just missed winning the title of Mrs. International by only one point. My husband was a good provider and I was thrilled to be able to be home with my daughters. Everything looked perfect—on the outside. But on the inside, I was conflicted.

It was Mother's Day Weekend in 1996, and my intuitive husband gave me the gift of a much-needed weekend stay alone at the Sundance Resort in Utah. He put together a beautiful basket of all of my favorite treats, tea, and a new journal. I was truly at a crossroads in my life. I was very unsatisfied with my current religion, which was very unsettling to my husband—a devout member of that religion. On Sundays I'd started attending another religion's church service after the morning service at our own. Our marriage, though we never fought, was sexless and passionless and had been for years. It was "fine," though.

I went to Sundance to reflect on my life, to get some answers, and to make some decisions. I decided to go on a hike shortly after I checked in. Everything in nature spoke to me on that trail that day. In fact, the download I received from God/Source/the Universe/Higher Self twice on that same hike was so profound, it not only answered all of my heartfelt questions, but also became the foundation of a book I was inspired to begin writing entitled *The Mountain Speaks*.

As I set out on my journey, I was deeply struck by the breathtaking view of Mount Timpanogos. As the sun shone on the remaining snow that early Spring, I stood in awe of its beauty and majesty. In that moment the thought entered my mind that this peak, this majestic summit, was how I had always envisioned my life. Never had I even considered having a ho-hum life that was just OK. My favorite quote at 17 was another classic from Thoreau, a lesson he learned during his time on Walden Pond:

> *I went to the woods because I wished to live deliberately, to front only the essential facts of life, and see if I could not learn what it had to teach, and not, when I came to die, discover that I had not lived. I did not wish to live what was not life, living is so dear; nor did I wish to practise resignation, unless it was quite necessary. I wanted to live deep and suck out all the marrow of life, to live so sturdily and Spartan-like as to put to rout all that was not life, to cut a broad swath and shave close, to drive life into a corner, and reduce it to its lowest terms....*

That summit was the perfect reminder of how that quote still lived within me. I have always lived deliberately—consciously aware of everything I put into my body, my mind, and my spirit. And I did the same with my children. I have forever been intent upon living in such a way that if I were on my death bed that I would have no regrets. To me, nothing would be worse than approaching death and realizing that I had wasted my life living another's dream, having given up on my own, and thus not living at all. I vowed to my young Self to never live a life of resignation and to "suck the marrow" out of every moment. The very top, the summit's peak—nothing less would do for this Aries-born Fire Horse. And yet, something was definitely amiss.

As I began to head up the trail, I immediately saw a wide open, meandering path that was very alluring, but I was going on a hike, and you have to go up, right? So though my heart wanted to go left, my mind said up and to the right. At that point in my own spiritual journey, I tended to listen to my mind first; the heart was something I didn't yet know or fully trust. "Ok," I agreed. It's what I always did. Discipline first. Take the long way, explore every other road before I'd allow myself any kind of frivolous fun or to go down the road my heart "knew" I really wanted to take.

As I hiked up, I noticed the path narrowing and I could no longer hear the bubbling brook. To the right was a steep cliff and to the left was a thick forest of trees. The only path available to me was literally "straight and narrow." It was hard and I began to resent the path. Every step on that now difficult path I likened to my marriage. We'd been going to counseling, talking to our ecclesiastical leaders, I'd even made suggestions of intimacy, and it all just felt heavy. I kept thinking that at some point on this arduous upward climb, I'd be able to see the peak again and find the path up, as I was hoping would be the case in my marriage.

So, I kept going like a good lil soldier and I finally arrived—at a dead end. And what was awaiting after all my hard work and effort up? A small clearing with a few aspens and some leftover dirty snow.

"Hmmm," I mumbled to myself. "It's pretty…I guess."

It was no mountain peak—that's for sure. I stood there, looking for something redeeming for all of my hard work, for some return on all the effort I'd invested. Tears began to run down my cheeks as the words, "It's fine…" fell like a lead weight in my heart. Then came these devastating four words, "…just like your marriage."

The life drained out of me as I received my answer in that moment. There was a heaviness that followed that comes when you know what you have to do, but haven't the first clue as to how to do it. You don't know how it's supposed to look or what will become of you on the other side. Regardless of the outcome, I was crystal clear, divorce was imminent. Having climbed the path I felt I was "supposed" to take, a somewhat pretty clearing and dirty snow, a.k.a. "fine," was the best I could hope for in this marriage.

There was no way I was going to resign myself to a life of fine. It wasn't who I'd ever been, though it was who I'd become. I re-committed to mySelf that day that I would never again settle for "fine," nor would I create another life of "fine."

The story of that revelatory hike doesn't end at the dirty snow. The culmination was actually quite epic, and could not have been a more accurate foreshadowing as to how my life would unfold after having made my decision. More on that later. Suffice it to say, if you are looking for answers, the Universe is always speaking to us in a myriad of ways. Your truth can be found as readily, if not even more reliably, by reconnecting with your heart and giving it the final vote. Go down all of the logical paths if you must, traditional therapy, reading all the books, speaking with church leaders, parents, or friends, trying to revive your sex life, etc. When you have exhausted all of those venues to no avail, I highly recommend going within, getting real with yourself, and taking a listen to that cute, brilliant heart of yours. It always knows the way.

### The Fine Marriage—The Hardest to Leave

The Fine Marriage can be the hardest divorce of them all. "Fine" should be good enough for you, *they* say. After all, your marriage is probably better than half of the married people that you know. There's no abuse, you're both semi-respectful of each other, no major blow-ups—everything is just…well… fine. So what if you rarely have sex, there's no big spark any more, or you rarely have a heartfelt conversation. You have kids, a house, a life, and a 401K. Why upset the apple cart? You know the rancor and judgment you will most definitely incur from family, friends, clergy, and possibly even your therapist if you tried to get out of your "Fine Marriage." "A marriage like yours can totally work," your hopeful therapist says, enthusiastically!

Often in the Fine Marriage we allow our own self-doubt, naysaying and fatalistic ways to keep us stuck right where we are. We tell ourselves we're not enough, we'll never find anybody that wants what we want, we'll never find anyone to fall in love with us. We're too old, too set in our ways, not accomplished enough, no longer attractive, or we are the ones that are too picky. We fear even a short-term decline in our happiness, so we rationalize and justify our own inaction. Eventually laziness and comfort take their place on the podium next to security and fine.

In the Fine Marriage, it often takes the overwhelming pull of a third party to get us in touch with our long-lost inner fire, our healthy desire, and our passion—all to assist us in understanding that there may be something more nourishing for our soul—to teach us that it isn't bad or greedy to want more, or to long for your heart to sing about the person you are sharing your life with.

Without that passionate pull, many stay in a Fine Marriage for years and years because nobody "did anything" wrong. It's hard to "justify" leaving, you think to yourself. Our fear of what others will think of us, and what we may think of ourselves is often the biggest nail in the coffin keeping us in a space that doesn't light us up anymore.

We talk ourselves right out of making a change because we give inflated priority to being comfortable and seemingly secure. Yet with all those warm blankets, you can't seem to shake that chilly feeling of being dissatisfied. You long for something more…more intense, more alive, more connected. Instead you are just going through the motions, telling yourself that you are the problem. You *should* be happier and way less greedy.

Maybe you started an in-depth study of a topic that has re-lit that fire inside you. Or perhaps you started to actually want to practice the discipline you learned in college, or finish that degree. Or maybe someone else has unexpectedly rekindled that flame in you. Sometimes all it takes is even the possibility of a small fling or the hint of an office romance—whether it happens or not—to generate enough spark for us to realize that something more for us may actually exist.

Be brave. Have an honest chat with your spouse…it's likely they may be feeling the same way. Chances are, neither of you may have much to complain about so the conversation can appear somewhat unnecessary, almost unthinkable—laughable perhaps. The fact that you even picked up this book, speaks volumes though. Your courage to approach the topic of divorce, may come as a relief to your partner.

If not, and your other says they're still into you, ask them to prove it. Maybe there's been some miscommunication. However, if staying in the marriage is far from a "hell yes" for you because you don't feel happy, alive, on purpose or truly in love, it most likely won't be a "hell yes" for them either. Having the conversation will at least enable you to find the way back together, or perhaps be unified in your decision to split.

If you find yourself routinely going through thoughts that hold you back from even considering divorce, thoughts like "I'd never find anybody else at this age," "he/she is a good person," "they're the mother/father of my children," "it's going to be hard to split everything," "I'll have to live with only half of everything I've worked so hard for," "I don't want to start all over," then let me ask you this: would you want anyone to stay in your life if these were their thoughts and their only reasons for staying with you?

Personally, I would rather live my life alone than be with anyone for whom the answer isn't a "Hell, fucking yes!" about being with me and I with him!!

If my person isn't as in love with me as I am with mySelf, please go. Go find your person because I'm not it. Take it all. I couldn't give a fuck about the material bullshit if it comes attached with a mere pathetic toleration and not mutual passion and appreciation. I'm a passionate being. Mediocre is not the way I want to do anything in my life, and most certainly not with my most intimate relationship. I can be happy with less than my ideal home, car and possessions if I have my person that I'm crazy about by my side. We will create everything we desire together. And if not, we'll just be too happy to care.

## Chapter 4

# Transcending the Muggle Slumber

*You see in the world what you carry in your heart. ~Unknown*

Let's talk about my snarky lil term "Muggle" for a moment because I intend to continue using it throughout the book. I want to spell out, perhaps with less snark, what I truly mean when I refer to people and/or their behavior in that particular way. It's a little heady at first if you're not familiar with the work I'm about to share, but I'll do my best to make it easy to understand. If all else fails, you have permission to just skip this chapter and come back to it at a later time—or never. First, allow me to back up.

You may be familiar with David Hawkins' Scale of Human Consciousness. If not, I highly recommend any of these books: Power vs. Force, where the chart first appeared, and these other two life-altering books that expound upon his consciousness scale: Letting Go: The Pathway to Surrender and Transcending the Levels of Consciousness. I have been applying this wisdom in my writings, classes, and coaching for well over a decade and so have countless others. It is profound. *See Appendix A.*

In his seminal body of work, Hawkins calibrates, through kinesiology, a guide to understanding the levels of human consciousness—or, more simply, the lens through which we see the world. The lowest level is that of Shame which calibrates at a 20. It progresses up through various levels to Courage at 200, and advances even further to Love at 500. The scale culminates at the highest levels of Enlightenment, which calibrate from 700-1000. In our pursuit of personal self-improvement, spiritual advancement, and enlightenment, Hawkins' map clearly lays out the terrain to be navigated along the journey of ascension.

Sound a little nebulous? What does that even mean, to transcend the levels of consciousness? And what does this have to do with your marriage, you may be asking? I get it, but please hang in there with me because understanding it has the ability to transform everything—or at the very least, to understand why you and your partner are the way you are.

To transcend levels of consciousness means going from living a life of shame, guilt, apathy, fear, anger, and pride, and feeling like life is miserable, evil, hopeless, scary, antagonistic, and demanding, to something entirely different. It means moving beyond all your bullshit to a life that is not only feasible but hopeful, harmonious, meaningful, happy, peaceful, and free!!

That's it. Simple, right? Want in? Easier said than done and some of you may just need to GAFDA before it will ever happen.

In reality, how this scale plays out in our lives is that we typically reside in and resonate at just a couple of the 17 levels that correspond to our baseline emotion. The vast majority of people in the world calibrate under the level of Courage at 200. That means that most people see everything in their life through a lens of shame, guilt, fear or all of the above. As a result, they blame everybody else for their problems and have zero personal accountability. But, again, it doesn't have to stay that way.

Life, and hence relationships, improve exponentially with every progressive move up that scale. However, in order to make any significant change in life, you will have to find a way to rise to at least the level of Courage at

200. If you are hovering at the bottom near Shame and Guilt, you will attract more experiences into your life to be ashamed of and feel guilty about, and you will project your blame on to everybody on your path. It will always be someone else's fault, or you will be so down on yourself and despise yourself so much that you will be consumed with what a despicable person you are.

If you are one of those constantly angry buggers, you will continually be attracting people and experiences that piss you off, aggravate, and infuriate you. When you manage to rise to the level of Courage, life will begin to look feasible, and you will feel empowered to take positive action in your life.

If you were to jump up to 350, the level of Acceptance, now that's a game-changer. At this level, you are able to accept "what is." You are able to accept life as it comes, and suddenly life becomes more harmonious and you become more forgiving of yourself and others.

So when I say "Muggle" or refer to "Muggle Behavior," I'm referring to those whose consciousness frequencies are below 200 and they *think* they know, and are right about, everything. For them, there is clearly someone else to blame for all their troubles, even though they may be enslaved to their cravings and riddled with regret, anxiety, and despair. They are fighting off being consumed by a whole host of toxic emotions like rage, jealousy, insecurity, low self-worth, and apathy. This lower level of conscious awareness is what creates real shitty partners that do super shitty things.

However, if you are earnestly on the path of truth and enlightenment, seeking purpose and meaning, most likely your path up the levels of consciousness has already led you down to the depths of the profound work of uncovering your own dark shadow and subconscious behaviors and beliefs. If you are not a poser, preferring to spiritually bypass your shit by waving some pink unicorn wand of "love and light" across your entire past, you will have seen with clarity many of these negative behaviors within yourself and are already working on being accountable for them. If you are serious about this work, you will do everything in your power to understand the origin of these negative behaviors and then to integrate, transmute or purge them.

I have found that doing this kind of awareness work, a.k.a. shadow work, is one of the best ways of transcending these lower levels of consciousness. In so doing, you will have naturally transcended your old self, i.e., the old lens through which you saw the world around you, and many of your less-than-favorable ways of being. And, thus, you have transcended the levels of consciousness. Congrats! You are growing!! Now it will be easier to create the reality, and the relationship, that is ideal for you.

Relationships of power and beauty find a hard time existing at lower levels of consciousness—indeed, it's nearly impossible. At lower levels of consciousness, where the ego is overly involved, love is identified with possession and control, which creates a fear of loss and leads to jealousy, rage, blame, and obsession. At the higher levels of Love and above, the source of love is not dependent on external factors, i.e., The Other (or Others). When operating from the frequency of Love, one behaves in a way that is nurturing, supportive, and forgiving. It is the level of true happiness. And as such it does not seek to own, force, coerce, control or manipulate. At this level, one is accountable for themselves and their actions, does not point the finger of blame outside of themselves, and finds that love is available everywhere. A perfect recipe for building an amazing partnership.

If your partner is on board and you've both been doing the work to clear your shit to reveal a more authentic you, you will be better equipped to save your marriage and build a more sustainable one if that is your mutual desire. Or you may just find that you have entirely different goals then when you were both in a lower place, and now you are ready to move forward—solo.

If this is the case, and you're both clear about it, you will be able to part peacefully knowing there is no shame in moving forward and apart with (gasp!) mutual care and an abiding respect for each other.

This is ideal and a much-preferred way to end a marriage. But maybe you've tried to share this with your significant other and they want nothing to do with your new path and your "woo woo" ways. They're of the opinion that everything is just fine the way it is, don't rock the boat. Or they are stuck in a belief that nothing will ever change no matter what they (or you) do. Both of those responses are based in fear, with a preference for burying their heads in the sand in the hope that your relationship will just miraculously fix itself. It doesn't work like that.

When I use the term "Muggle Slumber," I'm referring to those at a level of consciousness who have no hope of their world being any different than it is in this moment, no belief that they can effect change in themselves or the world, and no vision of a life other than servitude to the Man and the Matrix. These are not the droids you're looking for and not the folks for whom this book is written.

Hawkins makes the distinction that the ego-self favors *involvement* with the Other to serve its own wantings and cravings, while the higher Self favors *consensual alignment* to serve the relationship itself. Involvement can look like being controlling, demanding, in somebody's business, telling them what they can (and can't) do, tracking them, and/or invading their privacy due to a lack of trust. Consensual alignment looks like having similar goals, assisting each other, and being harmonious. It has a feeling of expansiveness together as opposed to a feeling of contraction.

Imagine that for a moment. Breathe in what it would feel like to live in expansion, growth, freedom, love and mutual support. How might that feel? Does your marriage feel like that?

This elevated way of being is the possibility I am holding out for both parties involved. However, if one of the partners remains in a different state of consciousness and refuses their own flowering, it will be next to impossible for them to stay together if the Other evolves. They will no longer be an energetic match or of a similar vibrational frequency. It will become like two magnets repelling each other, instead of coming together. They will energetically spin right out of each other's space.

Even if both partners rise to a more authentic version of their Higher Selves, they may still feel they have different interests and decide to part ways. The good news is that when both parties are at this level, an amicable split is not only possible—it's probable.

So, as discussed, when I say Muggle Slumber, I'm referring to those remaining in their egos, stuck and unwilling to budge, or entirely unaware and unconscious of their own low levels of consciousness. Got it?

*Chapter 5*

# Going Beyond Shame

In a more conscious world, surrounded by a bunch of self-aware peeps, there will be no shame in divorce. It will simply be a life change, like changing religions, jobs, towns, houses, going to college or having another child. Major life changes connote transformation and movement—not shame. Each of these changes are often accompanied by tremendous forethought and each deserves respect—not judgment.

You've heard the axiom, "The only constant in life is change." Why would this not also apply to marriage? Considering the current divorce rate, it obviously does. So get over it. Divorce happens.

I don't know about you, but I don't have a single divorced friend that wishes they were still married to their ex. Usually, in that rare case, it's due to some weird obsession, and everyone that knew the couple would say they were better off apart. For those healthy marriages that do last, most go through several iterations, continually evolving to match their growing needs, desires, and evolution.

But let's talk about shame for a minute. On the scale of human consciousness, shame is the lowest vibration of all of the emotions. It beats out guilt, apathy, grief, and fear. Shame actually leads to guilt, depression, despair, and even suicide. While guilt is about something you may have done, shame is turned inward on the self and is about who you are. Guilt says you made a mistake; shame says you *are* the mistake. Feelings of being flawed, defective, disgraced, disreputable, broken, and wrong accompany shame. When you operate at the level of shame, you believe that god despises you, you are miserable, and you live in a state of constant humiliation. FUN!!

Shame has been used since time immemorial by religious institutions, governments, cultures, communities, and families to keep people in check and for the benefit of someone else's ideals. Shame has people behaving in ways contrary to their own nature. We are shamed almost from birth that we shouldn't cry, get angry or act in ways our elders tell us are inappropriate. As a result, we no longer trust our own intuition, we question our feelings, and we buy into the fact that some person, institution, government or religion knows what's better for our lives than we do. It is an unconsciously agreed upon, societal form of slavery.

People that live in guilt and shame are easy to control. When "the mass of men lead lives of quiet desperation," the powers that be can pretty much have their way with us. We don't have the energy to get off the couch and go change the world. Our creativity and passion gets so squelched—who has time to create a biodegradable replacement for plastic, or alternative energy sources or save the rainforest? We just sit back comatose, unfeeling, unaware, addicted to all manner of useless activities to avoid our own pain.

We've become robots, fulfilling our duties to god, family, and country all whilst being dead inside. We shame ourselves for ever wanting more—which is exactly their plan. A world of free, happy, passionate, creative people may also be free-thinking—and that might be dangerous.

> *No society wants you to become wise: it is against the investment of all societies. If people are wise they cannot be exploited. If they are intelligent they cannot be subjugated, they cannot be forced into a mechanical life, to live like robots. They will assert themselves—they will assert their individuality. They will have the fragrance of rebellion around them; they will want to live in freedom.*
>
> *Freedom comes with wisdom, intrinsically. They are inseparable, and no society wants people to be free…no society likes people to use their own intelligence because the moment they start using their intelligence they become dangerous…*
>
> *In fact, a wise man is afire, alive, aflame. He would like rather to die than to be enslaved. ~Osho*

Somehow we've elevated the "Shame Police" to a place of self-righteous honor instead of relegating them to the hells they attempt to create for others—and where they belong. We've been sold a bill of goods about shame and it's time to take our power back! But before you get too excited and grab your pitchforks, this is not an unconscious rebellion. It will actually require more effort on your part than biz as usual. There is personal, individual work to be done before we can even think about changing the world—or getting a divorce.

First of all, it will require your own acknowledgement of your personal responsibility in perpetuating the shame bullshit. "What does that look like," you ask? Any time you've told your kids, spouse or anyone else what they *should* be doing, how they *should* be feeling, or how they *should* be behaving; anytime you've treated the people in your life as your personal property; anytime you've made up somebody's mind for them or made a decision for someone that was not yours to make; anytime you've used God and what God/ Jesus might think of someone to get them to behave… ughhhhh. I could go on for days, but you're getting the idea, yuh? When you do these things to others, you are reinforcing the slave-culture shame programming.

We do all of the above to our Selves—we actually shame ourselves when we don't feel, think or behave in all the ways we've been programmed by our families, church, culture, and neighborhood. Only when we are able to recognize the programming, step out of the Matrix, stop judging ourselves for doing what we love, and embrace who we truly are will we ever be able to offer that gift of acceptance to another.

So what does this have to do with divorce? Awareness. Awareness of your behavior and how you contribute to the shaming and damnation of people considering divorce. Time to fully grasp that there is no more shame in divorce than there is in changing religions. Oooh…sore spot there!! Have you ever plain left or changed your religion? Whoa! I have. And yes, I was not only shamed and shunned, but was ostracized and had my kids taken from me. Ouch.

Humans can be brutal. This is what deserves evolving. To me, changing religions was nothing more than graduating from kindergarten, junior high, high school, and then college. As I gained further light and knowledge, I moved on. I progressed. My expansive soul, that could not be contained by shame, was simply evolving. Period. The end. This can very easily be applied to divorce. We cannot expect anybody to be the same person they were last week, let alone 20 years ago.

Casting shame or judgment on anyone for choosing to end a marriage, regardless of however long or short it may have lasted, is not your job. I don't care if you're the mother or mother-in-law of the bride, the couple's priest or their own children. Their relationship, or the demise thereof, is not your business to judge. So stop! Shaming someone to stay where they don't authentically want to be solves nothing but your own ego desires to maintain the status quo for *your* benefit and comfort. Resist your urge to point fingers and play the "make wrong" game. YOU are not the law, and no one appointed you judge and jury. You simply cannot know for someone else what they are going through unless they tell you—and even then, you may never know the whole story.

What if you convince someone to stay—let's say your son or son-in-law—because he "made a commitment," has children, will be damned by his religion, lose his empire, etc.? If he reluctantly complies, you may have just created more harm than good. If he truly has no desire to remain in the marriage, discontent may lead to unhappiness, lack of productivity, vitality, and eventually ill-health. He may become more prone to affairs, addictions, and various ways of checking out. Thanks, Mom.

It's not your life. Stay in your own lane. If somebody wants your advice or opinion, they will ask you. Make sure if they do, you refrain from promoting your own agenda and seek instead to understand before opening your pie hole. Do your best to support other people's choices, though they may not jive with your own. Learn to share your opinion without any attachment to having somebody do what you want them to do. In fact, lose the idea all together that you know best for anyone else's life other than your own. Let go of pushing your agenda! Make peace with the idea that the exact opposite of what *you* think is best might just be the *right* thing for someone else—for reasons you may never know.

Above all, trust that all is unfolding perfectly for everyone involved, though you may not understand that right now. Send love. Be supportive. Stay in your lane. Nobody—and I repeat, Nobody!—wants you to "should" on them.

## Chapter 6

# Trust Your Heart, Not Your Stories

*"I regret following my heart," said nobody ever!* ~ Laurie Frazier

Your heart is the gateway to your Soul. Did you know that according to Greg Braden, your heart contains 40,000 sensory neurites that can think, feel, and learn *independent* of the brain? The heart's electrical field is about 60 times greater in amplitude than the electrical activity generated by the brain. Its magnetic field is the strongest rhythmic field produced by the human body. Unlike the brain, the heart has no judgment or ego, and is without fear. Pretty cool, huh?

All that seemingly trite bs to "follow your heart" and "follow your bliss"…it's a thing. It's more than a meme on Insta and it isn't anything to be taken lightly. If you go through life never tuning in to what your heart has to say, you will have missed the entire point of your life. Yuh…it's like that.

And newsflash, the voice of your heart is *not* the voice of your parents, spouse, children, church leaders, life coach, therapist or even Jesus, Buddha or Krishna. It is the voice of your very own Soul, your Higher Self, and it contains all the mysteries and secrets as to why you are even here. It's no accident that it is the first organ that develops in an embryo. It's your very own internal guidance system. To ignore it, to put your heartfelt desires aside for what you've been programmed to believe you are "supposed" to do, or "should" desire, is to deny your very being.

To quote Morpheus in the Matrix, "To deny our impulses is to deny everything that makes us human." If you find yourSelf on a little higher frequency than the average blue-piller, I'd say it this way: "to deny our *heartfelt desires* is to deny everything that makes us human." To be human also includes being spiritual. In fact, we can't really *be* spiritual any more than we can *be* human, as it is just something that we are. You can't really tell a squirrel to just *be* a squirrel—it is inherent in his very being. We need only remember that the nature of our Soul/Being is eternal.

There is an epidemic in our Western society. We have forgotten who we truly are—that we are powerful beyond measure, that we have a mission and a purpose that only we can fulfill. Life is sooo much more than your 9-5, the nightly news, and a mortgage. We did not come here to be blindly devoted to another's programming. Upon awakening, you will recognize all of the ways your soul has been imprisoned and, therefore, impoverished. You may experience a strong urge to liberate yourselves from the veil of unconsciousness.

> *I believe we are a species with amnesia, I think we have forgotten our roots and our origins. I think we are quite lost in many ways. And we live in a society that invests huge amounts of money and vast quantities of energy in ensuring that we all stay lost. A society that invests in creating unconsciousness, which invests in keeping people asleep so that we are just passive consumers or products and not really asking any of the questions.*
> ~ Graham Hancock

What are those pesky lil questions, you ask? They're the ones you avoid because you don't *really* want to know, because to acknowledge what you discover may cause you to have to take some action or make some major changes in your life. And change can be scary. Ya know what's scarier…staying stagnant, stuck, and enslaved. Living a life where the lights are half-on til they go out completely, slowly dying in a prison of your own making because you are unable to speak your truth.

Many of you refuse to speak your truth because you tell yourselves that you don't know your truth. The truth is you won't even ask the questions because deep down you already *do* know. You think if you can just avoid crystal clarity, you can continue in your half-awakeness and half-heartedness which is exactly where the term "ignorance is bliss" came from.

But is ignorance really bliss? Is pretending really blissful, or does it feel more like survival? It's much easier to feign happiness without that crystal clarity. Just allow the din of all the other voices to outweigh your own. This is what it looks like: your mind has a belief that you are supposed to stay married against all odds, though your heart is screaming otherwise. So, to avoid the unmistakable voice of your heart, you turn up the volume of the programming that repeats, "you're doing the right thing, you're doing the right thing…."

Then your brain chimes in with all the other voices that let you know, in no uncertain terms, how you believe you will be perceived by all those that matter to you—and, surprisingly, all that don't—if you were to do otherwise. And you start coming up with more noble-sounding thoughts to diminish the voice of your soul a little more like, "I made a commitment…how will this effect the kids…I'm being selfish…" and on and on it goes until the raging flame in your heart becomes nothing but a flicker that you dismiss as the desires of the flesh. Then you give yourself a pat on the back for "choosing the right." But did you, really?

~ ~ ~

Here's what else "ignorance is bliss" looks like: you have the hunch that your partner may be having an affair but instead of confronting them, you metaphorically put your head in the sand or stick your fingers in your ear with more noise, "la, la, la, la, la…." Somehow, you think if it remains unacknowledged then it doesn't exist—but the heart always knows. So more noise is required to squelch your intuition and keep yourself safe from the truth. But are you safe, really?

One woman I know had been married for over four decades. Her husband had a very successful business, had held many "important" positions in their church, and always seemed attentive to her and the children. But she knew something was off. "It's nothing, it's your imagination." She kept telling herself, until she couldn't any longer. When she finally did even a tiny bit of digging, she found her husband had been cheating for years. He'd had many different affairs with multiple women, some of which he had even hired and promoted in his business (nothing like a little afternoon delight at work). He'd bought these women jewelry, given them company cars, taken them on trips—all the while she stayed home and took care of their five children.

What do you think she did when she found out? Nothing. The Self-betrayal was strong with this one. "To rock the boat would be bad," she thought. "It would hurt the children to find out," she rationalized. "He would lose his status and positions at church!" The Horror!

Her programming had her believe that her only responsibility was to ensure that nothing changed the status quo of her family. So she blindly pretended to play along…for years. The dutiful wife, knowing that each business trip and late night at the office weren't spent alone—that much of the money he earned wasn't being spent on the family, but on his latest fling. She betrayed herself, and in so doing she betrayed the people she claimed to be protecting…her own children. But hey, she kept her family "intact."

~ ~ ~

Trust your own intuition, trust it enough to act on it. The problem is that we've been completely socialized into *not* trusting our own intuition, natural abilities, inner knowing, and intelligence. We prefer our desires be carefully tucked away in some dark corner so we can't even access how we feel about things, what we want, what or whom we authentically love or who we truly are. We tell ourselves that it's just easier this way, and way less messy.

We live our lives in the shadows of other's expectations while rejecting the true Light of our own soul and heart. This is slavery—to look to another for approval, invalidate your own Self, and put your life in the more "capable" hands of someone else, be it an individual, church, government or society.

What this truly is, is lazy. You don't need a rule book to know it's not OK to take somebody else's stuff, or their life. As a conscious, eternal being you do not need another to tell you what is right for *your* life. There isn't one rule for everyone that says if you got married you should stay married. It's different for everyone. Only you know if your marriage can be truly transformed, and by that I don't mean putting a simple band-aid on it with another trip to the therapist, ecclesiastical leader or the Bahamas.

If you brush away all the faux clouds and doubts and tune in to your heart, you will just know. You already do know. You're just afraid. You are the only one that knows if your relationship is toxic to your soul. Only you know if you are or *will ever* be lit up by your partner or if you will always feel like you have to dim your light around them.

Only you know if you (or they) are merely tolerating them (or you), attempting to thrive on scanty rations of affection, or if that person will ever be able to truly fan your flames or not. Laughing, eh? "Fan your flames?!" Your partner has no clue as to how to fan your flames, you say. Maybe that's because they don't know who the fuck you are, either. You've been pretending so hard, for so long, to be what you thought *they* wanted you to be, that they have no clue who's under all of those masks. Whose fault is that?

Whenever we pretend to be that which we think others want, it is rarely sustainable. It will suck the life and vitality right out of us. It is not easy to be that which you are not—and it is even more difficult to step into the truth of who you really are…at least initially. I promise you though, once you do, it will become easier and easier to remain in your authenticity. What will become difficult is returning to your old fake ways once you have experienced the happiness and freedom of living a life of your choosing, So…put your hand on your heart, take several breaths, tune in to your heart space and ask yourself some questions.

Am I in love with this partner?

Am I able to be my authentic Self with this person without dimming my Light?

Are my dreams supported in this space?

Can I be truthful with this person without fear?

Would my partner love me if they knew who I really am?

Looking into the future, is this the person you want to wake up to in five years or even next week? What do you think this person loves about you? Is that the truth of you, or a façade? Do you feel like you are a better *you* with this person by your side, or are you more a fraction of your true Self in their presence? Are there parts of you that you feel are rejected or would be if you unleashed them?

And to be accountable, where is it that *you* have created the disconnect between the two of you? Is there any resentment that you could let go of? If you were to forgive them for any perceived wrong doing, would the spark come back? Where have you closed off your heart, and why? Do you think it would make a difference if you opened it again? Is there someone else you'd rather be with? Can you love your current partner as much as you do somebody else? Could you let that other person go completely to dive wholeheartedly back into your marriage without feeling like you just lost a piece of your soul? When you think of the next few years with your current partner, does it feel heavy or light?

Time to get real. Would your heart be better served by moving on, or by staying together? If you let go of all of your should's and ought to's, how (you believe) your children may be effected, what your church has to say, and all the opinions of others—what would your big, beautiful heart say? In other words, Fuck your rules, what does your heart say?

"But how do you know it's your heart," you ask? Easy. Your heart doesn't tell stories, nor does it justify its answer. Justifying your decision is what your *mind* does, and normally that's just an exercise in convincing yourself to believe what everyone else is telling you.

The heart is clear. The heart just knows. And it doesn't need an explanation. Vanilla or chocolate? Stay or go? The answer is immediate, and it needs no justification. I choose chocolate…because…no! I choose chocolate because I fucking choose chocolate! Because it is the truth of my soul. Period. The end. Nobody is wrong here.

The heart chooses what the heart chooses. To ignore it is to fight an unending battle for the rest of your life by going against it. Notice all the stories you will have to create when you do go against your heart. Just notice. "I'm staying *because* the children…*because* I made a commitment…*because* of the lifestyle…*because* Jesus, etc." FFS!!

The heart wants what the heart wants and it isn't bad and it isn't wrong. Your heart is the gateway to your Soul. It always knows the way. Within your heart and its unequivocal clarity lies your courage. When you find that, there will be no stopping you.

> *Never regret anything you have done with a sincere affection; nothing is lost that is born of the heart. ~Basil Rathbone*

Remember who you are, that you are eternal—but that this earth life is temporary. Trust your heart, not your stories or the programmed voices in your head. Choose which one you will allow to be your master: your Divinity and Higher Self, or the voice of the masses. Figure out the difference. Your life is waiting.

# Part Two
*Everybody Changes*

## Chapter 7

# You're Not the Person I Married

There are changes that people go through over the years that make them different than the person you said "I do" to. Some of those changes may be deal-breakers for you, and that doesn't make you a bad person. It makes you, YOU. Everything in life changes—to deny that is to deny life itself. So if those changes don't continue to work for you, you have the right to make a new choice as well.

The entire institution of marriage deserves a massive overhaul, and we can start with the wedding vows. Let's consider this vow, *"In the name of God, I, _____, take you,_____, to be my wife/husband, to have and to hold from this day forward, for better, for worse, for richer, for poorer, in sickness and health, to love and to cherish, until we are parted by death. This is my solemn vow."* Hmmmmm...what exactly does "for better or for worse" mean? Can someone define that for me? And "until we are parted by death"?!?!? Where else do you take such a vow? Can you think of any other area of your life that you double pinky swear to do something for the *rest of your life*?

When you enter the legal or medical profession can you imagine saying, "In the name of God, I, Laurie, take you, the legal profession, to be my chosen career from this day forward, for better or worse, until death we are parted"?

Or how about with our religions? "Dear Catholic Church, I, Laurie, take you, Catholicism, to be my one and only avenue to the Divine, from this day forward, til death we are parted." Or with our best friends? "I, Laurie, promise you, Bebe, to be your bestie even when you're a whiney lil bitch for decades, talk incessantly about every dude that remotely smiled at you this week and bore me to tears every time we get on the phone, forever and ever besties til death do we part." Noooooo!

So why, oh why, do we think things should be different with a romantic partner? This person could be your rock, may light your fire, inspire and/or elevate you—or they may repulse, demean, bore or even damage you. How can we understand and accept that just about every other little thing in our lives may change, but we must take a vow *to our death,* not to ever, *ever* change this one thing called "romantic" love and marriage? Surely that can be more fickle than our chosen career path at times!

What if we made a vow to *ourSelves?* A vow that went something like this: "In the name of my Higher Self, I take you—cute, beautiful lil Laurie—in this incarnation, to progress the evolution of my Soul on Planet Earth. I pledge to follow my curiosity and pay attention to what makes my heart sing and enlivens my mind. When something feels heavy or off, I promise not to ignore it, but to take full accountability for it and either transform the situation to one that is more harmonious with my Be-ing or let it go if it is not in the highest and best interest of all involved." That's a pledge I could get behind. If more people listened to the truth of their heart and actually communicated their feelings, that would be an incredible foundation for any relationship, or society for that matter.

But we are never taught to honor ourSelves and our own hearts as much as we are programmed to care for and devote ourselves to another's. Not only are we taught that another's needs are more important than our own, but that we are also beholden to the whims of our church, government, and tribe—often at the expense of our own wishes and desires. "Self last," is the hallmark of being a decent member of society. It's unconsciously (and mistakenly) ingrained from a very young age.

Speaking of youth, most people enter the world of marriage when they are in their early 20's—and some right out of high school. Your brain is still in the process of forming until you're about 25. Your personality is still developing. Most are still very attached to their parents—their parent's religion, belief system, and often their finances. Some have never lived outside of their parents' home or run a household themselves. There is a lot of living to do in that space, a lot of self-discovery that has yet to occur.

When we are in our 20's most are still trying to be the person we think we are "supposed" to be—the person everyone expects us to be. We unconsciously believe that we need to fulfill everyone else's dreams and expectations for our lives. We do our best to behave ourselves and make everyone proud by following the script handed to us. That script may look different for different genders, cultures, and religions. It may be some variation of going to college, or getting into the family business, fulfilling some type of religious service, getting married, buying a home and having children. We believe that these are the "right" things to do, and rarely even entertain the idea of something different or ponder if those expectations are even true for us individually.

That is what comprises the blue-pill machine of our lives. Seduce people into behaving like robots, program them in their youth, and by the time they start to think for themselves it will be too late for them. They'll be enslaved with a mortgage, a thankless job, a passionless life and, perhaps a few kiddos—making it all the more challenging to break free and live a life of their own choosing.

Free people who can discern the whispers of their own hearts and souls are a rare breed. Free people are rebellious—and nobody wants that.

When we are in our early 20's there are so many choices we've never even been presented with, like what kind of house would I keep if it were mine? Would it be as messy as it is now if mommy weren't around to clean it? What kind of roommates do you prefer: quiet or loud, social or withdrawn, clean and tidy or is messy and unorganized OK so long as the dishes are done? Do you even know how to cook? Will you be attending church every Sunday, even if nobody is expecting you to go?

And forget about your sexual proclivities. You may have just barely started fucking. How are you supposed to know what you even like yet? If you were one of those that "saved yourself" for marriage, there's a whole new list of preferences you have yet to discover and acquire. What is it that turns you on, how do you warm up, do you need a lot of foreplay or do you want to get right to it? Missionary, doggie style or 69? Gay, straight, bi-curious, transgender? Sub, dom, or any other particular fetishes? Do you even know yet?

When you get married that young with so many unexplored opportunities and unknown preferences, do you even have a clue about who you are, what you desire, and what will make you happy? Do you think your preferences will shift over the years? Do you think your beliefs and viewpoints may be updated over time as a result of new information and life experiences?

Is marrying that young inherently bad? No. Intimate partnerships are one of the best arenas for your growth and evolution. Just realize that you will inevitably change and transform, and so will your partner and the world at large. Be prepared to grow together or grow apart—both are ok.

With all the countless opportunities for growth in our society, it's truly a miracle that anyone stays together forever—happily anyway. We've been sold some Disney-esque fantasy of the happily ever after façade. Walt Disney himself said that "Progress is impossible without change." The goal here is not to stay the same, it is to evolve and ascend. When one partner is committed to progress and the other to status quo and a don't-rock-the-boat mentality, it will almost NEVER work.

I'm guessing if you picked up this book, you are the grower, the changer, the one that's bored af, the one who wants more out of life. Am I right? If so, there may not be a simpler reason for just pulling the plug than this one—that you simply grew apart over time. Completely understandable.

If you've been the non-changer in the relationship and you are looking to heal, fix or remedy the situation and save your marriage, it's possible, but it will require some real transformation on your part. And it may be a far cry from "partnership as usual." Transformation is quite different than making a few changes. Change is like getting up at a new time each day, or choosing to work out. People make "changes" when their spouse has had enough and they're begging them not to leave. It's only done for the other and "in order" for them *not* to leave. As a result, "change" lacks true authenticity and staying power.

Transformation is forever. It's the difference between the actual ingredients in a pan of brownies and how they come out after you mix them together and bake. They are irrevocably changed. You can never extract the whole egg or the butter because it has become completely *transformed* into something brand new. A mere change can return to its former ways. Transformation requires a much deeper exploration and is something one can only do for themselves. Stick around, it may not be comfortable—taking full accountability for yourself never is.

And if you're the one committed to being the status quo-er in the relationship, and you picked this book up because you are ready to dump this person that you no longer recognize (because they are not remotely the person you married), that's ok too. You may be much happier staying in your comfort zone alone or finding a similar Muggle to status-quo with. Just know this: if your "person" has progressed to a new belief system, whether it be religious, philosophical, political, spiritual or a less conservative world view, and they are happier, there is no way in hell that they will be returning to their former selves.

As Oliver Wendell Holmes, Sr. said, "One's mind, once stretched by a new idea, never regains its original dimensions." Oh, you may be able to shame and guilt them to the point of returning, but it won't be authentic, and if it isn't authentic it will not be sustainable. Force, as a means of getting what you want, is always a short-lived solution. Sooner or later people will continually be drawn to what feels more resonant for them.

So maybe you are feeling guilty because when you got married you promised some things that may no longer be true for you. You promised to be a particular religion, you said working out would always be part of your lifestyle, you said you were a vegetarian, you thought you knew what your sexual preferences were, you thought you believed similar things about how the world works, and now... things have changed for you.

THAT'S OK! You're not a bad person. In fact, if you had not changed you would be a stagnant and stuck person, a set-in-your-ways person. It's good and wise to question your beliefs. It's healthy to listen to other points of view, and when moved, explore and do your research to determine if that new belief you were exposed to makes more sense than the one you previously held. That's called being open, being okay with not knowing everything, willing to learn and grow, not being threatened by differing opinions—that's maturity. That's wisdom.

Things happen. People change. It doesn't make them bad or wrong—they just grew. You don't call someone bad because they wanted to graduate from kindergarten. You expect them to do so. Many people now change careers after years of schooling and decades of practice, or even just a few years in their originally chosen field. Why? Does it matter? Because they changed their minds. That's why. They found something else that they *prefer*, maybe something that sets their soul on fire.

I don't believe in iron-clad arrangements, ones like "I'll stay with you forever, no matter what." Life is in constant flux, why would our relationships be any different? It's OK to not be OK with your partner's change and do something about it…like leave.

If you want to stay together, you will need to grow together. When you think you know someone, you are no longer curious about them. This begins the demise of our relationships. If you think you know how your partner feels about certain topics because they told you when you were dating—you don't know them. People's views, perspectives, opinions, and beliefs change over time, often more than once. Because of our lack of intimacy, we grow apart without even being aware that it's happening. We don't even know who we are sleeping next to each night. Until we wake up one day and there is a chasm so wide, it can't be crossed.

If you want your marriage to last, you gotta keep up. You gotta stay intrigued by and connected to your partner. If you don't, someone else will, and they will feel more seen for the truth of their current self, while you are still clinging to an older version. As a result, you will get traded in for someone who sees who they are here and now, and is more resonate with their current Self. You snooze, you lose. Fail to evolve and get left behind. Cling to your antiquated traditions blindly and stay asleep, while your partner is opening their eyes and becoming more conscious, translates to a restructuring of sorts, a.k.a. divorce.

Are you the same person you were when you got married in your 20's—or even last year? No. And you may no longer be that person your partner signed up for. Simple as that. If they're just not that into you any more, are you going to be happy guilting them into staying? If they'd clearly prefer to be somewhere else, are you going to hold them back? Is that love or is that co-dependance, addiction or fear perhaps? Does someone have to be the bad guy in every break up?

Let's consider some of the ways people change over time, how it's ok that you've changed and why it's also ok that your partner may want to leave as a result of that change, and how nobody is wrong for any of it.

## Chapter 8

# Somebody Got Fat

Oh, the fatties are going to be pissed about this one. I can hear them all shouting, "But, but, but…" Isn't it crazy how we fight for our limitations and weaknesses? "I had 5 kids," or "I'm menopausal," or "I have hormone issues," or "I have chronic fatigue, Epstein-Barr, Crohn's disease, etc." or "I have a full-time job," or "I don't have time or the money to work out, eat healthy, take care of myself," or "Obesity runs in my family," or "I have an eating disorder," or "I'm depressed," or "I'm on medication," and on and on the excuses flood.

Tough.

For every excuse you give, there are countless others with the same issues that have managed to stay fit, get fit, lose weight, and take care of themselves and heal. Your *excuse*, I don't care what it is, is just that: an excuse. It carries no weight…hahaha….but you do.

I'm sorry, were you counting on the fact that your partner made a commitment, no matter what? Get real. If you were a size 4 when you got married, and now you're a size 12, by definition, *you've changed*. And I can promise you, even *you* don't find you quite as attractive anymore.

What happened? People have kids and get back in shape—unless they're lazy. Most people work, some are on medications, and some of us have legit hormone issues. Loving ourselves (and our partners) means figuring those puzzles out. It's normal to put on 10 to even 20 lbs. between the ages of 30 and 60. It's not normal, however, to put on 30-100! There, I said it. What that says to me is that your "give-a-shit" factor went waaaaay down.

Did you think that just because you had the relationship nailed down or you're married, that they couldn't leave so it didn't matter if you let yourself go or not? You didn't think that you needed to take care of yourself anymore now that you got the guy or girl? So you got lazy. If you were single, looking for a mate, would you do that? Isn't it interesting when people get divorced they lose weight, get in shape, and cure their formerly "incurable" issues? Why is it that we want to look and feel good for strangers but could care less about our significant other?

Weight gain, like most things with your health, has an emotional beginning. When we are carrying excess weight, we are inevitably carrying excess baggage on some level. There are things we need to let go. There may be a layer of protection that we thought we needed, toxic emotions we may be harboring, or some person or thing we deserve to forgive. If you are grossly overweight, you most likely have issues and you deserve to tackle them. Our outer self is merely a reflection of our inner Self.

Some spiritual peeps and leaders want to deny all things of the flesh—they say it's the condition of your soul that matters, not your body. I'm here to tell you that's bullshit. We came to this Earth school specifically to get a BODY!! To be able to experience all of the joys (and challenges) that come with it. The condition of our bodies are a direct reflection of our thoughts, beliefs, and spirit. When our bodies aren't working properly, along with seeking medical advice, we also deserve to discover what is going on mentally and emotionally within ourselves. As we heal the way we think and attend to our emotional issues, most often our bodies correct themselves. The body never lies. It's your ally. Treat it with respect.

Don't you want your partner to enthusiastically choose into you each day? For them to wake up and be happy you are the one that is lying beside them and the first thing they see? Or are you just of the mind that they have to stick around for better or for worse—no matter how pathetic you allow yourself to get? "He made a vow," she says stomping her feet, hands on disappearing waist. "You should still love me even though I've gained a few pounds." They may love you, but it doesn't mean they're still attracted to you or desire you. Expecting that to be the case is called taking someone for granted. It sucks.

Remember that Vow to Self we discussed in the last chapter? The one where you take full accountability to restore things to harmony when something is *off*. Wouldn't the condition of your body apply to this Vow to Self? If you're not committed enough to yourSelf to manage this aspect of your life and take care of *you* in this way, how can you expect anyone else to do so?

As previously stated, don't go changing "in order to" please anybody else—it will never last. If you've let yourSelf go, first ask yourSelf some questions. What's going on? Where have you not been taking care of you and why? Listen to all of your excuses with compassion, then let them go. If you are truly ready to love yourself enough into your own physical and emotional well-being, let the transformation to being fit, healthy, and strong begin.

And while we are on the topic of losing weight for another, let's not kid ourselves that we are doing anyone any favors with the sympathy weight gain either. Spending more time in the buffet line is not a very well-thought-out plan to demonstrate your love. Nobody thinks it's cute that you both have decided to "grow" together, like having matching pajamas or something. And if you're just letting yourself go because your partner is—ewww. Have some self-respect. How about helping them get fit instead of joining the fattie ranks. That says I love you much more.

In a more conscious relationship, I not only take care of myself for me, first and foremost, but I am also aware that I made a commitment to join my life with another's. My not taking care of myself physically, mentally, emotionally, and spiritually will inevitably create undue stress and burden on my beloved. Obesity is a contributing factor to many diseases and makes every other condition worse. If I become incapacitated because of my weight, my betrothed will be expected to take care of me. Not only that, but my weight may inhibit any number of other activities, like something as simple as going on walks, hikes or playing with the kids. When I take care of me, I am showing my partner that I also love them.

If you've gained a lot of weight, or have completely abandoned healthy practices, just fix it. Everyone can eat better than you currently are, regardless of your budget. Everybody can inject more movement into their day. Everybody can take a good long look at the emotional issues causing their physical ones and decide to do something about it. There is access to free information everywhere to manage all of the above. If you're not taking advantage of these things, you are the only one to blame for it. If you are doing nothing to better your condition, don't whine when your mate finds a fitter, more fun version to hang with and leaves your fat ass.

And what about sex, how does weight gain play a role there? For one, the weight-gainer is most likely going to be self-conscious, their self-esteem may plummet and neither of those happen to be good for the libido. So now you might avoid sex. Or, on the flip side, maybe you're more of the entitled type and you think it's still your partner's duty to fuck you no matter how much weight you gain or how unattractive you allow yourself to become. Good luck with that long-term. Nobody wants to fuck a fattie.

When I say "fattie," I don't mean someone that's 5 or even 20 lbs. overweight. Nice curves are sexy on a woman—and some women prefer a little bit of a "dad bod." Women's weight especially can fluctuate 5-10 lbs. in the same month. That's called variety for your mate. No, I'm talking 30-

100 lbs. Think rolls…and rolls. Like, "Dude, where's your dick?" If you can't see it because your gut hangs down that far in front of it…c'mon, man. That's not ok.

When I say "fattie," I'm also talking about an attitude of someone that has fully embraced a lifestyle that has zero concerns with eating healthy, being active, and taking care of themselves. Someone that has given up on the idea of their body ever looking or behaving any differently. If you have completely given up on yourself, what makes you think your partner won't as well?

If you are the one that has to deal with your overweight partner, understandably you may be the one avoiding sex. You will be shamed if you admit that you are no longer attracted to your spouse, and made to feel like a bad person if you are no longer interested in sex with them. If you let this be known, you will be the bad guy/gal. You will be reminded that you made a commitment for better or for worse…til DEATH…not until obesity. The shame will be projected onto *you* for being shallow—not them for being lazy. Be prepared.

It's one thing to be patient and supportive when your partner is making an honest effort—or just had a baby, is recovering from an illness, etc. I am all for compassion, I promise. It's another thing all together when your partner has just given up, continues to eat shit food and makes no attempt to exercise. When this has gone on for years, I'm sorry—it's unacceptable. Time for an honest chat.

Why would anyone want to be intimate or have sex with someone who is so blatantly displaying such a lack of self-love and respect? When you know you are taking care of yourself the best you can, that confidence and Self-love shines through. That's fucking sexy, regardless of your body type.

~ ~ ~

And speaking of sex…

Chapter 9

# Somebody's Libido Changed

*Perhaps it's appropriate for the sex chapter to begin with a confession:*

*So just as I'm about to be done with this book, my editor says, "Ya know, your sex chapter is so...well...textbook. It's the only chapter you wrote in the passive voice...it doesn't even sound like you."*

*Ughhhh, I reply. So we discuss, we edit, we come up some things to "spice it up" and I add a few things, but it still feels "blah."*

*Soooo allow me to just out myself here. Pondering all of this I realized, with assistance, that being embodied, being sensual and sexual...well...it's the "hole in my game." And that's ok. I've spent my entire life, and countless previous lifetimes, in my upper three chakras...in my head, consulting with the Gods, reaching for higher knowledge and wisdom...with barely a thought given to sex. Not like I haven't been in relationships and had plenty of it, but it has never been my driving force, and nothing I ever think about until I'm actually making out with my partner.*

*Over the past 15 years I've learned to connect with my heart and my feelings, which allowed me to let go of my Ice Queen persona and become truly vulnerable and intimate. Yet still...I must confess that my sensual side is the frontier I've yet to really do the deep dive in...so at the risk of delaying the publishing and waiting another 10 years to return and rewrite this chapter—with the depth of experience that I've written others—I ask for your understanding with the lack of pizzaz here.*

*Though I believe whole-heartedly in what I've written, admittedly, it's a little lacking. I'm not good at "faking it" so instead of having somebody else re-write it for me, it just is what it is. I'm sorry. Please forgive me. Thank you. I love you. I too, am on a journey to elevate my own FQ.*

Sex...it's a big deal. Our sexuality is a major part our well-being, self-expression, and connection to our creativity. Issues in this area affect us at a core level. To ignore this aspect of your relationship is like sticking your head in the sand and just crossing your fingers that everything will turn out OK. Good luck with that.

Unless mutually agreed upon, most relationships cannot survive without their being some kind of satisfactory sex life for *both* partners. And "satisfactory" doesn't really cut it either.

"Hey Joe, how's your sex life?"

"Oh...it's satisfactory. Thanks for asking, Bill" Ewww.

That speaks volumes. Who wants a "satisfactory" sex life? The only people that would possibly dream of a satisfactory sex life are those of you that have *no* sex life at all! I think we can safely say that a "satisfactory" sex-life is nobody's wet dream.

And if you married young, or had little to no sexual experience prior, how do you even know what a satisfactory sex life is? For some, their wedding night is the first time they've *ever* had sex. Some religious folks get married just so they *can* have sex for the first time (at least guilt-free sex). This dichotomy alone—that in one moment sex was bad and one of the worst sins one could commit to all of a sudden on your wedding night it's not just okay, but actively encouraged and expected—can be difficult to reconcile.

How does one go from Victorian-era prude to sex kitten overnight—or even knowing how to feel "sexy"? It can be a tough chasm to cross. Some never do. The early programming of sex being dirty, shameful, sinful, and for procreation only isn't easily let go of just because you said "I do" in your house of worship.

Unfortunately, in our schooling and at home, when it comes to sex, most of us don't get more than a reproduction and anatomy lesson. When we think of sex, most simply think of intercourse. We are not taught the subtle arts of sensuality, touch, massage, foreplay or imagination. We don't realize that there are as many ways to do sex as there are people on the planet.

And while straight-forward communication with our partner's may be challenging, communication about sex is rare AF. Why? Because it's terrifying to most people. How do you start talking about something you were never supposed to talk about? Imagine if you wanted to explore something that seemed a little "unusual" or if your preferences had shifted, or you developed a lil fetish—that conversation may never happen. Without on-going communication, and especially given a limited knowledge in this area, we are doomed to failure.

Typically when you marry young, or start having sex, nobody's handing you a "how-to-sex" book beforehand. You're thrown into the bridal chamber with your beloved, and are expected to get naked and "do it." It's kind of barbaric when you think about it. The expectations are high, yet we rarely buy the books, take a class, go to a workshop or talk to a sex therapist about it—even years or decades later. "You should just know how to do sex, right?." And what if somebody sees you buying that book, or you know somebody in the sex class?! Horrors!!

Couples like this tend to get in ruts. "Well this seems to work for her, so I'll just keep doing it." Meanwhile, "it" hasn't been working for some time now, but she doesn't have the guts to tell him. Wouldn't want to hurt anybody's ego, or worse, have them tell you what *you're* doing that doesn't work for them either. Just keep biting that tongue.

It's not surprising that sex (or lack thereof) is one of the leading causes of divorce. We can't even talk about it. It's easier for some to just walk away and pray the next partner they meet will just be more "compatible" And for some, "compatible" may simply mean that they don't want sex *as often* as their current partner does.

Our sex issues may not be as simple as they seems on the surface—two people having a difference in their libido levels. It may appear that way because the way you've been doing "it," is no longer appealing to one of you. So somebody keeps saying no…or avoiding sex all together.

As a result, you may end up thinking that sex is just over-rated or not all it's cracked up to be, so you slowly start shutting it down. You have a myriad of excuses, none of which are real—from caring for the kids, a headache, deadlines, your tired, etc. When the real truth is, whether you're conscious of it or not, you're dying inside from what feels like a lack of love and attention.

Sex is very intimate. If I don't feel seen by you, if we have piles of things we can't even discuss, if I feel like you don't care about my needs, be they sexual, physical, financial, emotional or otherwise—or if my dog just died—and you want me to "perform" for you, which typically equates to having intercourse and you getting off…

Well…"not tonight honey."

And this goes on until a sexless life is just the way it is. Most either expect their partner to just deal with it or they blindly believe their partner must not be interested either. Neither makes an advance thinking the other has no interest. Or one is complaining about the lack, which puts pressure on the other and the whole situation just becomes worse.

If this is the case, it doesn't necessarily mean that one of you is a sex fiend and the other frigid just because of the *amount* of sex you seem to desire. Don't try to make each other wrong for this. There is always so much more going on here. We all have different needs. Sex is a fundamental part of life and one that both of you deserve to enjoy.

For some, physical intimacy is the way they express and feel loved. When the other partner is always avoiding or saying no to sexual intimacy, feelings of rejection and abandonment can arise. Feelings of inadequacy get planted on a deep level and resentments may grow.

When couples ignore this aspect of their relationship and marginalize the sexual needs of the other, it never bodes well. For example, if it's your hubby's desire for you to give him the occasional blow job and you can't bring yourself to do that—ever—and even the thought of it disgusts you, don't be surprised if he finds somebody that will. Many of my male clients have shared that they routinely perform oral sex on their wives but yet it is rarely—if ever—reciprocated. Not cool ladies. That's called entitlement, and it's never attractive.

To love a man is to worship his cock. Yes, I just said that. I'm going to speak in generalities right now, so chill. I have found that men seem to be much better at worshipping their woman's body—devouring us whether we're on our moon or not, enjoying the extra pounds that come and go, exploring every inch of us and just being present with our ever-changing bodies. Women, however, seem to be much more particular—and often squeamish. Disgusted with the slightest "man smells," putting their mouth on his cock, or licking his balls. "Save that for the prostitutes," wives say. What some women don't understand is that being repulsed by your man in this way feels like rejection to him. Yes, it works both ways ladies.

Can it just be ok that you don't want to do some of these things? Sure. Like I mentioned previously, we all have our preferences. I think it's important to at least *try* the things your partner would like before you judge and make a decision. If it's not for you, it's not for you. I like to say, "I'll try anything three times…"

And newsflash: when it comes to sex, intercourse alone is not the be all end all. Sure it may have been initially…when you were both young and the hormones were raging but as we mature, so do our tastes. Strawberry Boone's Farm may have been great when you were underage and sneaking booze in high school, but it's not going to cut it a few short years later.

Perhaps your partner isn't interested in sex because they don't feel an intimate connection with you anymore outside of the bedroom. Maybe you rarely make quality time for them, yet you want them to be ready at a moment's notice when you need some sexy time. And if you are the one with the unquenchable libido, ask yourself what you could do long before the act. Could you clean up the house, light a few candles, maybe make dinner for a change?

Men, if you want your woman to "worship" that cock of yours, you better find out what turns *her* on and if you are meeting her emotional needs. Where are you going out of your way to serve her, ease her burdens, and make her life easier? Are you able to appreciate her body in non-sexual ways—like touch and massage? Could you take some time in the bedroom just pleasing her, without a thought about yourself on occasion?.

Do you make time to really listen to her? Do you share *your* heart and intimate feelings?

Everybody desires love and attention. How can you expand your repertoire? Make it your mission to find out together. What are you curious about? What do you want to experience? If your sexual relationship is not working for just one or both of you, it probably won't survive if something doesn't change.

Really? Is sex *really* that important? Yuh…it is. Don't be pissed at your partner if you want nothing to do with sex and he has an affair or starts looking at porn and takes care of himself. Speaking of which…

It may amuse you that I even have to mention this, but listen, if your man or woman feels the need to pleasure themselves, that's *their* business. Good grief. Micro-manage much? Some religious people I know (remember, I live in Utah) can't even tell each other about it without shame, accusations, guilt, and desperate calls to their mother to find out what to do? I say this because the second you have to start hiding things from each other sexually, you've got problems.

Beyond your masturbation confession, are you able to share with your partner what fantasy you had running through your mind while you were taking care of yourself? What it was that turned you on? Is that something you can share with each other? Because it can be really hot when you do.

But what if your partner was actually looking at porn, not just fantasizing? Oh my! Have you ever discussed it? Do you care if they do? Would you like to look at it with them? And I get that a "porn addiction" is an entirely different thing. When a man or woman prefers the computer screen to the real thing, then "Houston, we've got a problem." But that's not what I'm talking about here.

So, in a normal situation, here is what won't work: your husband admitting that he occasionally looks at porn and likes to masturbate and you going into anaphylactic shock over the horror of it. Maybe you caught him looking at porn, maybe you caught him touching his wee, maybe you've heard your old all-male church leaders tell you how angry it makes Jesus when boys do that, and now it's all happening right before your virgin eyes. My advice: Don't panic. Calm the fuck down.

Oral sex. Vanilla Sex. Kinky sex. Fetishes. Tantra. Karma Sutra. Porn. Masturbation.. Whether all of it is on the table or none of it is or some combination of it, if you don't talk about it openly and without a knee-jerk, religious or puritanical judgment spasm, how can you know you're on the same page? And how can you know you're still on the same page even two months from now, three years from now, after the first kid, after the last kid, after menopause, etc. The point is you likely don't even know where your partner is on any of these sexual proclivities if you don't talk about it. Hence, you can't even say if you'd be willing to participate in their desired level of frequency and/or kinkiness.

I cannot stress enough just how important it is to stay current with your partner sexually. To check in from time to time—or every time. It's important that your partner can come to you with a new sexual fantasy, new position, or experience they would like to have and know that it won't be immediately shot down. For your other to know that it's OK to be adventurous and to explore together. Do you have that kind of communication? Are there sexual topics or activities that one of you has made taboo? Maybe you need to revisit those. I'm not saying you need to engage in them, but at least be able to hear your partner out, see what it is that turns them on about that particular thing, and how you might fulfill that fantasy in a way that's more palatable and exciting for both of you.

So, before you start complaining about what she won't do that you want, and what he tries to do that you hate, or somebody's libido changing...start by examining whether *you* would want to fuck you, if you were you. Ask yourSelf, "Am I fuckable?" Would I want to fuck me? Be honest with yourself. If *you* met you on the street—would you raise an eyebrow or keep walking? Do you feel like you "got it going on"? Do you feel sensual? Do you like your body? Just know that if you're not that into you, no one else is going to be either.

## Up Your FQ

But what if…you upped your FQ? Huh? Well, you've heard of IQ as a measure of your intelligence. And most of you have heard of EQ or emotional intelligence, those who display empathy, think before they speak, are helpful yet can also handle criticism, and forgive and forget. Well, I think there deserves to be an FQ—a Fuckable Quotient.

What's your FQ/Fuckable Quotient? Here are some things that could go into the FQ metric: Are you attractive, or have you completely let yourself go? Are you playful, or very serious? Are you comfortable or at least willing to explore things you've never done, or are you a status-quo, don't-rock-the-boat type all the way? How sensual are you? How intimate are you willing to be?

What is your sexual energy like? Sensual and erotic? Playful and fun? Sexy and alluring? Kinky and adventuring? Warm and inviting? Are you able to move through and play with more than one of these energies, or is it one frequency for you at all times?

Like the software of a computer, a strong FQ requires regular updates and upgrades. Be willing to learn more about yourself, your partner, and sex in general.

Respect is also HUGE in connection with our Fuckable Quotient. Do you respect you? Are you proud of yourSelf? I know that for mySelf, if I lose respect for my man, I have zero desire to be intimate with him. So conversely, the opposite would be true as well. If I'd gained a lot of weight, stopped being creative and productive (in other words doing the things that make me feel alive), I would no longer respect mySelf, and I probably wouldn't feel like fucking *anybody*. I'd be down on myself—low vibe. Who wants to hang with that? That respect loop is super important.

For virtually everyone, regardless of when you started having sex, your marriage signifies that this is the last person you may ever have sex with again…and then you die. So…it helps to communicate your evolving needs, desires and fantasies with your partner. It helps to be able to stretch your comfort zone, to be flexible, adventurous, and nurturing. The best aphrodisiac is to be accountable for yourself and your own happiness, and to not project your bs onto someone else. When we are owning our shit, we're super sexy. When it comes to sexuality, it's all about the evolution. Evolve or die, they say…or potentially be replaced!

And lastly, if you truly are on purpose and on fire about your mission, you know why you are here, and you're excited to go change the world, that's a beautiful, high frequency. That frequency deserves to be matched with similar fire, passion, and creativity. If all your attempts to create a win-win in the "sex and intimacy department" of your marriage fall short, and you're clear sex with your current partner will *never* be what you deeply, authentically need and desire, then just get a fucking divorce already. Sex is way too important to your well-being and vitality.

Whom you share your sacred sexuality with makes an enormous difference in the overall quality of your life. If you're excited about your life, but not about your partner, it might just be time to exit stage left.

*Chapter 10*

# Somebody's Core Beliefs Changed

What do I mean by core beliefs? It's different for everyone—but for most, it's foundational. Like your religion and that of your family. For many, core beliefs may include politics, education, culture, lifestyle, sexual mores, and even diet. Some humans choose their mates solely on the basis of some shared beliefs they have regarding how they should live, what's valuable to them, what they believe to be true, and what isn't.

When there has been a significant shift in core beliefs for one partner and not the other, there is often an upset in the equilibrium where previously there'd been a commonly held point of connection. Perhaps you were both liberals in college, met at the Young Dems Club, and have been quite politically active throughout your married life. Now one of you has become disenchanted with the more extreme leftist ways of censorship, medical tyranny, and government control that seem to border on Communism. They've seen the "error of their ways," and are finding more resonance with conservative principles of free speech, less government reach, and economic freedom.

Maybe it's your religion that's extremely important to you and you made sure to marry someone that felt the same level of devotion to that particular sect or religion. Maybe you believe that the only way to heaven is to return together with your partner, intact as a family unit. Perhaps your entire identity and daily life is built around it, from prayers, sadhana, ritual, celebrations, tithing, weekly gatherings, Bible studies, church friends, callings, confession, fasting, yearly pilgrimages, holy days, etc. It may be the rock and foundation that your whole world is built around.

One day your beloved tells you they no longer believe in said religion. They've been struggling, done a bunch of research, and now they're interested in another spiritual tradition, or none at all. They inform you they will no longer be participating in their previous rituals or attending your particular place of worship.

Maybe it's simpler than that and your partner just decided they want to be vegetarian—no more burgers, summer steaks on the grill, or hunting weekends with the boys. While you were brought up in a home full of carnivores, and are used to eating meat at every meal. Perhaps after years of pledging yourselves to the swinger "lifestyle"—enjoying more than the occasional threesome and yearly lifestyle Booze Cruises in the Caribbean—your partner just informed you that is no longer "a thing" for them. They want to join the ranks of the monogamous—with you—and *only* you! Wait, what?!?

Well…ok then. Looks like you have some choices to make. If your identity is truly wrapped around your politics, religion, lifestyle, etc., and you believe your way is the *only* way, then do everyone a favor and set your partner free. You will never be happy. You will be ashamed of your partner in your place of worship, political groups, family, social media, etc., and in yourself for "allowing" them to stray in such a way. You will most likely make their life a living hell. It will result in lots of guilting, shaming, and make wrong. Heaps of fun for all involved.

Only you can decide what is more important to you: Your religion, politics, lifestyle—or your partner. Is it more important to you that you are married to this *particular* spouse, or just *any* spouse that's a devoted member of your religion, party or belief system of choice? When identity is tied to our beliefs, we can feel threatened and make knee-jerk reactions out of fear.

If, however, you have not tied your identity to any of these ideologies, and they just happen to be your preference, you may be able to respect your partner's exploration. If you can honestly support them in their change of heart, not make them wrong, and allow them the space needed, there may be hope. If you can actually be curious about their shift, ask them questions, and go down that rabbit hole with them, it could actually add a new dimension to your relationship.

If you are the open and adventurous type, this can also be viewed as an opportunity to re-evaluate your own beliefs. You can see whether you chose into them blindly in the first place due to birth and its simply become comfortable for you, or if you have honestly done the work necessary to form your own opinion and consciously chosen practice. Maybe you'll discover that said belief, practice or party is no longer a match for you either and you may want to join your mate, or go down an entirely new path.

You get to decide where you fit on that spectrum. Be honest with yourself.

If you are the one that has shifted beliefs, how important are your *new* beliefs? Do you desire a partner willing to go down that path with you, or are you ok going it alone? If your current partner has no tolerance for your shift, is that something you can deal with? Are you able to find a space you can arrive at together and have some crossover? Is it ok with both of you if this particular area of your life just becomes completely separate?

I understand that these can be big issues and that individuals often have strong feelings and opinions surrounding these ideologies. If you can't accept the new change without contempt, whining, shaming, and/or complaining, then do everyone a favor and GAFDA.

Remember: You're never wrong for changing your mind, or wanting what you want. That's just evolution. People change. We grow. We acquire new information that leads to new thoughts and beliefs. Those new beliefs lead to new actions and ways of being that feel more suitable and resonant with our new growth. Neither side is wrong for staying in their beliefs or making a shift…it's just what is now. A simple, "We're here now…now what?" will suffice.

At higher levels of consciousness, both parties comprehend that they are not defined by their positions, possessions, beliefs, practices or relationships, etc. At lower levels, that is not so clear. They "are" their church, their beliefs, their stuff, their proclivities, their relationship style, and their opinions. Even you, their partner, are part of how they define themselves. They don't know who they are without all of those "identifiers." So when you make a change to one of their core identifiers, their whole world may feel unstable. If you're rooted in these beliefs, all this stuff matters. When loyalty to an institution or belief is above the loyalty in your heart for your partner, change or misery is inevitable.

At levels of consciousness above 200, life becomes clearer—and less petty. You love your partner for who they are—their essence. You don't define them by their position, prestige in the world, bank account or who they know. If they decide to change their religious affiliation, political party or lifestyle proclivities, you're able to roll with that with curiosity for their choices and mutual respect for each other's growth and transformation. It doesn't have to be a deal breaker.

However, if you are defined by the fact that you are a card-carrying Mormon, Muslim, Jew, Catholic, Democrat, Republican, Libertarian, Carnivore, Vegan, etc., and your partner has chosen out, well…it just may feel like the sky is falling for you. Instead of making your partner's future a living hell, it may be best just to release them with gratitude for the years you've spent of like mind. Just be honest with yourself and your partner and save yourself years of heartache. Deal with it…or don't.

## Chapter 11

# The Spark is Gone

"But the spark is gone," you declare in your whiney, powerless little voice. Get out of jail free card? I should get a divorce, right? No! Slow your roll. When a client—or anyone—says that to me, I will always turn that back to them. How's *your* spark? When did *your* spark go out?

What do I mean by "spark"? I mean that twinkle in your eye, that excited-to-wake-up-each-morning-and-do-*your*-life spark. By spark, I mean you're filled with vitality, fresh ideas, and joy to be alive.

In a relationship, that "spark" I'm talking about is not the same as sex—but without it, sex will be next to non-existent, or worse, the kind of duty-bound sex where you (or your partner) participate, but only as a means of getting off.

In a vibrant partnership, that spark looks like genuine joy waking up next to your person, a mischievous look from your partner from across a crowded room, a giddy feeling at the thought of them returning home after a long trip, pride in your partner's accomplishments, mutually shared goals, being flirty with each other for no reason, and a true concern for your partner's well-being and happiness.

The "spark" looks like a lot of beautiful things. If you've got it, you know it. If you don't, most pretend to be unclear about it. I had a client once that was trying to revive his marriage. He'd told me that his wife had been sleeping 12-16 hours a day since they got married. Yawn. He'd done everything in his power to bring back that spark. They'd done years of counseling, both individually and as a couple. He'd talked to his church leaders and friends for advice, kept having sex the way she wanted it, and couldn't figure out what was missing.

He had a good job and was a great provider for his family. To prove his loyalty he allowed her to track his phone at all times, and even deleted all of his female friends from Facebook at her request. This guy did all of the family laundry and the majority of the child care—making sure she also had at least one night a week for a girl's night. He even bought her a new SUV as a last ditch effort to generate the "spark" in her, to no avail. (You will recognize this archetype in the chapters ahead.)

I finally confronted him about it and asked point blank if *he* was actually in love with her, he paused, painstakingly long, then replied, "You know, we're really good friends." Hmmmmm…really good friends, eh?

"Are you really? If you could choose to hang out with anybody in your life for a few hours, would it be her," I asked.

"Well…no," his answer seemed to surprise even himself.

"So…it appears that maybe you too have lost the spark here," I questioned. (Perhaps, acts of service won't necessarily do the trick?)

There's a lot more going on here than a simple he said, she said. If your spark is gone—anywhere in your life—you have only yourSelf to blame. Anytime you are looking outside of yourself for the spark, you're looking in the wrong place. It never was, nor will it ever be, your spouse's job to make you happy or spark your interest. That's on you.

If I make only one point in this book it is this: if you have an issue of any kind, the first place you deserve to inquire is within YOURSELF. Period. The end.

In cases like this, I almost always (unless it's an abusive situation) recommend people slow down and start observing what is really going on. During that time, I have them work on themselves from *within* the relationship. Make sure they are doing their own Self-care and Self-discovery, and being fully accountable for how the relationship has been playing out. Where have they lost their spark? What is it that really lights them up? Are they doing and being all they desire to do and be? Are they living their best life? Do their dreams, goals, and the future they envision feel more possible with their current partner, or super heavy and less likely to ever occur with partner in tow?

I encourage people to stay in their marriage until they rediscover themselves and their own spark. If you choose to leave before then, you will create the same haze elsewhere. If you discover your truth later, you may find that *you* were the real problem and wish you had another chance. When you do your own work and have more clarity about who's been buried under a sea of people-pleasing and what is truly important to you, then…have a look around (with new eyes). Does the current dynamic fit with your more authentic version of yourself? And now that you are being more of the truth of you, how is the new you being received on the other side?

However that looks, it's time for a real heart-to-heart convo with your significant other to share your findings and see how they are feeling as well. You deserve to know where each other stands emotionally, spiritually, and physically. Burying your head in the sand may seem more comfortable than having the actual conversation, but you may end up finding yourself broadsided with divorce papers. Pretending all is well when it isn't may lead to all sorts of less than desirable outcomes: your partner seeking connection elsewhere, affairs, deception, and risking a life of quiet desperation while you suffer a slow death.

Instead, be brave, courageous, and compassionate. Time to get creative, responsible and actually CREATE the life you most desire. It's time for new alternatives to the old knock-down-drag-out divorce. New ways of uncoupling that don't involve the scorched earth, win-at-all-costs, attorney-driven divorces that ruin what could have been a mutually successful, consciously-created new entity. And by "new entity," I believe there are a lot more options than either to keep doing what you're doing or GAFDA.

One option may be that if you and your partner decide that neither of you care about the physical, sensual or romantic aspect, but still want to stay together—all good. It will be imperative though to keep an open dialogue as to whether that changes at any point for one or both of you. We are all allowed to change our minds. If and when that happens, you may want to see if there is a way to rekindle that flame together. If only one of you is interested in sex, you still have options. Would separate bedrooms be preferred or do you still like the comfort of sleeping next to each other? Are new partners allowed and to what extent? Will this be able to function as an open marriage? Will there be total transparency, or will there be a don't ask, don't tell policy?

What are the rules of this new space? Although some of these questions may feel unthinkable, it's all about being transparent and creating a new arrangement that you can both be happy with. If you both are able to maintain a positive energy moving forward together on new, more realistic and authentic terms—good for you! It may not be for everyone, but if you still love your family dynamic and enjoy being roommates, power to you.

There could be a lot of things that provide the "spark" in the dynamic. Maybe it's the kiddos that really light you up, and although your marriage may be less than ideal, it may be perfect for the next few years. If it's the lifestyle and your upscale neighborhood that ignites your flame, just be honest about it...it will work, until it doesn't. If you actually value materialism over connection, this really isn't the book for you. But hey...if together you can create a win-win where nobody feels compromised and you are free to be your unabashed Self—maintaining your own spark—by all means, work it out...at least for a time.

If, however, you continue to feel diminished, stifled, and/or contracted, GAFDA. If it's one-sided, there's bound to be resentment, contempt or mere tolerance on the other side. If that's the case, it will be best for both parties to separate. The one holding the negative emotions will be hurting themselves as well as the other, and the one to whom the negativity is directed, well...that just feels shitty. Why would you want to stay anywhere you're treated poorly? Raise your vibe and GAFDA.

Only the two of you can know what's best for your family. All I'm encouraging is total honesty and transparency about your needs, feelings, and desires. A new arrangement, made together, will always be preferable to deceit, deception, gaslighting, and manipulation. The two of you have the power to create exactly what will work for both of you!

Whatever you choose, continual open dialogue, heart-felt communication, and alignment to a shared goal is most preferred. This allows you to stay in the practice of consciously creating the relationship you most desire, a relationship in which both parties are able to sustain their own spark for life, and maintain a positive energy moving forward on more realistic and authentic terms.

# Part Three
*The Seven Deadly Archetypes*

## Chapter 12

# When the Dynamic Changes

Sometimes we enter into a relationship with a particular dynamic in place from the get-go, like being a Rescuer or the Rescued. More often, particular dynamics don't fully emerge until we "settle in" to a certain rhythm as a result of familiarity with each other—when one feels comfortable enough for their true colors to shine forth. If negative behavior continually goes unchecked, previously disguised narcissistic, controlling, entitled, and self-righteous tendencies feel free to rear their most heinous heads.

Other dynamics develop as a result of circumstances—like a betrayal of trust, falling out of love, boredom or the give-a-shit factor plummeting for some reason. Most of these dynamics clearly display an imbalance of power where one of the partners may feel like they clearly have the upper hand and there is no fear of loss on their part.

Although the results of such dynamics can be devastating and detrimental to the well-being of both partners, many couples will passively choose to remain in, accept, and resign themselves to these demeaning states for years and even decades. It can be akin to Stockholm Syndrome, where one partner begins to sympathize with their captor and almost believes they are deserving of such bad treatment or that the other just can't help it.

Please pay attention to the archetypes in the following chapters. If you are taking the brunt of one or more of these abusive ways, and have been for longer than you care to tally, you deserve to GAFDA. Your partner is a beast and you are a fool for putting up with it for another moment. If you really have trouble seeing it, I suggest you read these with a good friend, sibling or even an adult child and ask them if they see you and your spouse playing any of these roles.

All of the archetypes to follow—Rescuers, Dream Thieves, Punishers, Tolerators, Bullies, Control Freaks, Care Takers and the Chronically Ill— are all driven by a lower level of consciousness, mainly Pride, Shame, Anger, Apathy, Fear, and Guilt, respectively. For many of these blue-pill peeps, they are completely unconscious of their unconscionable behavior. If not *entirely* unconscious, they simply believe their other half *deserves* the exact treatment they are doling out for whatever reasons they've made up, and they feel completely justified in behaving in such a despicable manner.

If you have been accepting this poor behavior, most likely your consciousness level has not been any higher. You've most likely been riddled with your own shame, guilt, apathy, grief, and fear and have felt deserving of their abuse due to your own lack of self-worth. If you've picked up this book, that tells me that you are starting to wake up to the hell in which you have been living. If so, you've probably been raising your own consciousness and Self-worth, and may be looking for the courage to GTFO and GAFDA. Enough is enough, already.

If you need permission to GTFO, you'll find it as you read the shocking truth about your partner in the chapters that follow. This is in no way about pointing the finger of blame in anyone else's direction. We all create, by way of acceptance and expectation, how we allow ourselves to be treated by others.

My hope is that you will first be angry AF, then ashamed of yourself for putting up with this bullshit. Then…and I know this is a bit of a leap, but…I hope you will not only find forgiveness, but gratitude in your heart for the great life lessons that will come from this experience for the rest of your life if you allow it.

If you find yourself or your partner in the chapters that follow, all is not lost. What is required is simple awareness, self-honesty, and pulling your head out of the sand it's been buried in for probably too damn long. If you're the one behaving in such unconscionable ways—cut the shit. Your partner (and all human beings) deserve better. Time to examine why you've been such a lil bitch and either apologize and clean up your act or apologize and GAFDA if you have no intention of changing your shitty ways.

More than likely, you may be the one that is being treated poorly. Remember, no one else is to blame for behavior you have submitted to and accepted. Sometimes a stern conversation letting your little tyrant know you're done and will be on your way out if they don't shape up may just do the trick. You may want to suggest working with a therapist or coach if you are serious about working things out.

However, if you've already made repeated threats and requests to no avail, you may want to ask yourself what's still in it for you and why you're still hanging around. Examine your heart. If your son or daughter were being treated this way, what would you tell them? Love yourself as much, and make the best choice for you and your physical, mental, emotional, and spiritual well-being.

## Chapter 13

# The Rescuer

Let's begin with the premise that none of us are perfect and that there are times when we all deserve a little extra assistance. Maybe we are feeling down emotionally, perhaps we lost a job or someone we love, or we could use a little financial assistance to get through a rough patch. It happens to the best of us, and in those times it really feels good to have a partner that has your back. This is a two-way street and it's called "support" and being a good partner and a decent human. "We get by with a lil help from our friends," remember. But that's not what we're talking about here.

While most of these upcoming archetypes evolve later on in a relationship, for the Rescuers this is often how they enter. You could call them opportunists—but they hide it so well under their guise of "wanting to help." Rescuers have very low self-esteem, their survival depends on being on high alert for the needy, the victimized, and the helpless. Swooping in with their heroic deeds is often their ticket into romantic relationships.

If you're a Rescuer, your entire identity is built around you wearing that superhero cape. "Here I come to save the day!" You like being known as that guy/gal…the one who falls for the damsel in distress, marries the woman with seven children, puts her man through school or gives her jobless bf a place to live. You know the type, always coming to the rescue of those with "broken wings." In fact, most of their friends have rarely seen them in a relationship where the dynamic has been otherwise.

When this is your usual pattern, it becomes something for *you* to look at. You can lie to yourself by saying that you're just a good guy, but that's not really the whole truth. This isn't about helping them; it's about hiding you—sometimes even from yourSelf. It's a parasitic way for you to feel good about yourself. It's also a way for you to avoid your own issues and prop up your self-importance that you are desperately lacking.

As long as you're the Rescuer, you always have the upper hand. As long as you're the Rescuer, you are the "good one," and above reproach. As long as you're the Rescuer, you have the power because the other is indebted to you. You like the feeling of having the scales soooo tipped in your favor. You like being "needed," in fact, you actually prefer that your intended feels that they could never get along without you. When you put someone in the position of being dependent upon you, you don't have to worry much about them leaving you.

And there's never any need to look at the issues that may plague *you*—why would you? You're the motherfuckin' Rescuer! You're sooo busy being in someone else's lane, managing somebody else's life—there isn't time. And that's good. Because what you fear the most is that without all of your indispensable "rescuing," you would have no worth.

But what happens when your partner pulls themselves up and starts standing on their own two feet? Maybe they finished school, got their degree, and are starting to make their own money and are moving up the success ladder? Maybe they've been doing their own personal inner work, dealing with their past insecurities and healing old wounds.

Maybe they are finally starting to feel some sense of self-esteem, confidence, and courage.

Uh oh. Our lil Rescuer may feel threatened because their partner no longer feels inferior, small or needy. Thoughts of their own self-doubt may begin to creep in like: "What if I'm no longer the hero?" or "What if they don't need me anymore?" Are you going to become irrelevant to them? Will they still want you around?

This may be challenging to your ego, for it fears deflation by negation. Your fear of becoming irrelevant may overcome you. You may conclude that you prefer the savior role and that if your services are no longer necessary, your work may be done here. You may need to go find another damsel in distress or a struggling artist so you can assume your position of superiority and ease the overwhelming fears of inadequacy flooding your consciousness.

This is a self-esteem issue, covered up by your false sense of pride for being such a hero. And the payoff is pretty big for you, at least you think it is. You think that "saving" your partners has you looking like the Good Samaritan to outsiders. It doesn't.

What it screams is that you don't love yourself, and will allow yourself to be taken advantage of for a crumb of love. It says that in order for you to feel worth, you have got to have someone to need *you*, to be dependent upon *you*. Someone that couldn't live without all that you do for them.

This creates a total imbalance of power. And when the broken wing is healed, they actually feel bad for using you and they can no longer stand to stay. If the broken-winger does some true healing and conjures up some real self-love—and you have yet to do so—they will have no respect for you. Their "neediness" that you labeled "love" may no longer exist.

Again, there isn't a problem with assisting your mate, and sharing roles and burdens. But it deserves to come from a healthy and whole place, not an "in order to" place. What do I mean by "in order to"? If you are doing something "in order to" be the hero, "in order to" look good, "in order to" make someone love or desire you, "in order to" not feel inferior, "in order to"…you get the idea.

This is something you will have to honestly evaluate for yourself. Ask yourself if most of your relationships ended after the broken wing was healed. Ask yourself if you begin to feel threatened when your partner starts to succeed. If you fear becoming irrelevant, your self-doubt will create the very thing you fear.

If you can't handle an equal playing field, you're probably a Muggle. Your partner is stepping out of Muggledom and it threatens you. If you're going to give your partner grief for going out in the world and being the amazing gift that they are, or if you're going to be whining bullshit like "you never have time for me anymore," or "your career/purpose/passion is more important than me," then ewwww. Take your fake cape and go. You will be nothing but a dead weight around her neck if you can't cheer her on authentically.

If you feel more threatened by their healing than you are happy for their improvement and success, you are now the one with issues—or at least your issues are finally being exposed. Welcome to *your* work, sweetie. Savior, save theySelf.

If your partner has been the Rescuer, and s/he now has nothing but criticism for you with every forward step you take, if s/he puts you down and tries to keep you small so they can feel tall, then it's time to say thank you, make restitution, and exit stage left.

If you confront your Rescuer with transparent communication and all they want to do is make you feel bad for all they've done for you (and you feel like the proverbial crab being pulled back down into the bucket), run, don't walk…time for your Rescuer to rescue themselves.

## Chapter 14

# The Dream Thieves

You have dreams, goals, and a beautiful vision for your life! Maybe you've been talking about your dreams for years—maybe even decades—but you've never pulled the trigger. Perhaps you're just waking up, surveying the scene of your life with new eyes after having taken the red pill.

"What is going on here," you wonder to yourself as you take a conscious look around at what appears to be a wasteland. "This is not my beautiful life," you sigh. Maybe it's your job/ career that feels the most inauthentic, like the biggest noose around your neck, and you've decided you are finally done with it. You're clear it doesn't light you up, it gives you no sense of purpose or fulfillment, and you're ready to go do something that holds more meaning for you.

Enter the Dream Thief.

There are actually two types of Dream Thieves. The first we'll call DT1. This Dream Thief comes from a place of fear and scarcity, paralysis, and shame. They've squelched and choked out their own dreams, probably long before you met them. More than likely, these Dream Thieves either work shitty jobs or have never finished their education. They are often hiding behind some excuse like "I'm taking care of the kids," or some sort of illness or incapacitation that conveniently doesn't allow them to work—be it physical or emotional—while you bring home all the bacon. If they actually have a job, it's one they feel safe in, they rarely ask for a raise or seek out bigger and better opportunities, and they never rock the boat. They're like scared lil mice, they prefer their small yet consistent crumbs of existence (typically the ones you provide for them) to the mere thought of a moment of discomfort that may ensue whilst you pursue your greatest passion. Your dreams terrify them.

There's another genre of Dream Thief (DT2) that simply doesn't want to be out-shined by you or have you reach your dreams before they do theirs. Though they do their best to hide it, you always feel an unsettling air of competition coming from them. For these Dream Thieves, every brilliant success of yours equates to some weird internal failure for them. It's baffling because you're partners, right? You love and adore them and want their every success. When one of you succeeds, you both do. Isn't that how it should be?

These Dream Thieves can be kind of sneaky. They like to mask themselves in several different cloaks. They call themselves, "The Voice of Reason," or "the sane one in the relationship," or "the one who has to pay the bills"—even if they're not the one to make the money. All this under the guise of your collective best interest, of course.

I once had a man in my life that could never tell me I looked pretty. This was in my early thirties when I dressed up in beautiful suits each day to go to work with 39 men in the construction industry, and I was the only woman. I got plenty of compliments at the office, but all I wanted was my husband to notice me. When I confronted him about it, his response dumbfounded me. He told me I was the most beautiful woman he'd ever met but that somehow, if he told me so, he felt less valuable. WTF?

Another man I dated started working at the same company with me. I was recognized right away and repeatedly asked by various teams to speak to their networks. He complained to me, "Why do they keep asking you to speak? Don't they know I'm the professional speaker?!" It was a company I was passionate about that represented everything I knew and loved. His DT2 jealousy and interference in my success was a total killjoy for me and was eventually what led to the demise of our relationship.

Yet again, whilst at a dinner party, a young man asked me about meditation. He knew I was a Chopra Certified Instructor and he wanted *my* advice. Now what would a good partner do in this situation? Compliment the young man for coming to the right source, or at the very least allow me to respond to the question asked of me, right? Oh, but no…my latest DT2 partner interrupted my response mid-stream, quite aggressively, to let this man know that *he* knew that contemplation was much better than meditation and that, basically, I had no idea what I was talking about.

Funny enough, on the ride to that event, it was me that was sharing with him a talk I'd found by David Hawkins on "contemplation"—and apparently, he was now the expert. It was no surprise when this same partner tried to insert himself as a 50% partner on projects I'd dedicated my life to. His jealousy of my wisdom and subject matter expertise killed any hopes of working together.

One client told me that during couple's therapy, his then-wife complained to the therapist that he was constantly reading self-improvement books. Gee…can you imagine, books on improving your business, thinking positively, being a better dad, setting new habits, and goals, etc. The therapist was confused as to why this would be a negative thing—many of her other clients would've loved it if their husband cared about self-improvement. "It's like he has a pathological need to be better. Why can't he just be happy? It's like I'm not enough for him," was her telling reply.

Diagnosis: Dream Thief. Recommendation: GAFDA. It shouldn't be a big surprise that his wife made their divorce a living hell. He went on to find the love of his life, someone that shared many of his dreams, and together they started a successful business. Go figure!

Perhaps *you* are the bloody Dream Thief and your aspiring partner is done with your life-sucking ways. Maybe they have big dreams like being an entrepreneur, running for public office, or moving out of the country. Perhaps they want to sell your big home and run off to be humanitarians building schools in third world countries, or perhaps they're a doctor and they want to leave their practice for their childhood dream of being an artist. Whatever it is, it scares you to death, you hate the idea, and you want nothing to do with it. Or perhaps you feel threatened that you may lose the lifestyle you've been accustomed to or that they may be moving ahead without you. If that's the case, check yourself. *You* are the problem.

If you're a DT1, you somehow have the mistaken notion that because they're *your* spouse and "property," you have the sole authority to squash their dreams if those dreams don't feel accommodating or safe to you. So you've been telling them for years why their dreams are far-fetched, stupid, and why they'll never work. Some of you may have also resorted to making them feel selfish for their dreams and guilting them for the very thought.

Meanwhile, DT2's are busy single-handedly undermining their partner's confidence, and consciously doing things to sabotage their spouse due to their own envious shadow-self. Sometimes it's overt and in your face, e.g. "As if you could ever accomplish that!" Other times it's more subtle, like discouraging you from getting a job at all, or making snide comments like, "You're traveling so much for work, the kids forgot what you looked like," or "All the other moms were at the school play," or "Must be nice to be paid that much money/get that award."

DT2's, how much vitality and passion do you need to drain before your partners have no ambition left? How much of your jealousy and insecurity must they endure before they are forced to choose between a peaceful relationship with you or their own dreams and success?

DT1's, how long have these poor partners of yours been acquiescing to your pleading to just stay at their high-powered, stressful, great paying gig til you can buy that house in a better neighborhood, or keep that boring job at the bank—it's stable and it makes you feel safe! So what if it's draining their life force? You deserve to be taken care of!

Just as the Rescuers operate from a place of smallness/ unworthiness and lack self-love and self-validation, the Dream Thieves suffer from a debilitating lack of self-confidence, shame, jealousy, and entitlement. To the Dream Thieves it's all about making them feel safe and/or important. Their spouse is nothing more than their slave. How many years have you already held them back? Stop it!

It's selfish and it's total bullshit.

If you have in any way attempted to hold your partner back from their dreams, you are small, weak, and pathetic. No doubt your partner has been bending over backwards for you, tamping out the flame of their own cherished desires to please you and demonstrate their love. How gross that loving you means they are relegated to half a life. You are most likely the type that is never happy or satisfied no matter what they do. And if I had to guess, you rarely show your appreciation for them living a lackluster life so that *you* can feel safe and secure. Eww.

Well, all good things must come to an end. If your big dreamers have finally told you they're moving ahead with or without you, and/or they're tired of your constant undermining of their dreams—better shape up. If you can't handle a change in the comfortable dynamic to which you've become accustomed without being a whiney lil bitch, and continuing to make your dreamer miserable, do them a favor—and go! Just go!!

You have the right to kill your own dreams, but not another's. Their life is their own. Dream Thief, no one owes you a life of servitude because they said, "I do." Oh…you have kids and a mortgage? Maybe *you* need to get a job and start making a bigger contribution to all the things that YOU desire. Maybe you get to downsize so your beloved can be more fulfilled and happier. Oh, your big house is more important? Thought so. Go find another slave, honey.

You have no right to dampen a partner's vibe that outshines or perhaps out-earns you. How sad that you can't be happy for or share in your partner's success. While your partner is being happy, full of vitality, and passion doing something they love, you choose to be a miserable ogre? These two energies are diametrically opposed. You are not a vibrational match. Go find someone else that will be easier for you to outdo and rain upon so you can feel better about yourself.

## Chapter 15

# The Punishers

Let's talk about the Punishers. This is a juicy one. Might just be my favorite to expose.

The Punishers don't just become Punishers because YOU have transgressed. For the Punishers, holding grudges and grievances is a way of life. They habitually feel slighted, powerless, and on the defense. The very existence of your misdeed is the thing that grants them power over you. (It's as if they magnetized it right to them.)

The Punishers come from a place of anger, resentment, and contempt. They feel justified and entitled to their vindictive, punitive behavior. They all have an air of self-righteousness about them. They are your judge and your juror. You fucked up, and they are never going to let you forget it. In their mind, they are completely spotless and without blame.

Maybe you feel genuine remorse about your transgression. You've confessed, said you're sorry, changed your behavior, and all you want is to be back in the good graces of your beloved. You've done everything in your power to turn things around, yet still no warmth coming from the Punisher. When will your penance ever be enough for their blood-thirsty souls?

Perhaps *you* are the Punisher and your partner has transgressed in the past. You believe this has given you license to now keep them right under your thumb, which is where you've always wanted them in the first place.

Sad truth Punishers: You don't trust anybody, least of all yourself. And this has given you a legit reason to micromanage, control, and be bossy. Apparently, nobody's ever dared have you look at yourself or how you may have, in any way, contributed to your partner's so-called transgression, huh? Fact is, you point so vehemently in their direction, you don't even see the three fingers pointing back at you. That's called projection, honey.

Somewhere in you, you may feel inadequate in some way, or like it's your fault, or that you could have been a better spouse—though you would never admit any of that. The fact is, the Punishers feel powerless. Maybe the Punisher has done something (gasp) that they're not very proud of, even if it's just being a lackluster human. Maybe if they wag their finger loud enough at their partner, no one will see their own shortcomings.

But wait, now your partner's finally fed up with jumping through your ridiculous hoops to get back into your good graces. You went overboard. You were mean-spirited and self-righteous. Now they're revolting and taking their power back. Perhaps they told you to shove your lil tracking device up your ass. Perhaps they've changed all their passwords that you forced them to give up, or they even hopped back on social media—another of your demanding no-no's. Maybe they are now going outside of their prescribed boundaries for a couple of hours at a time and not telling you where they're going! Horrors! Perhaps they've even stopped having their checks automatically deposited into *your* account!! "Unacceptable," you shout!! Too bad. To forgive is not to punish. To withhold love isn't either!

Looks like your little reign of tyranny is up, princess. Time to take your crown off and put your scepter down. Your loyal subject has woken the fuck up and has left your servitude for good—if he's got half a brain. Face it. It would drive you completely insane if he weren't forthcoming with his every whereabouts. Imagine if you couldn't tell him where he wasn't allowed to go anymore. What if he decides he's going to start going out for drinks with the guys after work? What if he wanted to go on a golf weekend with a buddy? You'd lose your shit without 24/7 surveillance. You know this rebellious attitude is never going to work for your insecure lil Muggle self.

A person who can think for themselves and finally realizes that all the shame that's been inflicted upon them is bullshit, can be a dangerous lil ball of fire. Once your dude gets a taste of freedom and gets to hang out with the big kids, where he is no longer treated and monitored like a child—good luck reigning him back in. Time to find yourself another slave to make you feel safe, sweetheart.

And here's what's really twisted: you Punishers secretly *want* your partners to transgress, because you just love wearing that crown—and having something to lord over them is the only way you know how. You inherently feel unsafe and are deeply mistrusting. You actually *expect* people to be untrustworthy, unreliable, and well…liars. You appear so shocked when this is *exactly* what you get. For you to feel remotely comfortable and safe you have to hold the power. That doesn't make for a loving relationship.

Not all Punishers are created equal. While some Punishers will use your transgression to control and monitor your daily life, other Punishers will say they'll forgive your transgression, but they never forget and they treat you accordingly. You will forever be on trial, and will most likely never experience the warmth or affection you once knew with them.

They may not behave like the little tyrants mentioned above; instead, you will just die a slow death—like a once loved, but now forgotten houseplant. You have eternally fallen out of favor with them and they can't authentically shine the light of their love in your direction. You will have to subsist on indirect sunlight and random, infrequent waterings. Don't expect things to change.

People subjected to a Punisher will normally try hard to get back into the good graces of their partner and regain the love they once had. To make up for my own transgression, I once told my husband that he didn't have to work anymore, and that I'd take on the majority of the household bills. I even told him I'd help buy a particular program for a new and exciting career he desperately desired. I foolishly thought that if he were happier in a career of his choosing, maybe he'd warm up to me again. Didn't happen. He continued to shut me out and when I saw that things would never be the same, I checked out as well.

Some Punishers like to share your wrong doings far and wide—the more people know, the saintlier they feel for putting up with your evil ass. One client's spouse, after he admitted an affair, demanded that he write an email to her entire family detailing his transgression and asking for forgiveness—from them! You read that right—*all* of them. She then insisted that he send it to *his* siblings, aging parents, and ecclesiastical leaders. She said that if he didn't, there would be no chance at their reconciliation because she "wouldn't feel safe." Wow, right? Talk about cruel and unusual punishment. Clearly, that was not about safety. It was about humiliation and control, and it was a shitty thing to do.

But what a payoff for her! The entire family will see her as the family saint/martyr, she gets to exercise total control over her partner, and can play the Punisher card at will. "Do the dishes, cheater!" "Let me track your phone, betrayer!" "Eat my pussy, bitch!" As crazy as it sounds, most comply—at least for a while. Until they realize that *nothing* will satisfy their insatiable tyrant. The Punisher will always milk their victim status for as long and far as you will let them.

~ ~ ~

Is this the way you want to live? I get you did that thing…and you still feel horrible, but how long do you have to suffer? If you've been a good boy or girl for years and your partner is still unable to get past it, that's not ok. Time to have a talk with your Punisher and ask if they will ever feel genuine affection towards you again. Don't settle for the Punisher's standard answer of, "Well, I'll always love you…but…" That is no existence.

And I'm not saying to just tell your partner to "get over it." Some things take a little time to heal. However, If you have real remorse, have apologized, and are serious about not only staying but re-creating your relationship—but your partner continues to withhold their affection and treat you like you deserve to be taught a lesson—that's not how we do. There are much more conscious ways of dealing with this.

I don't care what it is that you did, you don't deserve to suffer endless punishment, humiliation, and control. If you believe this is your lot and that no amount of good behavior is going to shift their chilly ways, it may just be time for you to GAFDA before you sin again while looking to end your drought.

## Chapter 16

# The Tolerators

This next archetype is kind of a silent, slow-death killer—the Tolerators. This one doesn't happen overnight. It's a slow, subtle burn, so it's harder to detect.

Here's how it goes: you connect with someone that was super enthusiastic about you initially. They couldn't wait to see you after a day apart, complimented you on your amazingness, was appreciative of your efforts, spoke highly of you to family and friends, and now…all of that is a distant memory. They don't acknowledge you when you walk into a room, and rarely say thank you for anything. You can't seem to do anything right in their eyes, and you can't even remember when you got a compliment or an unsolicited kiss. Sound familiar?

You're not feeling the warmth in the room, in fact it's been quite chilly. You keep trying to figure out just what it is that you did wrong, because you get the feeling they'd be happier if you just stopped breathing. Unlike the Punisher's transgressors, you've done nothing but be an adoring fan. Yet, they prefer their friends, family, co-workers, kids, and even pets to your company. They seem to rejoice when you're not around, and they treat total strangers better than you. Their eyes can be seen rolling as you discuss a topic you're passionate about with someone new. Their contempt is often palpable, though they may not say a word. Those that *really* know them, know the look well.

The Tolerators could care less about tracking your ass down. You could stay at the office all night, have a big smile on your face while texting a potential fling, or spend hours online in the evenings. They won't care if you're looking at porn, your new girlfriend or heading out on a hunting weekend with "the guys." They won't ever check your phone, and won't read your diary if you intentionally leave it open in plain sight.

They've checked out—on you. You are about as interesting to them as last week's newspaper. You know better than to interrupt their show, ask a favor or inconvenience them in anyway. Forget about asking them for sex, they have zero interest. You have become merely an unliked accessory, a necessary evil. You have been relegated to the shadows of what feels like *their* life, *their* home, and even *their* family. They leave you out constantly and when you question it, they off-handedly and innocently say, "Oh, I just thought you wouldn't be interested." Like they were saving you from some dreaded activity—when all you wanted was to be included.

Because they aren't blatantly mean, or prone to name calling, you tell yourself they're just stressed, going through a phase or that it's not so bad—you've been treated worse in other relationships. You subsist on meager crumbs of inauthentic affection from them and call it good. They may even feign appreciation when you bend over backwards for them. You're always the one bringing offerings in the form of acts of service or surprising them with gifts of their every heart's desire, like a cat dropping a mouse at the foot of its master. "Do you love me now? Now will you pet me?"

Tolerators are classic gas lighters, always pretending they are innocent or shocked if you dare question their love. The Tolerators demand your undying love and loyalty and have high expectations of you—though you dare not have such of them. The Tolerators truly believe that you are fucking lucky just to have them in your presence, and that *they* are doing *you* a huge favor by not leaving you. Unfortunately, you typically agree.

Why do these Tolerators even stick around you wonder? They must love you, right?!? Wrong. There is always a payoff for these "eye rollers." Tolerators stay because you continue to support their sorry asses in all manner of ways. And…you're just so damn nice. They have settled in to a very comfortable life with you. They've got it made, and they know it—though they'd never tell you that.

Another reason the Tolerators stick around is that some of them are highly concerned about how they'd be judged for leaving such a *good* person, i.e., you! For some of the holier Tolerators, their religion did a great job of programming them that enduring til the end was the only ticket into heaven. So endure they must. Or they stay, though they can hardly stand you, because they need you for something—like watching the kids, mowing the lawn, paying the bills, or simply kissing their ass.

The Tolerators are probably the slickest and the hardest to detect by their partners, who are incurable optimists and rarely think a bad thought about anybody. The Tolerators behave very well in front of others. They typically have good jobs/careers of their own, no trouble finding romantic partners, and have a decent standing in the community. Because of this, they make it quite known (subtly, of course) that they don't need you and they have options. Unlike the Bullies, Punishers, and Control Freaks who can be spotted by others from miles away, most casual onlookers would never detect the Tolerator's evil ways. In fact, the Tolerators often brag to their friends about everything you do for them—*how sweet.*

However, to their closer intimates, besties, and adult children, it's a little more obvious—because they too have been their slighted victims. The Tolerators care only about themselves and are very fickle and superficial. Those close to the Tolerators (like their grown kids), know they are not the folks you can rely on for help at 3 a.m., or that will even drive your kids (*their* grandkids) to school if it inconveniences them in the least.

The Tolerator has a lot of expectations of their partners. They not only expect to feel very comfortable financially, they really want someone to almost worship them, wait on them, fulfill not just their needs but all the extras. If you're their partner and not fulfilling this for them, you'll be quite useless and on your way out. Make no mistake.

If this is your life, you've slid into the Merely Tolerated Zone. It's a far cry from feeling accepted and embraced. You long for some kind of validation, for someone to really see you, and a real heartfelt snuggle would feel like a cool drink of water in the Sahara.

I was about to tell you, "It's not you, it's them," and that the Tolerators do this to everyone they end up in long-term relationships with, but…since I'm being honest, let me tell you how it *is* you—*and* them.

I have yet to meet anyone who was okay with being merely "tolerated" that didn't have major self-esteem and self-worth issues. Most likely in your family of origin you were the people-pleaser, peacemaker, perhaps the middle child that went unnoticed. You never got in trouble, did what you were told, did well in school, but rarely got acknowledged for all your efforts. Your older or younger sibling were the troublemakers, rock stars, or total fuck ups—and they got all your parent's attention.

You are a really good person—always have been. Initially your partner was forthcoming with the compliments and it felt soooo good for someone to finally see your cute lil Self. The problem was that you were almost shocked by it and could hardly imagine your luck that such a god/goddess could possibly fall for you. You wanted to do everything in your power to remain in their good graces. However, the story you have about being in the shadows, rarely acknowledged, and your overriding low self-worth, has brought out exactly what you feel you deserve in your partner's treatment of you.

Maybe you are finally coming to the realization that being alone would be better than the silent hell you are living. Time to stop tolerating your Tolerator and give them the boot. GAFDA!

No? Too scary? More than likely, you are terrified of being alone. Here's what you can do to turn things around.

Be sure to do your own work to uncover your personal beliefs and stories about yourself, and work on your own self-worth issues, or you will simply re-create an all-too-similar situation with somebody else.

The fact is that though your Tolerator "acts" like they don't need you, it's a total façade. They have massive self-esteem issues themselves, and although you've done your best to shower them with love and attention, the Tolerators don't feel the least bit lovable and can hardly stand themselves. In some ways you are perfect mirrors for each other—you're just much nicer. You tend to find your value in service and they find theirs in "being served."

When you start to learn your worth, make a stand for yourSelf, and stop being a pushover, I promise you it's going to be attractive, and perhaps a bit threatening to your partner. Your Tolerator won't know what hit them. They have a lot more to lose than you do—bet that never occurred to you. I'm not telling you to behave like them—just start taking care of *you* first.

Whatever acts of service you perform for them, make sure it's what you genuinely *want* to do and not in order to "earn" their love. The Tolerator is going to have to step up their game a notch and start attempting to prove *their* own worth and why you should keep *them* around. It will be a nice change for you and I predict it won't take very long for you to shift this dynamic back to equilibrium.

Whatever you decide, moving forward with some self-awareness and self-esteem (whether you stay or go), will only be beneficial for you in the creation of the next phase of your life and relationship.

## Chapter 17

# The Bullies & Abusers

Here's one of the not-so-subtle archetypes: the Bullies and Abusers. The Bullies come from a place of fear and severe insecurity. Think of the kid that is being ridiculed or beaten at home, who then takes it out on the kids at the playground. Think about that same kid who may have been bullied by older siblings, or physically abused by his dad, who starts working out and gets bigger than most of the population so nobody can hurt him ever again. Or who becomes the biggest shit-talker and badass verbal abuser around. It's all a façade of protection, grown from a place of fear and inferiority.

Because of their low self-worth, they feel they have to threaten and demean their partners to keep them feeling a little lower than themselves at all times. They don't want their partner's feeling like they could possibly make it without them. Like the Rescuers, the Bullies prefer you to be dependent upon them. It keeps the imbalance of power right where they prefer it.

We often look at those in relationships with a Bully/Abuser and wonder why they stay. We may even pity them or worse, judge them harshly for doing so. Most likely, the Bully didn't reveal themselves right away—they may be an ass, but they're not stupid. If they went all in with their hurtful tactics early on, you'd run. The Bully's evil super power is to slowly erode your sense of Self.

The Bullies will tell you that you're wasting your time with your job/career, that your friends are shit, and that you are a loser for choosing such idiots. The Bullies will have you quit your job, give up on your business, and isolate you from your friends before you even know what's happening. Pretty soon you don't even recognize yourself. Try envisioning who you were before meeting them and who you've now become. The difference may be startling. Where did your Light go? Where are your former interests, passions, and dreams? Beware: when you finally get the courage to leave them, you may feel like a fraction of your former self for a while. Don't let that stop you. You will recover.

If you live with a Bully, you are always cautiously tip toeing around them—doing your best not to set them off. You often have to ask permission before you do anything. "Is it ok if…I turn on the light, get up early, eat the rest of the ice cream, go on a retreat with my gf's?" and so on.

The Bully is often critical and name calling—they may berate you for the slightest thing. "You idiot why did you light incense in this house?" "You stupid bitch—you put a red shirt in with my whites, now all of my clothes are pink!" "Are you going to go whine about it to your sister?" "I can't believe you didn't pass that test." "When you hear a noise like that you need to take the car in, now we have to replace the whole transmission, you fucking moron." "Keep eating that and you are going to be as fat as your mother!" "I am so tired of this disgusting food—this is what we had on Monday." Wow. Bullies can be harsh that way.

Once the Bullies have you isolated, walking on egg shells, and worn down, you can expect the manipulation to continue on an even more insidious level—so you won't even consider leaving or getting any help. The Bullies are great gas lighters as well and will have you thinking their behavior is all your fault.

The Bully/Abuser can be heard saying things like, "You will never find anybody to love you the way I do." "You will never be able to make it on your own." "You wouldn't survive without me." "Nobody else would put up with your schedule, your weirdness, diet, kids, etc." "No one will take care of you the way I have." Do any of these sound familiar?

This behavior can be generational and become so normalized that some think it's just the way it is—there will always be the powerful and the weak, and to keep yourself safe you need to know your place. A friend of mine recently recounted an incident with his elderly mother. She had been verbally abused, accused of wrong doing, and screamed at for the better part of an hour by her oldest son. Had my friend not found her sobbing, he probably would have never known what had happened. His mother recounted that just before the end of this Bully's tirade, he told her, "You can never keep anything to yourself. Everybody knows you can't be trusted. You'll probably go straight to your sister and blab—everybody hates that about you. So why don't you just keep your mouth shut for a change." Manipulate much?

You may be asking why this grown women let her own son speak to her that way. Maybe it's because her husband of 40 years had verbally abused and belittled her for their entire marriage. And why did she stay married to that Bully for so long? Who knows, but here's a list of some of the usual suspects: because they're a member of a particular religion and they got married in a church/holy place; because they had kids; because she didn't know how she'd support herself and her kids by herself; because she'd been programmed by her family, church, and community that divorce was bad; because, because, because....

Her husband had passed on before this happened, but obviously not without passing on his dirty tricks to his eldest son. And old patterns can be hard to break.

~ ~ ~

Stories like this are everywhere. If you are being verbally and/or emotionally traumatized and terrorized, that's not ok. Just because they don't hit you, doesn't mean they aren't leaving scars—emotional scars are often worse. I sometimes wished my abuse had been physical instead of emotional—at least physical bruises go away. It's not ok to be belittled, demeaned, made fun of, ridiculed or called offensive names.

If you are being physically abused, there is absolutely no excuse for it—whether you are a man or a woman. Get out. No religious ceremony or "til-death-do-us-part" vow is worth risking your own life or well-being for. God/Jesus/Buddha/ Krishna won't hold it against you if you GTFO or have your abusive partner removed from your life and worry about the actual divorce later.

And for fuck's sake, if your spouse/partner is abusing your children in any way, I don't care if it's their biological parent or a stepparent, you deserve to get your children to a safe place. Do not turn a blind eye. Believe what your children tell you, though it may be the worst thing you can imagine hearing. Kids don't typically lie about these kinds of things unless they have an extremely manipulative parent that is out to get you. It is absolutely unacceptable for you to keep your kids in an environment like that. And how could you possibly love anyone that wants to hurt you or your babies?!?

If you are in a relationship with a Bully, let this book be the permission you deserve to step out of the manipulation, abuse, bullying, and belittling and back into a life of your making. You are more powerful than you think and you *can* choose out.

These Bullies are often, though not always, alcoholics and substance abusers, which further aggravates their bullying and projections towards you. The Bully is also the archetype most likely to choose brute force to beat you physically, sexually, and/or emotionally. That's why I've also dubbed them the Abusers. It's unacceptable. Run, don't walk, and get a fucking divorce already…along with some good therapy to figure out why you've accepted this abuse for so long.

And yes, I'm going to ask you to do your own work around this issue…but only after you get some distance between you and the Abuser. First of all, abuse wreaks of a lack of respect and major control issues. Ask yourself where you may have been lacking respect for yourSelf? What part of you thought this kind of behavior was ok or if you felt like you deserved it in any way whatsoever? Where are you controlling and need things to be your way? Not necessarily with others, but in what ways are you that exacting and demanding of yourself?

Yes I know, people stay in these situations because of money and their perceived inability to provide for themselves and their children if they leave. As big of a deal as it seems, your physical and emotional well-being will always be worth more than the money. The peace of mind that comes from leaving a house of chaos and terror is priceless. You will all be better served in a dinky apartment with your lives intact, than the mansion on the hill where everyone fears for their lives.

There is always a way. When you take steps in the direction of creating a better life for yourself, the universe will rise up to meet you in ways that will initially shock you. As you learn to take care of *you*, daily miracles will abound as a result of living a more conscious life.

## Chapter 18

# The Control Freaks

Although there are plenty of control issues going on with the Bullies, Dream Thieves, and Punishers, the Control Freaks typically emerge early on and deserve their own category.

It's not because you did anything wrong that merits punishment, or that they necessarily intend to dash your dreams, it's just that Control Freaks think they are the boss of EVERYTHING—including you. They can be heard saying things like, "He who makes the gold, makes the rules," "I'm a banker, I'll handle all of the finances," "You will not be going to a, b or c, or doing x, y or z." "Don't wash the dishes like that, do it this way." "God told me what you need to do." And "You are going to stay home and take care of the kids…no wife of mine is going to work," to name just a few.

The Control Freaks are always right and you are always wrong. They know everything and you know nothing. You don't do anything right in their eyes unless you are agreeing with them, and deserve to be treated just like a child. They prefer you with no money of your own to spend, sometimes no car, and almost always no voice or opinion. They want you to get their approval for everything.

~ ~ ~

The Control Freaks like to micromanage—tell you how to cut the vegetables, how to wear your hair, and which area of the zoo you should see first and which exit to come out of when you're done. WTF? And I'm not talking about just helpful suggestions either—their way isn't just a good way, it's the *only* way. They will tell you what you can eat, when it's time for a haircut, and how to reprimand your own children. They want to choose your outfit when they take you out, correct your grammar, and tell you how to act with their family or at the office party. These Control Freaks will have you take down every picture on social media of you and anyone but them, and delete any pic of you they find too sexy or unsavory, all to prove your undying devotion to them.

If you did any of these things in a way other than they have "requested" (I use that word lightly because we all know it's more of an expectation than a request) they will either give you the silent treatment, a look that expresses their disappointment and disdain for your lack of obedience, or flat out admonish you for not fulfilling their "request." If you forget to do something they have "requested," you will have no question about how disgusted they are with you.

The Control Freaks will let you know, in no uncertain terms, that they are the boss of you and that you should feel quite fortunate they have agreed to be the keeper of such a floundering idiot as yourself. They will make you wonder how you ever managed anything in your life on your own before they arrived. You should kneel—and don't forget to be grateful!

There's something a little un-human about the Control Freaks. Most of them are really lacking the compassion gene. Because they feel so inherently right about their beliefs, opinions, how things should go, and how you should live your life, they almost can't understand how or why you'd have any problem with them telling you shit. How could you feel anything but gratitude for their spectacular guidance? Their EQ, a.k.a. emotional intelligence, is also severely lacking. They have next to no capacity to be conscious of another's feelings, or how to read and react to social cues—let alone any real self-awareness or empathy. They "know" how things should go, how we should behave, and how we all should think.

In fact, they are so unconscious of their controlling ways, they are often completely ignorant of how they show up in public with their mates. The Control Freaks actually think the people around them approve and think they are doing their partners a favor. A friend of mine told me of just such a doctor… whenever his wife started getting too loud for his taste, he would glance in her direction, slightly raise his hand, and she would immediately stop—mid-sentence. Silence. With the look of a child that just got reprimanded. He had the mistaken notion that nobody noticed. But apparently everybody noticed, and talked about it behind his back.

I've had girlfriends that talked about their dad taking the cheese off their cheeseburger and telling them it was for their own good so they wouldn't get fat. Or guys whose dad told them what sports they were going to play and what their major would be in college if they expected him to pay. Classic Control Freak—knows what's best for everyone.

The Control Freaks can't even stand to allow you your own opinion if it doesn't jive with theirs. I was once involved with a man I dubbed "The Commander," as if that weren't telling enough. He had the nerve to tell me that my adult children, whom I consciously chose *not* to vaccinate as kids, would never be allowed around his grandchildren if they did not submit to being vaccinated now (pre-covid, btw). He bombarded me with all his scientific articles extolling the virtues of vaccinations, attempting to prove what an imbecile I was for making such an ignorant decision.

I tend to agree with him—not for my maternal, conscious choice, but for allowing myself to be convinced to move all the way across the country and leave a life I loved. The Commander proceeded to dismiss me after a month of living with him with the only explanation being that I was too strong-willed, free-spirited, and smart. Translation: I see I'm not going to be able to control you, mold you, or convince you to see things my way; therefore, this will never work. This is the same guy that said to me in shock, "Nobody has ever spoken to me like that," after merely speaking my truth and telling it like it is. Dude had a military background and had been a CEO of the city zoo for over two decades, and was used to his every word being agreed with and obeyed. How did I not see that coming?!? A friend of mine was quick to point out upon my return, "He keeps animals in cages for a living—what did you expect?"

When you're with a Control Freak long-term, you get used to being seen and not heard, and rarely speaking in public in their presence—though you are expected to laugh at all of their jokes. You are never to side with anyone that disagrees with your Control Freak, and never, ever do anything to outshine them.

The Control Freak's fragile ego feels easily disrespected and they are quick to suspect others of disliking them. Over time, they will even have you distance yourself from—or flat out disown—close friends and even family members that don't pay your Control Freak the proper deference. You are not to associate with such dissenters. They demand your loyalty be with them alone, By severing these relationships—even if it's with your own aging parents—you prove your loyalty.

I've heard stories of religious Control Freaks whose favorite tactic is to play the "God Card" whenever it serves their cause. They piously inform you that "God told me you are supposed to study medicine," or "I had a revelation…you are supposed to marry me," or "The Spirit told me we need to become vegans," or "This atheist friend of yours is a bad influence on you," or "As the patriarch of this family, you need to stop working outside of the home," or "Jesus said we need to have more sex (or stop having sex)," or…you name it. Nobody can argue with the "God Card."

Ahhh, those lil cuties. Unlike most of the other archetypes, the Control Freaks don't really need you. They will cut you loose after the first few signs of dissension. If you've been with them for any length of time it's because you've been fairly well-behaved. The Control Freaks prefer to be alone as opposed to being challenged. They're rarely any good at intimacy because that would require sharing their heart, which they've yet to find. Vulnerability is not a trait in their wheel house because that would place them on equal footing with *you*, which they want nothing to do with. Nor do they believe you to be capable of such a feat—it would shatter their illusion of superiority over you.

If you ever want a relationship with some kind of equality, where your opinions are valued AND you feel free to move about the world and breathe at the same time, you may just want to GAFDA. These folks aren't typically open to self-improvement suggestions because they believe they're perfect already—that's for fuck-ups like us. Run don't walk. There is a rigidity here that can rarely be adjusted without a psychotic break to their fragile ego structure. Most Control Freaks would rather die than admit any wrong doing or give up any of their perceived power over you. Save yourself. GTFO.

## Chapter 19

# The Caretaker & The Chronically Ill / Addicted

Trigger Alert! Please know that when I speak of those with chronic conditions, I'm talking about those that have resigned themselves to believing:

"This is just how it is,"

"I can't do anything about it," and,

"My condition will never change."

I'm referring to those who have a sense of entitlement due to their condition, who show no appreciation or acknowledgment for the extra effort it takes everyone around them because of it. I'm pointing to those who assume no personal accountability for their own health and well-being. Many are still blaming their condition on bad childhoods, traumatic relationships or something that "happened to them" in a distant past—real or imagined (or just plain made up).

While the Chronically Ill may experience legit symptoms, the majority of chronic illness is a result of internal issues, toxic emotions, and unprocessed trauma. Most of which could be dealt with through deep therapeutic inner work and dedication to proper, high-frequency nutrition. I strongly believe that if one is truly desirous of better health and committed to their well-being, they can experience complete healing and a return to wholeness.

I loosely include in this category the lazy drunks, pill poppers, chronic drug users and alcoholics because they create similar issues for their Caretakers as the Chronically Ill. Their similarities are quite striking. The Chronically Ill, like most addicts, typically can't hold down a job for long (many don't even try). They both have to be cared for, put to bed, picked up after, and often driven and shuttled everywhere they go. Both struggle (or feign struggle) to clean the house or adequately care for their own children, and you can forget being bothered to have sex with their partners on any kind of a regular basis. Their vitality and energy levels are so low you have to scrape it up off your shoe.

Most Chronically Ill, as well as the Addicted, claim they want to change, at least they are constantly promising to get a handle on "their condition" …next weekend or next month, or just…sometime. Their Caretakers soon learn to relegate these promises to fantasyland.

And what about these Caretakers? How did they end up in this chapter with that whole host of nefarious creatures like the Abusers and the Punishers? Caretakers sound innocent enough. Is nothing sacred?

When I say Caretakers, I'm not talking about caring for someone with a short-term condition or temporarily acute situation, like somebody who got in a bike accident and is immobilized temporarily. That's part of being a kind human and a decent partner. I'm talking about those who, after years and even decades of dutiful service, continue blindly sacrificing their own life, happiness, and vitality while their partner continues feigning debilitation, never even entertaining the thought that life could be any different for them.

The shadow side of these cute lil Caretakers would be the martyrs, silent sufferers, and enabling cowards, with a side of savior complex. The Caretakers are under the impression that nobody else can help their partners but them. They believe themselves to be solely responsible for their partner's physical and emotional well-being. Or they just believe so deeply in the concept of sacrifice that they will put their *entire* life on the altar of marriage to serve someone in perpetuity that really has no thoughts of ever trying to get better and actively participate in the marriage.

In reality, the Caretakers are nothing more than enablers to their long-term sufferers. It goes without saying that the Caretakers end up shouldering well more than their share of the marital and household duties. Not only are they typically the bread winners, but they often assume the majority of the child care. Waking up littles, bathing, feeding, and carpooling them to school because their partner can rarely get out of bed at such early hours and conveniently retires before the bedtime rituals begin.

The Caretakers are also known to pick up the slack around the household when they get tired of the over-flowing dirty laundry, piles of mail, filthy floors, and mountains of dirty dishes. When they can no longer stand to wait for their ailing partners to do something—*anything*—like clean an overdue filthy toilet, or change a child's soiled sheets, these lovely Caretakers finally just do it themselves.

They have been so nice, and they've taken such good care of their "disabled" Chronically Ill partner for sooooo long, their other half has no motivation to get well. They have it so good, why would they wake up, get better or put any real effort into their own healing? If anything new pops up that they don't feel like doing, they just feign *extra* tired, agitated or not well, and the Caretakers around them instantly pick up the slack for these pitiful souls.

And that is the dark side of the Chronically Ill or Addicted—they often behave like narcissistic victims and unappreciative assholes.

For as chronically fatigued that they *claim* they are, many of them manage to find huge reserves of magical energy when it comes to doing something *they* really want to do. Here are a few examples from various Caretaker clients over the years. (Remember almost every one of the Caretakers in these stories did all of the above—they were the sole bread winner, cared for littles, and did the majority of household chores.)

One client's wife claimed to have suffered for close to 17 years from an illness no doctor would even diagnose. She couldn't be disturbed to get the kids ready for school in the morning…but when it was triathlon time, she jumped out of bed to go train for her races. Yet she couldn't manage to wash the dishes or even keep her side of the room free from piles of clutter and garbage. How?!? That same wife had plenty of energy for games when visiting family, but would suffer sudden exhaustion when it came time to start cleaning up. She demanded her husband stick up for her and defend her honor when anyone spoke poorly of her or dared to point out the coincidental nature of her "condition."

Another man I'd been working with in the course of our sessions mentioned that on a recent family trip one of the children needed some medicine. To save time, he asked his "chronically ill" wife to go get what was needed at a nearby drugstore while he bathed and packed up all four children to be ready to check out. She said she couldn't possibly manage that 15-minute round trip drive herself. Yet a few weeks later, this same client tells me his wife travelled from Utah to Oregon with their children. I asked if they flew, as it was easily a 12-hour drive.

"Oh no, she drove," he obliviously replied. I was flabbergasted.

"Aren't you afraid for your children? What if she falls asleep on the drive?" I asked.

His response, "Oh, she always has plenty of energy to go visit her parents."

"And you don't find that odd?" I questioned in disbelief. Can you say abuse? Taken advantage of?

How is it even possible that these Caretakers could be so ridiculously subjugated to the whims of their Chronically Ill? Unfortunately, the Caretakers often operate from the energy of guilt. These are the folks that think everything is their fault, they could've done better, and they'll never be good enough. Instead of exploring what all that inner turmoil may mean or where it comes from, it's easier to fill that space with being useful, feeling needed, and caring for someone else. The Caretakers, being inherently good people, feel guilt-ridden for any slight wrongdoings, and especially for any desire to leave their chronically pathetic spouse.

These kind folks often suffer in silence, hiding their misery from the world. If they were to make their discontent known, they would be thought of as schmucks. After all, they married for better or for worse, right? They took that vow seriously, that's why they feel *extra* badly about even the thought of a life of their own. Ahhh the guilt that would be invoked to leave!

The fortunate Chronically Ill recipients in their care know this and are well aware of their Caretaker's sense of duty. Speaking of those psychic lil parasites…did I call them narcissistic victims and unappreciative assholes? Hmmmm, yes, I did! Just watch the massive reserves of energy they will suddenly have access to when they come at me for that!

It's so interesting to me why people will continue to fight for and defend to the death the validity of their condition, negative thoughts, and limiting beliefs about themselves and their life. Imagine defending why you can't manage *anything*, from doing the laundry, to having a job, to caring for your own children, to…fill in the blanks.

"I just can't help it" they pitifully declare. But they *can* help it. And If they truly wanted to, they would. If you don't believe me, go participate in a week-long retreat with Dr. Joe Dispenza or listen to Bruce Lipton on the Biology of Belief before you come at me. Or better yet, head to Peru and do a little journeying with some plant medicine before you say another word. There is *always* a way out.

The Chronically Ill have plenty of energy, make no mistake. They just choose to spend it fighting for their illness or addiction—fighting to keep the Caretaker in their service. Instead, maybe the Chronically Ill could pause first and make a list all of the *many payoffs* that come your way as a result of your "condition." That's right, I did say PAYOFFS! There are sooo many—and you know it.

Sometimes the payoffs are obvious—as in your spouse taking care of abso-fucking-lutely everything. Sometimes the payoffs are slightly more subtle. You will find some using their Chronically Ill status as a free pass for getting fat or "losing" their sex drive. Others may need extra money from their Caretakers because they can't possibly work—but hey, they still need their nails and lashes done. The Caretakers can't even bring these payoffs up without sounding like total assholes and the "forever sick and tired" know it—more payoffs. Are those payoffs something you're willing to give up in favor of your well-being? Didn't think so.

Why did I call them narcissists? Even their children have to grow up quicker, with the older kids taking care of the younger ones and doing more than their share of the chores. Everyone in the house has to be quiet because poor mommy or daddy is always needing to rest, sleep or just not be bothered in the middle of the fucking day. They are so consumed with their *own* issues that they can't even see that their over-worked partner may actually have some needs of their own. You can't possibly be expected to fuck your partner or be a contribution to making *their* dreams a reality—let alone yours. Oh, that's right, you don't have dreams/ ambitions any more—and why would you? Being constantly "served" and waited upon feels like you've achieved the status of royalty.

For these chronic underachievers, to even *notice* anybody else has needs, let alone acknowledge them, would mean they'd have to take some accountability for their own well-being. Feigning powerlessness is much easier and allows for unaccountable irresponsibility. Ponder that for a minute. It's *never* their fault. They can't help it if they're tired all the time and can't drag themselves out of bed. Really?!

You can see where I'm going with the unappreciative assholes comment....

For all these Caretakers do to support their partner's unmotivated asses, and the efforts they go through to make life more comfortable for them, you'd think the Caretakers would be more appreciated and revered for their sainthood. On the contrary, they get treated like doormats. And those they serve typically feel somehow entitled to their partner's efforts by virtue of their marriage license.

Instead of expressing their gratitude, the Chronics are more often inclined to expressing their disappointment that *more* was not done for them. Openly and authentically acknowledging these kind, Caretaking souls might wake them from their trance of servitude and possibly slow down their obsequious behavior. (Nobody wants that!) A sincere, heartfelt thanks would actually require that the Ill take some responsibility for their own healing if they *truly* wanted to ease the burden they have heaped on their unequally yoked other.

If they were not drowning in their own self-pity, and truly loved themselves *and* their partners, a solid effort would be made towards healing, and true appreciation would be overflowing. However, I've yet to meet one of these Caretakers that felt fully seen and appreciated by their partners for their heroic efforts.

Caretakers, it may be time to grow a pair and GAFDA if your partner is unwilling to make an honest effort. You've sacrificed enough of your life. Stop worrying about what others will think of you and make a heartfelt choice for a life of *your* choosing. You are just as much a victim, suffering in silence, secretly hating your life of unappreciated servitude.

Just keep in mind that when you start to get serious about making a break for it, inevitably your partner's "condition"—and then their behavior—will take a turn for the worse. Big surprise. The "sick one" will see it coming from a mile away.

When the always-kind Caretaker gets serious about leaving, they wouldn't think of doing so without bolstering up their lifeless partner in all the ways that they can possibly think of to set them up for a successful life on their own—and without them. The Caretaker may help the Chronically Ill get a job, finish their degree, encourage (and probably pay for) additional professional training—whatever it takes. Because that is what a Caretaker does. But don't be fooled, it won't be enough.

Be prepared for a plethora of new catastrophes to keep you in your guilt-ridden trap. The Chronically Ill couldn't possibly handle a divorce right now when their favorite grandmother just died, they have a big test to pass next month, or the holidays are just around the corner. They couldn't possibly handle the childcare even *half of the time* on their own because they are such an emotional wreck. They can't possibly handle working full-time, you'll have to support them for the rest of their life. On and on it goes. The Caretaker feels trapped, and justifiably so. That Caretaker mindset is *exactly* what their manipulating, chronically pathetic/ill partners are counting on.

This is never going to change. Your partner has it too good with you under their thumb and they know it. If this is your lot, and most likely has been for years, and you feel used, undervalued, and unappreciated, here's an idea: start taking care of yourself! Nothing else you've done thus far has helped them.

You Caretakers may not want to hear this, but the *best* thing you can do for them is to leave them. Trust me, they'll figure it out quicker than you can imagine. Remember the client whose wife "suffered" for 17 years with an undiagnosable disease? Can you guess what happened the minute he (finally) filed the divorce papers? Yup, she was miraculously cured! (She wouldn't want the judge to think she couldn't care for the kids—it might cost her some child support money. More on that later.)

Speaking of being cured…another warning.

Before these poor, lifeless souls will let you—their meal ticket—walk off into the sunset peacefully to your own sovereign life, be prepared for them to fight you to the death.

"Whaaaa?!" you say. "They can barely get off the couch!" Don't say I didn't warn you.

For them to find anybody else to do everything *you* did, they'll have to pull themselves out of the mire, at least temporarily, to find, lure, and hook themselves a new slave. That could be a lot of effort—and effort is something they just cannot abide.

I have seen this type viciously turn on those who tirelessly cared for them for decades. I've seen the previously incapacitated file false restraining orders so the partner couldn't get back into their own home, and then sell all of their things and max out all their credit cards—all in a very short period of time. I've seen the Chronically Ill use their victim status to turn entire families against their former Caretaker, make up blatant and horrific lies about the other, and rack up exorbitant attorney fees fighting for every drop of blood they haven't already extricated from their former servants.

Those that couldn't be bothered to get kids ready for school in the morning will be claiming *you* are the horrible parent, and *they* deserve full custody! This seemingly lifeless bunch can rally to raise the roof when their slave attempts a peaceful exit, and their comfy life is threatened. Beware!

And one more thing Caretakers, before you hitch your wagon to another project you'll never be able to "fix," you deserve to turn your attention back towards yourself. Learn to start meeting your *own* needs with as much attentiveness and diligence as you did your unappreciative slave owner.

*Chapter 20*

# A Little Self-inquiry Before You GAFDA

If you are the guilty party here, the one playing the role of Rescuer, Dream Thief, Punisher, Tolerator, Bully, Control Freak or Chronically Ill, and your partner is on to your little charade, your days are numbered. When they wake up to the truth that they deserve better, you will soon be on your way out.

Consider yourself lucky you lasted this long. It's ok, you're going to like them even less when they take their power back, grow some balls, get sassy with you, and tell you to go fuck yourself for your shitty behavior all these years. That kind of independence, free spirit, and strong will won't be any fun for you at all! You're really nothing more than a slave owner.

Don't worry, fortunately for you there are plenty of Muggles looking for masters. You'll land on your feet, until your next slave wakes up. I may be your worst nightmare because I'm on a mission to liberate these slaves, like I've had to liberate mySelf and countless clients.

But who am I kidding, these people aren't reading my book. Just like they aren't coming to me for coaching. In their opinion, they're good—nothing to see here. Everything is going according to plan....their plan. They have it made—thanks to you.

I'm here for YOU.

If you are on the short end of any of these previous archetypes, I have compassion for you and a question: what the fuck have you been thinking all these years?! Many of you have been living with similar situations for so long that you don't even understand what an energy drain it has been on your Soul. However, the buck doesn't stop with pointing our fingers at *them*...those creeps, those bad, selfish people. The buck may only start there because it's always easiest to see what's "over there." In reality, it ends with *you* and a deep self-inquiry.

Why have you tolerated this for so long? Why do you feel you deserve this kind of behavior? How was this OK for so long? Why have you been burying your head in the sand? Why have you not wanted to look at this? What part of you believes a relationship (no matter how bad) is better than no relationship at all?

What part of you is afraid to be alone, ask for a divorce, speak your truth, or say how you really feel? What part of you fears taking your power back or even knows what that may look like for you? What part(s) of yourself have you had to cut off, hide, pretend didn't exist, or have all but died within you to be in this relationship? How much trust do you have in yourself to just *be* yourself?

And if your partner hasn't been lighting your soul on fire, before you point your fingers "over there" and outside of yourself, ask yourself: do *you* light your soul on fire? Are you turned on by your life? Do you love your career? Do you have great relationships outside of your marriage? Are you excited about your personal growth and development? If the answer is no, then do your best to be turned on by *you* first.

If you've picked up this book I'm willing to guess you've had enough, and have been anxiously engaged in improving all areas of your life—and your partner may be just the opposite. Miserable, asleep at the wheel, ho hum, full of expectations you're not fulfilling, blaming you for what's wrong in their life, and basically just being irritable and unhappy. Nothing you've done, or attempted to share, has improved the relationship or seems to make any difference.

Just remember, nobody will ever show up to love us anymore than we love ourSelves. Sometimes by simply realigning ourSelves with our truth and self-worth, and connecting with some real Self-love and respect, our partners begin to shift like magic, especially when they realize their behavior is no longer acceptable to you. If these little buggers don't shape up after you've done your deep work, well…don't be dumb. You will be amazed at how much energy and vitality will return to you when you cut that noose off from around your neck.

If you are one of those that have strong, deeply ingrained beliefs and rules about how "good people" stay in their marriage no matter what, enduring until the end because you made a vow "until death do you part," or because you just never wanted to be "one of those people" that gave up on their marriage…I feel you. But only for a minute.

It would be heartless of you to leave these pathetic creatures, right? How will they survive without you? What would the others think of you if you left? Let all of those things go. They're all about judgment—your own and your perception of how you will be seen by others. Do you really want to live the rest of your days through that lens?

At some point in your waking up process, you will realize that *you* are the author of your sovereignty and the only boss of you. When you fully own your autonomy and realize that you are beholden to no one person or institution, you'll be able to make choices that are more in alignment with your most authentic Self. Does that mean that you'll never have challenges or heartache? No. But those challenges will become more authentic and not neurotic; therefore, they can be dealt with and managed with confidence and an inner Light within, knowing that you are living on purpose and there is no obstacle that you cannot overcome.

This is not narcissism or even self-indulgence—though other's may try to convince you otherwise. It's called Self-care, Self-love, Self-preservation, and just plain taking care of you. And, if you have been living with any of the aforementioned archetypes, it will be the best thing that ever happened to them, as well. It may give them pause to look at themselves. But that's not your business. Stay in your lane and stop saying yes to being treated in ways that insult your Soul. And when all else fails, GAFDA.

# Part Four

*Self-Betrayal & The Real Infidelity*

## Chapter 21

# Self-Betrayal: The OG Sin

> *You can't escape from what your heart actually aches for no matter how hard you might try. The brain hardly ever wins. The core does. ~Victoria Erickson*

Before we dive into all there is to say about infidelity, let's take a look at something most people miss and rarely look at under these circumstances: where the real infidelity originates, long before any "act" takes place. When someone cheats on us, or we feel we have been betrayed in some way, we often find ourselves getting washed up in a chaotic sea of rage, jealousy and grief, calling in the make-wrong troops, and eager to point the finger of blame in the other's direction. We rarely look at where those other three fingers are directed. That is…at ourselves.

The first act of infidelity is always that of Self-betrayal—a lack of self-trust, refusal to listen to the voice within, ignoring the red flags and inner promptings, and keeping your truth and Light hidden.

The greatest betrayal of Self happens when we agree to dim our Light or to be anything less than *exactly* who we are for any person, group or institution. We do it because we don't think we will be loved or accepted otherwise, and that whoever *they* are and whatever *they* stand for is worth the compromise. We are so desperate for love—but not our own—we give away all that we are just to chase acceptance. And we lose ourselves in the exchange.

Fear has us reprioritize someone else's beliefs, feelings, and ways of being as more important/valid than our own. We willingly cut off parts of ourSelves on the chance that we may be loved *more* if we can just be a way other than we really are.

If you want to end the cycle of betrayal, *Self-betrayal* is the exploration that's really worth contemplating, and the only thing that will make a difference. Let's take a courageous look at just a few of the ways we betray ourselves in partnerships, and clearly do not show ourSelves love in favor of the other:

When we agree to forgo our big dreams if our partner feels threatened—or we let our dream go completely so our spouse can pursue theirs.

When we give up our own education in favor of the other's, and never return for our own degree.

When we suppress, deny, invalidate or fail to communicate our own feelings so as not to hurt (or even bother) the other.

When we do all we can in anticipation of the other's needs *in order to* "earn" love and affection—even when those actions are not authentic for us. Meaning we don't really want to do those things for our partner, we just do them as a means to gain their love and acceptance.

When there's someplace else we'd rather be and don't go, and when there is someone else we'd rather be with and don't choose them—or give our heart a single vote—we dishonor ourselves

When we forfeit traveling the life path our heart yearns for because we feel our partner can't or won't support us, we cheat ourSelves

That's a very short list, but you get the idea. At some point we get weary of this, or even fed up, and many of us end up resenting our partners falsely because of it. Truthfully, the one to blame is none other than our cute lil people-pleasing selves. (FYI: Blaming another for *anything* will never get you *anywhere*. Blame will simply get you stuck in victim mentality from which you will never grow. There is zero evolution in pointing the finger of blame outside of yourself.)

Thus, for some to stay married, is the greatest betrayal of Self and becomes a lie to all parties involved. Yet for another to remain wedded and work things out may be their highest truth and desire. We cannot suppose to know or judge for another which may be the case. It's different for everyone.

We've been taught by our families, religious institutions, and communities to love our neighbors, our spouse, our children, and humanity—everyone but ourSelves. We've been conditioned that to love ourSelves or to put ourSelves first is selfish and narcissistic. We never get taught how to love ourSelves or how to tune into the voice of our own hearts.

The message that's communicated is that to serve the other's needs before our own is the noble and true path, and what it means to be a "good person." When we choose to link ourselves with another in holy matrimony, the expectation of self-sacrifice becomes even greater, and when children get added to the mix, that expectation grows exponentially.

Suddenly your life is no longer your own. The message is loud and clear that this domesticated behavior is all that will be accepted, respected or admired. To break free and act otherwise or stray from the norm (by getting a divorce), is to risk being shamed, ostracized or called shitty names. You may even lose family and friends and be cut off from your tribe. No wonder we have become so complicit. Nobody wants to be shamed, shunned or cast out.

And if you had that kind of courage to just get a fucking divorce already—do you even remember who you are anymore? We've been doing what we've been told for so long, buying into the idea of one-size-fits-all when it comes to what we *should* desire and what is *appropriate* behavior, that we forget our natural inclinations of what we authentically desire and who we really are. Many of us never knew—though we are crystal clear about who we are *supposed* to be and what is expected of us by our family, church, and friends.

As we buy into the programming, we become our own most effective captor. When we find ourSelves dissatisfied with the status quo and wanting more out of life, we often become self-condemning and shame ourselves for desiring anything different than what we've been programmed to accept as our lot. After all, who are we to have it all? Why do we get to choose out of the matrix and be happy when poor Joe next door is clearly sucking it up and doing his duty? And your sweet cousin has been in a miserable marriage for years, but at least she's comfortable and all her material needs are being met.

Gross. Be the change already. Pave a new road.

### The Real Battle Between The Dark & The Light

We have been lied to about the real battle between the dark and the Light.

We've been taught that the dark is the Light and that the Light is the dark. We've been taught that what our heart longs for is sinful and selfish, while to follow all the rules of church, state, and family is the Holy Grail—and if not *the* road to heaven, it certainly is the *only* road to acceptance from the fold. Choosing otherwise, in some cases, risks not only eternal damnation, but also complete rejection, excommunication, and extrication from all that we know and what feels comfortable.

So what is the dark, really? Let's start by looking at the meaning and etymology of sin, which is often likened to the "darkness" in Western society, sin actually means to miss the mark and deviate from one's path.

And though "sin" has been used to imprint shame and guilt for time immemorial, in truth, sin is not about a burn-in-hell-and-beg-for-forgiveness-moment. "To deviate from one's path" is to not be in unison with the Soul—to be separated from your higher consciousness and the Divine.

We miss the mark by following mass consciousness and social programming, and doing what we are told when it is not our truth.

True happiness comes from authenticity—authenticity of Self—being OK with loving what we love and allowing ourselves to follow our own hearts, instead of succumbing to the expectations of others. When we wake up to the truth of our hearts, we can finally see that there is more to life than the scanty crumbs we've been subsisting on under the guise of Light, good behavior, and expectation. Through this new authentic lens, your old life may *feel* like hell, because living in somebody else's ideal for your life *is* the *real* darkness.

Deviating from your own Soul's path, and thus truly sinning, may actually be *staying* in a marriage that has long outworn its original intention. Try it on as a possibility, that's all.

Here's the truth that no one wants you to know: We will not be receiving any gold stars when we reach the pearly gates for blindly following another's program or squelching the authentic desires of our hearts. We are not meant to be robots. We are human BE-ings that came here to feel, experience life, and learn how to follow our bliss. Only by doing so can we figure out who we are and why we are here.

Contrary to popular programming, our victory over the dark comes from being courageous enough to choose ourselves at the risk of appearing selfish and incurring the wrath and shaming of others. This confrontation between finally choosing to listen to our own Soul, or succumbing to the noise of the blue-pill world, is the real battle between the Light and the dark. It symbolizes what someone "on the Path" may expect to go through in definitive moments and important stages necessary for awakening, awareness, Self-realization, and enlightenment.

We triumph over darkness when we love ourSelves enough to choose ecstatic over satisfactory, devotion over duty, and freedom over slavery. Our journey into the Light begins when we cross the threshold of simply recognizing our own voice amidst all the others that have been shouting. When we allow ourselves to feel the gentle pull of our own heartstrings and acknowledge them as our own, the shadows begin to dissipate. When we courageously follow our life's passion and purpose, we are saying "yes" to our own becoming and to choosing the Light.

Following our bliss leads to greater creativity, vitality, and feelings of joy and gratitude for being alive. While blind obedience to all of your duties, should's, ought to's, and have to's—when those are *not* your truth—feels heavy and drains the life force slowly from every pore. That is what Self-betrayal feels like, and that is the difference between the Light and the dark, and what it means to "miss the mark."

When we think of people as "being dark," or that are "choosing the dark," we tend to think of murderers, rapists, thieves, or verbally, emotionally, and/or physically abusive people. Most of us don't wake up with the battle of whether or not to kill, rape or pillage each morning. We do, however, wake up wondering how much longer we can continue to go to a job that robs us of our creativity, or stay in a life-sucking, passionless marriage/relationship that is not meeting our needs. We wonder how long we can go on stifling our voice and opinions, pretending to like things we don't, and dislike things we love. This is the "dark" of which I speak. Disavowing your own Soul.

To the Muggle, the ego's desire to look good and be accepted and respected are so important, they believe their very survival/identity depends upon it.

As a result, many are willing to sell their souls to the devil in an act of Self-betrayal, just like Judas.

Judas, the iconic Biblical symbol of betrayal, turned over his best friend to an imminent and gruesome death for thirty pieces of silver. Ladies, have you ever entered into (or stayed in) a living arrangement with a man for the promise of financial security? Was it worth it? Have you ever tied yourself to someone in holy matrimony because you were afraid of being alone and the possibility of not finding anyone better was terrifying? Have you ever stayed in a job you hated because it made your partner feel safe, or entered a field of study that you had zero interest in because that's what was expected of you by your family? Are you staying in your marriage because you don't want to look bad by getting a divorce? It appears, in the above cases, that the preference of image, safety, and security over heart-centered authenticity wins the vanity and "dark" award.

What does it feel like to *pretend* you're in love with somebody when you're not? What's it feel like to feign happiness with someone when you're miserable on the inside? What's it like to act like you are still the same person you were 20 years ago? What's it feel like to live a façade every damn day pretending to be someone that you're not? Heavy? Dark?

These acts of Self-betrayal, if succumbed to indefinitely, will suck your Soul and destroy your vitality. Whether you're staying for the money and lifestyle, or because you feel it's what you're "supposed to do," but your heart's just not in it—both are false and Self-betraying.

Do you remember what happened to Judas? Oh, he got his 30 pieces of silver alright—and then he killed himself for his own Self-betrayal. In the end, whatever your 30 pieces of silver are, it will be worthless if you've abandoned your heart along the way. There is no dollar amount nor "noble cause" you can muster that is worth your Soul's betrayal.

Surprise! Your heart could not give a shit about your fucking reputation, what the neighbors think of you, or your precious possessions—all empty and meaningless when you are dying on the inside. The heart wants what the heart wants, and it isn't all money and status—unless you're a Muggle.

> *Sometimes it takes darkness and the sweet confinement of your aloneness to learn anything or anyone that does not bring you alive is too small for you.*
> *~David Whyte*

When you wake up to the beauty you are and realize you've allowed yourself to be unappreciated, unloved, and under the thumb of a Bully, Dream Thief, Punisher, Tolerator, or Chronically Ill…it's time to say no more. When you get that you've allowed your heart to take a back seat and you've missed your *true* mark—it's time to let go of any shame and guilt, take your power back, align with your truth, and come into the Light. Make a new plan, Stan. GTFO! Your allegiance belongs with your own heart, not your religion, your politics or your personal ego-identified dogma—with your Self!!

Get clear about who you are and what is most important to you, and be THAT! Realize that YOU are the love of *your* life. If you don't love you, you can't authentically love the other. If you can't be true to you, you won't be true to anyone else. The first and greatest love affair we ever have deserves to be with ourSelves.

There is nothing more glorious than a person stepping into their truth, acknowledging their greatness, and simply owning who they are with no apologies. We are made of literal stardust. It's in our DNA. We are pre-programmed to SHINE! We were born to stand out, to be unique, to follow our hearts and be our unabashedly big, bright, beautiful Selves.

If your partner can't handle this shift, and shift with you—or at the very least, not hold you back—it may be time to get a fucking divorce already.

## Chapter 22

# To Thine Own Self Be True

I went through decades of betraying mySelf in intimate relationships and the one thing that I know for sure is that the Universe/my Higher Self will always create for me the exact lesson I need at the exact moment that I need it. It hasn't always been fun, but it has *always* been for my growth and benefit. The painful awareness that came from betraying mySelf for another assisted me in knowing what was truly important to me.

It was like a refiner's fire of sorts. When I'd had enough suffering from putting my needs and dreams aside, I learned to love and value myself like I never had before. I could finally be true to me. Sounds simple enough, right?

"To thine own Self be true," some crazy half-wit poet said centuries ago. We've all heard that line, but do you know what came before it and after it?

Before "…to thine own Self be true," is this line: "This above all…." In other words, if you do *nothing* else! Allow me to elaborate for my old friend Will. "This above all—that is, above all other things, people, circumstances or situations—To thine *own self* be true!" For heaven's sake!

And why is that? Why must we be true to ourSelves at all costs and "above all"? Willie answers with his last, most brilliant line: because then "Thou canst not then be false to *any* man."

Let me Amercanize it for you, If you are true to yourSelf at all times and in all ways—you must not only speak your truth, but *be* your truth. If you are speaking, acting, and *being* your truth, you cannot be fake, inauthentic or false to any man, woman, child, situation or circumstance in your life. Not so easy now, huh? How does one get by in the world without ever being fake?

And why is it so important *not* to be "false" to anyone? First, for the obvious reasons—it's not cool to be a fraud. Second, and less apparent, because it hurts *your* soul. Not in the way that it's a betrayal and you are a bad person—but in a compromises-your-truth and eats-a-hole-in-your-heart and you-hate-yourSelf kind of way. That's all. Because when you live even a smidge less than your total truth, or dim your light just a tad, before you know it you're cutting off your right arm, the light goes out completely, and the self-loathing magnifies.

Why do we do it? Let me stick to what I know—mySelf. So why did I do it? I did it for a myriad of reasons. I dimmed my Light because I thought people would like me more if I didn't appear quite as fabulous and brilliant as I really am. I've even pretended that my core beliefs weren't as important to me as they really were for fear of abandonment.

For example, If I tell you who I really am, your beliefs may be different or diametrically opposed, and you may judge me and no longer want to be my friend, partner or lover. If I tell you how I really feel about love and compromise, it may scare you and you will want to run away before your perceived inevitable heartbreak ensues. I don't tell everyone that I believe I am the Sun's beloved and that He is mine because you will think I'm a nut job. And all the wise things

I've shared in the past will become empty and meaningless to you now because you think I'm whacked. Those are just a few reasons that I chose not to shine as brightly with certain people—I was scared. I loved someone or something and I wanted to be loved back. What are some of your reasons?

Buddha is attributed with saying, "There is no one else in the world more deserving of your love than you." If I am consistently putting your needs above my own, it will not be long before I start resenting you. If I keep doing that for you, I'm certainly not loving mySelf or owning the truth of me. I'm being only a fraction of mySelf—the piece I think you will deem acceptable, appropriate, and lovable. If I'm withholding my truth, I'm being inauthentic—living a lie—and deep down you know it. But you remain silent, *pretending* to believe my lies because part of you thinks you have won.

If I am untrue to my own core truth, if I agree to live less than I truly am so you can feel secure and I can feel safe that you won't leave me, at some point it will become too crushing to my soul to stifle that much of mySelf. And what started as something beautiful will soon be over.

This is how it often goes—we meet someone, we share our brightest Light, we share our heart, our truth, and ideals. We fall in love with all of that yumminess. Then fear of loss sets in, conditions arise, and the parameters and rules are carefully put in place. You are now not allowed to be as big, bright, and beautiful with anybody else. The compromise begins. You start to suffocate.

To tell this story more accurately and accountably, the person we are really resenting is ourselves, because we willingly agreed to give ourselves up. We agreed to things that were not *our* truths, but the desires of others. We agreed to play by *their* rules because of our fear of losing them and our own lack of Self-love. We end up hating ourselves for the inauthenticity of the *lesser* self that we agreed to be. We alone are entirely to blame for this. There was no coercion—just a perceived loss on our part.

~ ~ ~

Allow me to summarize: When you give yourself up and compromise your truth for another because you are afraid of loss, or want somebody to like you, you *will* resent them, and you will not garner their love, nor will you keep them because of it. They won't respect you for it, and when you get right down to it, you will see that it is *you* that you resent—it is YOU that you betrayed. If you need to tattoo it on your arm, "To thine own Self be true…" I highly recommend you do. At least energetically across your heart: To My Own Self Be True! For fuck's sake!

*Chapter 23*

# Infidelity & Accountability

So here is the topic I think you've been waiting for…though I doubt it will be the discussion you were expecting.

One of the more common reasons people get divorced involves infidelity of some sort. Many people upon discovering their partner has cheated, will begin the divorce proceedings immediately and shout it from the rooftops that they have been wronged without ever taking one look at themselves. I'd call that the Muggle's way—completely lacking in self-reflection, preferring instead to place all the blame outside of themselves and maintain their victim status.

There is no one-size-fits-all as to why people have affairs. It's different for everyone. There are those that will cheat on a partner simply because they've been given the opportunity, even when they're in a great relationship. There are others that have been in long-term affairs, living various double lives for years. There's no shortage of material out there to tell you that your spouse is a dirtbag, how to get even, and take them to the cleaners. I'm not here to address what they do in Muggle Land.

In the world I live in, there are always two 100% accountable parties. If you are on "the Path," or headed in that direction, this is how we roll. That is, that everything is happening for a reason and that whatever we think is "happening to us" on the outside, had its origins somewhere on the inside. For many, it may be the affair itself that wakes you from your slumber and puts you on the Path and on track with your life purpose. It's definitely a wakeup call for all involved.

Sometimes the Universe/your Higher Self has to dangle a shiny enough carrot for you to make a move or be extricated right out of your "fine," complacent life of stagnation. Sometimes that affair may be because either you're meant to be with that new person/energy, or to shake you and your spouse up into consciously choosing back into each other again after a major disconnect. Not always, but often it's just simply time to GAFDA and move on because you've both served your purpose together and are no longer moving forward or growing as a couple.

Some affairs occur to show you where you've been dead inside, living a lie and a life of resignation. Maybe you've been telling yourself and your partner the story that your kids/job/ life sap all your energy and your libido has just simply diminished. You may need something to show you that's not entirely true and, more likely, there's a deeper issue at play. Out of nowhere comes "Mr./Ms. Right" and what do you know—suddenly life is exciting and all you can think about is getting naked with them. No lack of energy or libido now, huh?

Obviously, your lack of energy and vitality had *nothing* to do with the physical workings of your body, or the perception that "you are just tired all the time." You're just tired in your relationship. You got lazy. Are you going to attempt to fix it, or will you move on?

We're taking a different look at infidelity, from some new angles. We've discussed the concept that before you were ever cheated upon, *you* betrayed yourself first. And this act of self-betrayal within, co-created the very thing you are pointing your fingers at outside of yourself and onto your partner.

Try on the possibility that what the cheating spouse did was an unwitting act of love for *you*, meant to put *you* on the life path you may have been avoiding.

Try on the possibility that "the cheater" isn't always the bad one and the cheated upon isn't always "the victim" and that everyone is playing their roles perfectly in this little game called Life. Or it just may be possible that you are simply a saint and your partner is an opportunistic, dirt bag. However, I encourage you to try on the other possibilities first.

If you do happen to be the so-called perpetrator/unfaithful party, you are typically the underdogs, cast out and shamed by legions of women (and men) and #metoo-ers. If you happen to be in the category of those taking accountability for themselves and their actions, way to go. You may enjoy hearing how your partner deserves to take full responsibility on their end as well. However, if you haven't owned your misdeeds, you have no right to take what I'm sharing below to justify yourself to your spouse and let them know that *your infidelity* is all *their* fault. Capiche?

So let's say your spouse cheated on you and you're claiming infidelity as your reason for divorce—or maybe you're not planning on divorcing, you're just planning to make your partner's life a living hell. Let's take a deep dive at what's really going on, shall we? My intention for the so-called "victims" of infidelity is for you to see where you have been lying to yourself and giving your power away. The opportunity here would be for you to see with new eyes how you may have created exactly what you've feared and how to stop being "at effect" in your life. My wish for you is to wake up to and claim your own inherent power, which will enable you to create a life you love—with or without your partner.

You may not like what I have to say, but if you're ready to make a change, radically transform your life, and stop being lied to, cheated on, and betrayed, then please have an open mind. I tend to be a lil harsh initially, but don't let that be the reason you check out without considering what I'm sharing. If taken to heart, and put into practice, you will find yourself so empowered by your own accountability that you will never consider yourself a victim again, no matter what happens in your life.

Many victim-like folks recognize the tremendous mileage they get from playing the victim role, from sympathy to control. The rewards are often so great, the shtick is hard to release. Many have lied to themselves and projected their shame, guilt, and worthlessness on to their so-called "perpetrator" partners for so long they actually believe they're partners are *solely* to blame.

However, somewhere in the dregs of your subconscious you know you have every bit contributed to this shit-show of a life. And if you really allowed yourselves to "see," you would understand that YOU, and only you, are the author of your story. It's the good news *and* the bad news. The bad news is, "Crap. I created all of this!?" But the good news is, if you unconsciously created your drama and chaos, you can choose to *consciously* create something beautiful.

So let's get real, any of the deep-seated insecurities, the low self-esteem, and all the trust issues you claim are a result of the infidelity existed *long* before you ever met the current "perpetrator" that did you wrong. In fact, I'm sure you have no shortage of childhood stories of rejection, abandonment, worthlessness, and betrayal. I'm willing to bet your partner is not the first s.o.b. you've ever encountered in your life. He will not be your last either if you continue to wallow in yourself pity, wondering just how you attracted all these horrible people and situations into your otherwise spotless life.

"Why does this always happen to me," you wonder. You've never cheated on anyone. You've been nothing but kind, loving, supportive, and forgiving—and everyone in your fantasy world agrees with you. You've got references, recommends, and testimonials of your purity. Barf.

I saw this seemingly innocent post on FB, that appears to sum up the Victim's Creed perfectly. The post had a cute lil forest creature in the Buddha pose with what seemed to be a harmless quote, initially. However, upon closer examination, it was more like a wolf in sheep's clothing. If you believed this bullshit, you would remain in Victim Land for time and all eternity and get eaten alive by life and the big bad wolves that seem to (randomly) keep crossing your path. Here's the quote, (it helps to read it in a mousy, powerless, pathetic tone of voice for full effect):

> *No, don't tell me you attract what you are. What if you're kind and you attract mean? What if you're honest and you attract liars? What if you're loyal and you attract cheaters? No, you don't always attract what you are. You sometimes attract people who are in desperate need of what you are. ~ Nashiha Pervin*

Flowing below the post were all the thumbs-up, likes, loves, comments of agreeing 100%, and #truth(s) that you would imagine on such a pathetic post—everyone from a disgruntled woman. One woman even said that she felt she had come so far in no longer attracting "assholey men" and that "this post validated to her, that there was *never* anything wrong with her, except for her self-sacrificing tendency to accept far less than she deserved." I know, I know, you agree, too—therein lies the problem. And it is exactly why you will continue on this path endlessly—until you own your shit.

Let me break this down. That quote is bullshit, ladies. Written by a victim, for victims, to keep you "safe." Not safe from bad men, oh no. Safe from being accountable for yourSelf. Safe from feeling *your* true feelings of shame and worthlessness that you continue to project. And safe from creating real transformation in your life that would make an actual difference and end this repetitive drama.

A client named Karen told me her boyfriend "betrayed" her and that he treated her poorly. I asked if she'd ever cheated on him? She said "no," nor had she ever cheated on anyone, she added.

"Do you treat him poorly," I asked. She said no, and in fact it was just the opposite. Karen's boyfriend was an alcoholic, so she had stopped going to school, working out, and taking care of herself just so that she could fully devote herself to taking care of him.

Would anybody call Karen a cheater? Clearly she's a saint, right? Kinda sounds like a lot of women, huh? Self-sacrificing in the name of love, right? Surely there's going to be a big payoff at some point, right?

"Well…you used the word '*betray*,'" I said to Karen. "Do you think you have ever betrayed *yourSelf*?" She looked at me puzzled.

I continued, "So when you stopped going to school, seeing your friends, and working out, were you valuing yourSelf? You let go of your own life, all that you loved and valued. Everything that was working for you, correct? That sounds like an act of Self-betrayal to me. Would you agree, sweetie?" Tears began to run down her cheeks.

"Absolutely," she responded, devastated by the weight of her new awareness. Then the truth dagger.

"So why would you expect your man (or any man) to treat you any differently than you are willing to treat yourself?"

Newsflash: Nobody will ever show up to love you any more than you are willing to love yourSelf. Nobody will respect you any more than you respect yourSelf. Nobody will value and appreciate you any more than you do. Let's be honest, when you sacrifice yourself, up to and including the extent that Karen did, you end up resenting and blaming the person you are serving—usually your partner. That resentment is misdirected. In truth, the person you are really loathing is you.

~ ~ ~

Here's how this works: if you are attracting liars, it doesn't mean that you are lying in the same way they are. But you are a liar—make no mistake. You are lying to yourself, by telling yourSelf that the liar you chose to be with really does love you. You are lying to yourSelf by believing what he says while ignoring your intuition and the obvious red flags that are screaming otherwise. You so desperately want to believe him. You may also be lying in other areas of your life, like to your boss, employees, parents, siblings, kids, etc.

If a person cheats on you or "betrays" you, it is because *you* have been betraying YOU in some way. If you were my client and we talked about it long enough, I would find it. You betray you every time you think your partner's needs and desires are more important than your own. You betray you when you stop doing the things you deserve to do to take care of yourself, in favor of taking care of someone else. You betray you when you don't know the first thing about setting boundaries for yourself or how to say no. You betray you when you apologize obsequiously when it's not even your fault and take the blame for things you shouldn't. When you only watch movies *they* want, only go to the restaurants *they* like, only have the friends *they* approve of, give up your career for theirs—hell, give up your life for theirs—YOU ARE CHEATING ON YOU.

You betray your partner and yourself when you withhold affection and don't share your feelings. You betray your partner and yourself when you act pissy because of some suspicion you're not even willing to talk about. You betray your partner when you share his infidelities with parents, siblings, neighbors or children. (Save that for your therapist or maybe one mutual friend.) You betray your partner when you don't appreciate all the good he does in an attempt to make amends. You may also be betraying someone else in a different area of your life all together.

So just because you may not be behaving or treating your partner/spouse *exactly* the same way they may have mistreated you, most likely there is no lack of lying, cheating or betrayal energy within yourself. You are no different than the one to whom you point your fingers. Everything you are whining and complaining about "over there" exists inside of you. Projection, Denial & Blame 101. Shocking, eh?

We teach people how to treat us by how we treat ourSelves and what we are willing to accept. Can you see that? These men or women are simply showing up for you the way *you* show up for you, and reflecting a trait within yourself that you have been unwilling to acknowledge.

I was reminded by a reader that many women are simply mimicking their mothers, aunts, and/or grandmothers—that we take our cues from how our family members behaved in similar situations and don't even know better or realize it. To that I say, the unexamined life is not worth living. If you are not consciously looking for and busting up old patterns of thinking and behavior, you will get exactly the same thing your mothers and grandmothers received. You can no longer blame your upbringing for your behavior when you are a grown-ass human. Time to wake up!!

Consider again, carefully, the last line of that earlier quote, *"No, you don't always attract what you are. You sometimes attract people who are in desperate need of what you are."* Unmitigated bullshit. The "cheater" does not *need* who *you* are. There are more than enough women to go around that believe they are doormats. There are more than enough women that are afraid to speak their truth and believe their voice will not be heard (and hence, it isn't). There are more than enough women that have been raised to believe it is their job to make their husband happy. Your husband/partner does not *need more of* that! Nor does anybody else on this planet!

YOU attract these people. And you do so because YOU need who *they* are to show up so YOU can see exactly how YOU have NOT been showing up for YOU. You need who *they* are to reflect back all the ways you feel unlovable and untrustworthy. You need who *they* are to mirror how YOU have been lying to and betraying yourSelf.

Stay in your own lane, clean up your own space of lies and betrayal. Treat yourself better—truly love you, and you will have a different experience from the men/women in your life.

I am not in any way excusing your so-called "perpetrator," though I could hardly call them that and would not do so in my own experience. I believe that people are always showing up perfectly for me to learn exactly what it is that I deserve to learn and to show me who they are. The very act of calling someone a "perpetrator" would instantly make me a victim, which clearly I am not—nor are you. You just don't know it yet.

## Chapter 24

# So Your Man Cheated: Why It's All Your Fault

*People do not believe lies because they have to, but because they want to. ~ Malcolm Muggeridge*

If you want to escape this lame cycle of victimhood, tyranny, control, and obsession, there are some simple—though not always easy—truths that must be established outside of Muggledom. These Truth Bombs were specifically written for the ones who feel "betrayed" so that they can take their power back and have some self-respect.

In this chapter, the pronouns I'm choosing to use are with the woman being the "betrayed" party and the man being the unfaithful one. We'll turn it around in a following chapter. However, though these particular examples are traditionally assigned to women, they can easily refer to some men. Read it however it applies to you.

Try these truths on like you would a new coat. See how your life would *feel* if you could incorporate each of these truth bombs below. Determine whether you would feel more peace and empowerment, and if it's a good fit for you. Keep those that work, put them into practice, and let the rest go—take the coat off if it isn't a fit.

**Truth Bomb Number 1:** People aren't property.

You can't own a man like you can a horse. Your marriage certificate is not akin to the title on your SUV. It doesn't matter if they are your family, your spouse, your children or your friends. You own no one but you—start acting like it.

Let go of your tracking devices and put down your short leash. Your partner is not a child! No amount of maniacal control is going to make *anybody* behave in a way that they don't like or that feels forced—not for long anyway. It's degrading, humiliating, and reprehensible.

I don't know a single soul—child, teenager or adult—that likes or appreciates being controlled or told what they can or can't do. Unless, however, they're into BDSM, in which case it might be kinda fun. But that's a different story.

Maybe you could turn your control-schtick into a game and get your hubby to think you're into some new kink where you are the dom and they're the sub. Under that guise, you could tell him to jump and he'd gladly say, "How high, my queen?"

**Truth Bomb Number 2:** Nobody but you is responsible for your happiness.

It's not your husband's job to *make you* happy, nor is he responsible for your ever-changing moods. Your happiness and even peace of mind is an *inside* job. They are *not* dependent on your partner's behavior, either. Your spouse is playing their role perfectly, by triggering you and bringing up all of the issues you've buried away.

I'm sure you've heard this one before: "Happiness comes from within." It's not an "over there" kind of thing. If you can't find your happiness independently, you will never know true happiness.

Happiness will always appear elusive to you whenever you *expect* any one person or thing outside of yourself to make you happy. If you are a miserable bitch, you will remain a miserable bitch until you figure out that you are the *only* one responsible for or capable of changing that. You give your power away every time you mistakenly place your happiness in another's lap. It doesn't belong there.

**Truth Bomb Number 3:** Nothing anybody ever does will make you "feel safe"—ever.

You know why? Because you don't feel safe within. Just like happiness, safety is something that is generated from within one's own being. It comes from knowing, trusting, and believing in yourSelf. If you don't feel that inside yourself, you have work to do.

You have the mistaken belief that safety is connected to how much you can control every living thing, person or situation in your little world—mainly your spouse. How's that been working for you? Feeling secure, yet? You can't control life. Life is going to keep life-ing.

Earthquakes and tsunamis *are* coming, whether you have told them to behave or not. Your job is to be unshakable from within yourSelf. "Safety" and security are an illusion.

**Truth Bomb Number 4:** You will always find what you're looking for!

We bring about what we spend our time thinking about. If you are dreaming of a red Porsche, you will start seeing them everywhere. If you obsess about finding evidence of your spouse having an affair, you will find it. But only always.

I'm certainly not telling you to ignore the signs, just to acknowledge your part in the co-creation. Ever hear somebody say with conviction, "I knew it!" once they'd discovered evidence of the thing they've been obsessing over? It's because they have an expectation of whatever they *think* they know, and they're always looking for evidence to prove themselves right.

They would rather have their theories proved correct, than have their spouse proven faithful. Their repetitive fearful belief is *exactly* what draws the desired outcome towards them.

I've had clients that had never been unfaithful in their life… until they got into relationships with people who were constantly suspicious and controlling. Eventually, some of these faithful folks ended up cheating, while the others just left the toxic environment. In such cases you have to wonder, was it really in their nature to cheat, or did their partner's ironclad belief that "all men are cheaters" create the very thing they dreaded?

Ask yourSelf if your constant suspicion of your partner's innocence may just have them declaring, "Fuck it. She thinks I'm cheating, anyway." Is that what you want? Is there anything in you that *wants* to find them cheating so you can be right? Think about that. Tell the truth. The payoffs can be tremendous. For one, you'd feel you had a legit excuse to be even *more* controlling and micromanaging. Maybe you'd feel "safer"? Or you could just GAFDA.

**Truth Bomb Number 5:** Your projected shaming of your partner is about YOU—not them.

If you can get everybody to buy into what a horrible person your partner is and that you are the poor victim of his behavior, maybe no one will look too closely at *you*. Maybe you can hide your own guilt and shame a little longer. Deep down this betrayal has brought up all of your own feelings of shame and worthlessness. Hurry and divert the attention—even from yourself.

~ ~ ~

Somewhere deep within, you believe that if you were a better wife, prettier, skinnier, smarter, etc., this never would have happened. Those excuses are bs—more lies you tell yourself so you can feel puffed up. Because if those reasons were the *only* truth it would make your hubby shallow AF, with *you* once again the pillar of purity and receiver of sympathy. Score. You could feign being sick and tired all the time, and you'd have a permanent hall pass from everyone for being a lackluster human. "Poor Molly…her husband cheated on her; she can't get out of bed." The truth is much deeper than that.

By pointing the finger "over there," you get to continue to avoid looking at the truth of yourSelf. It gives you another reason why you can't possibly be amazing. Blaming and shaming *him* for being the cause of all your misfortune is just another excuse for *you* to continue shelving your own dreams, avoiding your own greatness, and stepping into your own power that you're so terrified you don't have.

If you can blame somebody else and get your family/ community to buy into the fact that your life is sooo pathetic, maybe nobody will have any expectations of you. And maybe, if only momentarily, you can ease the noise of your own self-loathing, surely a result of your own failed expectations of yourself.

"It's all his fault," you cry! "Shame on him for doing this to me!" No—shame on you for giving up on yourSelf, for not handling your own shit (past traumas, toxic emotions, personal issues, etc.) such that they continue to resurface over and over in new forms This is what is meant by being so desperate *not* to see ourSelves…that we will create all manner of chaos, trauma, and distractions just to keep the truth of us hidden.

Your shaming of the other wasn't a bad plan—most people fall for the sob story. Typically it's pretty effective. However, it won't make a difference. That's not how we roll in the world of 100% Self-responsibility. In this world, it will always be self-examination first.

**Truth Bomb Number 6:** You need to trust yourSelf, NOT your partner.

You deserve to trust yourSelf to make wise choices, exercise discernment, and listen to your intuition. Your intuition has always been speaking to you, yet you've chosen to ignore it again and again. You bury your head in the sand in hopes your intuition is wrong. You have preferred lies to the truth, hence…that's what you've received. You do not want to acknowledge this simple fact, so you project your own lack of trust onto your partner. How convenient. If you want things to be different, learn to trust *you*.

Do you really need to trust him? Is that true? No! You need to trust your fucking Self! If you have a need to trust him, it's probably because you don't already—you are suspicious, you are worried, you have concerns, you believe he isn't trustworthy. Your great need to trust comes from your own insecurities, and your own desires to control people, situations, and events. What you resist, persists. You can't control anyone into trustworthy behavior.

People will always live up to your expectations of them. The more you believe him to be a cheater, the more you try to control and micromanage, the more you show him that you clearly do not trust him as far as you can throw/GPS him—guess what that creates? And guess who created that? You. Not the other. This is not rocket science, ladies.

**Truth Bomb Number 7:** If you spent as much time working on yourSelf as you do obsessing about what your partner is up to, you wouldn't be so worried about them leaving you.

Ever wonder why other women may appear more interesting to your mate? I know you'd like to go with the same old shallow reasons—younger, prettier, skinnier. Nope—that's too easy, and it's certainly not so for the man heading in a more conscious direction. He's drawn to those that are anxiously engaged in their lives, who's very presence has him feel invigorated and reminds him what it's like to be vibrant and alive. It's attractive to find someone that actually shares his ideas, curiosities, and inspirations—and doesn't treat him like a child. When's the last time you did that with your partner?

If all you've got going in that pretty lil head of yours is what your partner may be doing, and questioning him throughout the day about his whereabouts—you're boring...not to mention controlling AF. Chances are you put him in charge of your happiness long ago. If he's had any missteps along the way, he's clear you believe that your unhappiness, discontent, and resentment are all his fault. That's heavy, and not even accurate.

Those low-frequency emotions are your responsibility. They are the main contributor to your overall lack of vitality, malaise, and inevitable weakened immune system—not to mention how much negative energy they bring into your relationship.

Try on the possibility that your pain may be more about your own unexpressed potential than anything else. If you were to stop avoiding the responsibility of your own greatness and start spending your time deepening your character, developing your talents, pursuing your career, furthering your education, and prioritizing your Self-care, your own inner Self-worth would climb. You would have a sense of empowerment, you would start to feel alive again, and you wouldn't be so worried about your dude leaving you.

Why? Because YOU would have a life worth living! And guess what, dude would be way more interested in you all of a sudden—and so would everybody else. You would actually be free to choose whether you truly *wanted* to make it work or if you were done.

You would be *that* powerful. Instead of relying on guilt and shame to keep your man, you would see infinite possibilities available to you. You would have options.

**Truth Bomb Number 8:** If you decide to leave him, or he leaves you, and you don't handle your shit first, you will inevitably attract a new partner to play out your same victim drama.

If you continue taking no accountability and pointing your fingers away from yourSelf…

If you're thinking everything you just read was so mean and I don't know what I'm talking about…

If you feel you just need to find a better man, or better control the one you've got (ankle monitor, perhaps?)…

Well, good luck with that.

Everybody knows, the first step in any recovery program is to admit you have a problem. The irony here is that while many women send their husbands off to one of these groups to fix any number of problems, including sex, gambling, drug or alcohol addiction—they never dream of considering that they too may have a problem. Your man has probably already done that—and is attempting to atone for his sins. If you've never acknowledged what role *you* may have played, you will continue to repeat the saga.

Everybody wonders why sweet Molly continues to pick "bad men." Bad luck, I guess. No, Molly *is* the problem.

**Truth Bomb Number 9:** Zero victimization and 100% accountability is the only way to live an empowered life.

Nothing is an accident.

Everything that happens in your life is for your benefit and growth. Life is always happening *for* you, not *to* you. You have a choice to rise above your circumstances. Stop being addicted to your excuses, pain, and drama and love yourSelf enough to develop the strength to face the weight and responsibility of your own greatness.

We learn who we are through our challenges. Every life has tragedies and villains, sunshine and rain. You are *never* a victim. Your world is your creation—so own it, 100%. We are here to expand the evolution of our souls. Someday you may just thank this man for showing up perfectly for you.

*Chapter 25*

# Three Questions: Radical Honesty Required

That was a lot. #Sorrrynotsorry. I'm sorry, please forgive me, thank you, I love you.

But now that we're being accountable—and if you're still here after the last chapter—let's speak some real truth. I have some questions that you deserve to answer for yourSelves. Again, this is mostly for the ladies, but insert yourselves men, as it fits.

Ok. Let's pretend that 1) you actually took accountability for the results of your life, and that 2) you can see how your unfaithful dude has been the greatest gift for your personal growth.

The newfound clarity of your own accountability in this story of infidelity does not mean you have to stay in this relationship. There are still legit reasons why the relationship may no longer serve you—and maybe some of those reasons you haven't fully owned yet. It's just so much easier to point your fingers.

So here are your questions, ladies. And remember, only radical honesty will do if you're really longing to remain empowered and retain some sense of your newfound self-responsibility.

Question 1: Do you even know if you are still "in love" with this man?

Set aside any anger, resentment, jealousy or competitiveness for a moment and check in with your heart. Is he still your truth? Does this man still excite you? Are you lit up in his presence? Do you want to jump his bones? Do you have any respect left for him?

If not, do you really want to spend the rest of your days with someone you are not madly, passionately in love with, or that may not feel the same way about you? Or did you fall out of love with this man a long time ago? Maybe even before he was ever unfaithful and sought out another woman?

Question 2: If you're not in love with him, have you dutifully replaced love with some socially accepted moral high ground?

Has this partnership become an obligation held together by what you were taught by your mommy and daddy, or your religion, that you're *supposed* to stick with it no matter what? And being the good girl that you are, you're going to "endure till the end." Maybe your righteous plan is to wait till the kids grow up and then check out—surely God and the neighbors would sanction that? Either of the reasons above put you in a much better light than the truth I'm going to suggest next.

Staying for God or the kids maintains your sparkling morality. It's often the two cards you sneaky victims play, instead of admitting the real truth of the next question. And, if you are truly staying because of your religion or the children, would you want your partner to stay with you if that were *his* only reason? Does this not wreak of a little ewwww to you?

Personally, if any man of mine just wasn't that into me, I would've wanted him to leave yesterday! Force himself to stay with me because of some commitment to an institution, or to keep the kids happy? Yuckity yuck, yuck yuck!! Fuck no!

Question 3: Is there *any* part of you that is staying in this partnership because you are afraid you can't make it financially on your own?

That's the million-dollar question ladies (pun intended). Think about that for a minute, or ten. You deserve to *seriously* evaluate this question. Get honest, at least with yourself. If you had an incredible job or a few million dollars, would you be sticking it out with this particular person? Most women don't want to look too closely here, let alone talk about this out loud.

If you stick to your *"holy"* reasons for staying with your cheating husband, you get to keep this answer under wraps till your dying days. Nobody will ever know your dirty lil secret. The best you can hope for, if you're in it for the money, is to feign love while making the dude feel guilty for destroying your "perfect façade" of a family, whilst you now have the perfect excuse to not even fuck him due to your "trauma." All this while maintaining your desired "status quo." Score. #shitnobodytalksabout

Although this pathetic lil plan may work for a time while you sit home being a lackluster wife and mother, having all your needs met, and keeping your fears at bay, inside you are dying. You have resigned yourSelf to a life of quiet desperation—better hope you can keep your slave (a.k.a. husband) in check.

If this is the case, you're no different than the prostitutes he picked up. Only the prostitutes are being much more honest with him than you are—and probably more generous…for less. Tell me why he needs you, again?

Ya know what would be way better and exponentially more attractive than staying with someone you don't love or trust, just for the money? Owning your shit. Taking real charge of and responsibility for your life, instead of trying to hijack somebody else's. Remember who the fuck you are and take your power back. How about dusting off your dreams and ambitions and taking real steps in that direction? How good would that feel? Imagine the possibilities!

If you loved YOU, you would be doing *your* life, being a rock star, and he would have an interesting partner that was actually excited about her own life, instead of controlling his! Do you know how attractive that would be to your partner—and more importantly yourSelf?

And if you got honest and clear that you weren't in love with him, you would actually have the balls to leave or divorce his ass. What if this were the best thing that ever happened to you? Staying or going as a powerful woman, not a pathetic victim. You could do it with your head held high, acknowledging your role in the demise of the relationship, and parting friends, not enemies.

If that were the case, nobody would have any need to "screw anybody over." You could share your kids/pets and split your shit with a lil love and gratitude in your heart, knowing that you each played your roles perfectly for each other. You'd both leave with a little more wisdom than that with which you entered, excited to consciously create your new lives.

This is where that beautiful Hawaiian prayer of ho'oponopono comes in: "I'm sorry, please forgive me, thank you, I love you." Or if you prefer, my own simple mantra, "I love you. I bless you. I release you," usually said with a sigh of relief and always wishing the other well.

## Chapter 26

# So Your Girl Checked Out: You're Probably A Pussy. Time To Daddy Up!!

*To live is to choose. But to choose well, you must know who you are and what you stand for, where you want to go and why you want to get there.*
*~Kofi Annan*

Gentlemen, it's your turn—you didn't think you were going to be left out, did you?

How would you like to know 9 secrets about how everything you thought you were supposed to do to win a woman and keep her was, in fact, the fast track to losing her? Not only to losing her, but by doing these things you will actually reveal your lack of self-esteem and self-worth, your lack of conviction and a backbone, and your ultimate desperation. None of which are remotely attractive in the male species.

~ ~ ~

Want to know the real reason good women lose interest and may cheat? It's different than why you cheat. Quality women stray because they've lost respect for you in some or many ways. All of the following truth bombs relate to what men do, or don't do, to lose a woman's respect. And a loss of respect often means a sharp decline in attraction, which may eventually lead to your woman looking elsewhere—or not giving you the time of day in the first place.

One of the biggest ways you men lose respect is by being too nice—putting her needs above yours at your own detriment and against your better judgement. You seem to think that being "the nice guy," letting her make all the decisions, handing over all your money, giving her everything she wants, and putting her first was going to earn you unlimited brownie points. You were wrong. You've been duped.

You've got women all wrong. This notion that the more you give into her, let her have her way, and do what she says, the more she is going to love you, is bullshit. Strong, confident women don't really want a man that will cater to her every whim.

You may think she wants the bad boy, but that's not entirely true either. Here's what the bad boy's got over you. A so-called bad boy is "bad"—and, therefore, attractive—because he can't be pushed around or easily swayed. A bad boy is selfish and has his own interests first and foremost. A bad boy is not going to stop what he's doing because his girl wants him to hang her curtains or go rescue her fucking cat. He has a strong sense of self—even if he is a narcissist.

Dropping everything you're doing for something menial that she asks of you is one of the worst things you can do and the quickest way to lose her— that is, after she takes all your money, has you fix every broken thing in her house, yard, and car, and has you set up her website. It may take a minute (or years) for her to kick you to the curb because you are soooo fucking useful. However, while you're slaving for her, she'll be off sexting some bad boy from the gym in no time.

Wait…am I saying that doing things for your woman is a bad idea? No. Not at all. Is your head spinning already? Am I just proving the point that some women don't know what the fuck they want?

Here's the deal, the following truth bombs will help clarify:

**Truth Bomb Number 1:** A conscious woman will value a man that is more dedicated to himSelf and his mission than he is to her—at least initially.

Putting us above everything else in your life makes you untrustworthy. Don't get me wrong, we are not interested in being with a narcissist either. But if you're purpose driven, stick to it and don't let it go or hit the pause button just because we ask you to come shopping with us.

Yes, we absolutely love when you do helpful, considerate, and sweet things for us. However, we really do want a man that is committed to a bigger purpose and higher calling. We really don't want a puppet that we can control like some of our mothers did to our fathers. When you can control a man, he ain't a man. The very nature of man is that he is powerful, strong, assertive, and knows who he is. Anything less, and you lose us—or at least our respect.

And if you lose our respect, it is a downhill slope from there—one from which you may never recover. You need to wear the pants—or at least your own pants. There is nothing worse or more unattractive to a woman than a weak-willed or wishy-washy man. Ewww.

So, to clarify, it's not the asshole in the bad boy that women are drawn to—it's that he is self-directed and will not succumb to our whining, pleading or bullshit. Yes, we want and need your assistance at times—we depend on you to show up for us in these ways. But we really don't want you to do it at your own expense.

Your dedication to your own mission, business, children, and workouts are something we find highly attractive—sexy, in fact. Even if we complain about it. There is nothing hotter than man who's rock solid from the inside. Big difference from the bad boy who really doesn't give a shit about her or anyone else but himself.

You taking care of you and the things that are important to you, makes you the opposite of wishy-washy. When you refuse to stay up late with us, stay home from the gym, or eat the unhealthy food we make you—you make your truth clear by your actions. You understand that when you take care of you, you are much more capable of caring for those in your orbit. We now know what is important to you, and we can't help but respect it—whether we like it or not. Unlike the bad boy, we know that when we *truly* need you, you will show up for us too—because you show up for yourself. That's hot.

If you are just dating, don't do too much too soon! When you do, there's an energy of you trying too hard to get us to like you. Get rid of all the "in order to" energy behind your doings. Don't do anything for us "in order to" make us like you more, "in order to" get laid, "in order to" get something in return, or "in order to" show off. Do it from the goodness of your heart because you are able to and because you *want* to, with no ulterior motive—or don't do it at all. Just don't overdo it too soon.

**Truth Bomb Number 2:** Women don't want a man that will turn all of his decision-making power over to her.

Always have a voice and speak your truth.

Do not let us put pink pillows in our shared bedroom or allow us to decorate our home as if it's inhabited by a Disney Princess unless you approve, or you truly don't care. A man lives here, there should be some evidence of YOU—not just in your man cave, garage or one room that you squirreled away for yourself. Have an opinion! Make your home look like it's yours, too! Do not give all decision-making power to your woman.

If you truly don't like something, say so! Otherwise, every time you look at those fucking pillows, they will bug you and you may feel emasculated. Not because the pillows are pink, but because you no longer have a voice. Always have a voice! Speak your truth even if you feel you may risk losing her. Women respect men with opinions, whether we agree with you or not. (Just try not to be stupid.)

Also, do not allow us to tell you where you can and can't go or what you can or can't do. Do not let us deny you your boys' night, hunting weekend or golf trip with the guys. Men deserve the company of good men, just like we need our girl time. To not go, or not even consider it because you fear her wrath, makes you weak. You shouldn't feel like you need permission. Still, in a strong partnership, we consult each other when making plans—it shows respect, and it feels like we're a team.

The same goes with getting a motorcycle, guitar, racing cars or playing in a band. If it's something your lil masculine heart desires, you get to do it. Again, just don't be dumb. And it's great to be consulted. Just know that you get the last word—and thank you for taking our feelings into account.

You get to have women friends, too! Just be transparent. If you allow your woman to make you eliminate long-time girlfriends (real friends, not former lovers), you're a total pussy with an insecure tyrant as a wife or gf. If you are a good guy with nothing to hide this should not be a problem (even for you to be friends with former girlfriends). If your woman is that insecure about your affection or your trustworthiness, that's her issue to work through. She is not the boss of you. Just be transparent and don't be an ass.

**Truth Bomb Number 3:** We lack trust in men who don't spend time with and invest in their own children.

Be a man and Daddy up with the kiddos.

Do not absolve yourself from their rearing because you may be the bread winner and she is home with the kids. Do not let us teach your/our children something that you do not believe in or disagree with. Your offspring and how their young minds are being shaped and programmed ought to be important to you. When you are an active participant in the important things having to do with their development, that's notable.

If you are dating or in a second marriage, do not allow your new girl to get in the way of your relationship with your children by having you see them less, pay less child support, not attend their events or by disconnecting with them in any way. If your woman pulls the jealousy card with your own kids and tries to make you choose between her and them to prove your love—dump her, asap.

Do not allow your ex-baby momma to keep you from your kids, either. She may try—never make it easy for her. If you succumb, she will dis you to all her friends and family and talk about what a shitty father you are—even to your children in subtle, and not-so-subtle ways. They are your children, too.

If you really don't give a shit and think your life would be much easier if you didn't have anything to do with your own offspring—this book is not for you. Any quality woman that would be ok with you abandoning your own kids knows she will just as easily find herself rejected and abandoned. It speaks volumes about the kind of man you are—be prepared for the boot.

I once dated a recently divorced guy that was in a real battle with his ex, and the children were one of their points of contention. One day he and I were just leaving the driveway when his son called saying he'd broken a finger skiing and asked to be picked up from the resort. This guy blatantly lied to his son saying that he was working and that his mother was going to have to "figure it out." I was mortified.

"Go get him…we can hang out another time," I said. He responded venomously about his ex, saying that if she wanted the kids to herself so much, she was the one that was going to have to deal with them. My respect for him plummeted in that moment—and never returned.

A man who doesn't love and invest in his own children is not worthy of a woman's respect. Nor is a woman who attempts to keep a man from his kids. Children are not pawns, and to use them in that way is deplorable.

**Truth Bomb Number 4:** We really don't want a man that will sit quietly back while we spend his or *our own* hard-earned money frivolously.

Money is equivalent to power—don't give it all away. You will be seen as a pushover.

Do not throw money at us or let us spend yours, or our own money, haphazardly. Don't blindly give up 100% control of the purse strings. Be involved and know where the money is going each month.

Am I saying you need to control every dime? Hell, no! I'm saying have some clear communication about your financial goals and at least some loose agreement as to how you will spend your hard-earned cashola. Decide together which part of the budget is discretionary, what's for bills, and mutually agreed upon savings.

If she has her own job or source of income, know that it's hers and she has a right to do what she wants with it. But don't allow a double standard where she gets to control all of hers and your cash, too. That clever lil quip that "what's mine is mine, and what's yours is mine" is cute, but total bs.

When women (or men) have 100% discretion over the family income, it's an imbalance of power and though they may be thrilled about it, they won't respect you for it. It's dangerous.

Be helpful. Not in a judgmental way, but in an open communication kinda way. If you know more about investing or financial stuff, share your wisdom. Like most things, this is an area better served by both parties with some checks and balances to avoid resentments and maintain respect.

A man who doesn't care about how his money is being spent is not trustworthy. If you let us spend whatever we want without question, or buy us *everything* we desire, it feels like you are trying to buy our love and keep us happy. Though generous, it's a weak move.

We want to know that you have a bigger plan for our future and that you care where our money is going—like a smart man should. There is an interesting balance of power with money—don't be foolish, but don't be a tyrant either!

Same goes for your kids. Don't buy them everything their lil hearts desire in exchange for their love, or because you feel guilty for not spending more time with them. Instead, spend more time with them! Teach them the value of money, how to earn it, and why they deserve to save some of it.

Red alert, men! If your disinterested wife starts hiring personal trainers, getting plastic surgery, boob jobs, tummy tucks, Botox, and buying a new wardrobe all of a sudden, she may just be prepping for her exit. She'll need to look her best out in the single market. Funny enough, it's a thing. Just have a clue where your pennies are going. Be cognizant of behavioral changes with the finances. Sorry ladies :(

**Truth Bomb Number 5:** Don't let your woman permanently give up her career/schooling for yours—at some point, she will resent you for it.

Do everything you can to encourage her to get her degree, follow her passions and assist her in being independent. If she did give up her job/career to have babies or to put you through school, return the favor and get her back to school as soon as it's feasible. Watch the kids in the evening, pay for it, encourage her, insist! Take away every excuse that she may have to not complete her degree or master her craft. It shows your genuine concern for her and your confidence that you don't need her to remain "barefoot and pregnant."

You don't ever want her to stay with you because she feels she has no options, can't afford to be on her own or has no clue what she'd do without you. It feels much better knowing that she could do anything and be anything, and she still *chooses* you.

And what if something happened to you? You don't want her to be forced into some kind of menial labor job just to get by or feel like she has to marry some jackass to be taken care of. If you care about her, teach a woman to fish already. She may resist—push it! She will thank you later and respect you for it, whether she says so or not.

If you are one of those dudes that believes that "if she doesn't need you, she will leave you," then wtf!? Are you nothing but a paycheck? Is your sole sense of worth tied to your income? If that's the case, you should be worried. If you don't know who you are outside of that paycheck, then you are not a strong man. Your ability to provide, though sexy and desirable, will not cut it with a woman on an evolutionary path. Don't worry though, there are plenty of Muggle women that will have you simply based on your proven ability to earn alone—won't matter if you've let yourself go or if you're dumb as a rock in all other areas.

If you have insecurities about your wife leaving you if she no longer needs your financial support, then two things: 1) Why are you with this shallow being?, and 2) Why do you feel that's all you are good for? Time to work on your Self-love and worth. Get a life—have some interests outside of your work and your relationship. Do some inner work, see a coach or therapist. Know your worth outside of your income.

If your worse fears come true and she does leave you, good for you! Would you have wanted this shell of a woman to stay with you because you were her only option? Would you have preferred her feigned interest indefinitely to being alone—or to finding someone that is genuinely into you? Hint: YOU will have to be into you before anyone else ever is.

Let it be enough that you did something honorable by assisting her to take care of herself. Chances are she's made plenty of sacrifices for you in the past. Consider her repaid and move on with your head held high.

**Truth Bomb Number 6:** We don't want you to get too complacent in bed, or consistently be overly sweet and gentle.

Women like variety, too. We want to be taken by you and know that you are still turned on by us.

Just because your woman liked something 10 years ago, and it still seems to be "working," don't rest on your laurels. Spice it up! If you're curious, know that she most likely is too. What haven't you done together? Can you take a tantra class, try some different positions or different locations? Maybe one night each month it's all about her, and you take nothing for you. Maybe some role playing…meet at a local bar and pretend you are meeting for the first time. Try objectifying her a lil more…whaaaaa?!?!? Let me explain.

As much as you hear women complaining about being objectified by men, you'd think they totally hate it. But that's not entirely true. Hear me out. It's one of the reasons she turns to the bad boy. He has no problem telling her she's hot AF and what he wants to do to her amazing body. Though he may be brazen, there is no question as to his desire for her. Men seem to think that women just want to hear you declaring your love and devotion and telling her what a fabulous mother and wifey she is. While that's all sweet and good, and we do love to hear those things, to maintain her *sexual* interest you'll have to stretch a little more than that.

As a "good man," you may never dream of uttering things in her ear like, "I'd like to fuck your brains out," or "You are sooo hot tonight. I am going to skip the foreplay entirely and not apologize for it," for fear of rejection, or a slap across the face. It's exactly what she needs! While she really has no interest in the dirtbag random guy that says shit like that to her, to hear her husband/partner saying naughty things is a total turn on (unless your girl has become a nun—then you have other issues)! She already knows you love her. What she wants to know now is that you still *desire* her above all others—that *your* body craves *her* body. She wants to know that she still makes you hard at the mere sight of her.

A real problem in long-term relationships, according to Esther Perel, author, therapist and relationship expert, is maintaining eroticism with each other. Sometimes all the ooey gooey, nurturing love we have for each other, while comforting and blissful, can be a far cry from building arousal, passion, and desire. What you need is a good dose of objectification.

Instead of seeing your woman as just the wonderful mother of your children, or the brilliant, successful woman that she is, try also seeing her as your temple of pleasure, your gateway to sensual, erotic play. Send her naughty texts throughout the day. Tell her she has a great ass once in a while or that she looks super sexy in that black dress. When you get home whisper something in her ear that will make her blush in front of the kids. She'll be pulling you into the bedroom and locking the door in no time—and have zero need for that bad boy.

**Truth Bomb Number 7:** Though we want you to be intimate and vulnerable with us, don't be too emotional—and definitely don't be a whiny little bitch.

"I knew it," you declare, "we got bad information." Wait.

Just consider what you are sharing. There's a difference between serious grief and being a whiner. If your mother died, we expect you to cry and we want to be there for you and comfort you in all the ways that we can, whether it's a listening ear, sex, or good food. We got you. However, don't be a cry baby about losing a video, poker or softball game. That's lame. Determine to do better next time. Be a man.

We don't want to hear that Joe at the office disrespects you, that you lost some verbal war with your brother, that your momma has always favored your sisters over you or that someone at the bank was rude to you. The bad boy is never going to tell us any of that or that he's afraid he can't make his motorcycle payment next month. We don't want to see our man as weak— or whiney. Daddy up!

Never talk shit on yourself in front of us or say things like you'll never get a raise, progress in your job, lose weight, get healthy or make anything of yourself. Don't say you are a loser, stupid, broke, that you don't know why your girl would choose you or that she deserves so much better. This wreaks of victim mentality and is a total buzz kill. Ewww. If *you* think that, why should *she* think anything different?

Don't use your girl as a crutch for your pathetic need for self-validation either—she's not your mommy. Being needy is soooo unattractive. Fake it 'til you make it, dude. Or get a therapist, coach or guy friend to share that whiney shit with next time.

Sharing your genuine emotions or fears is totally different. It can be healing to share, and a bonding experience. We want you to be vulnerable with us and share how you are feeling about our relationship, things that may be bothering/ worrying you, and concerns that you may have.

We don't want you to be a robot, we want to feel your deep passion and share your heart felt sadness and grief—just don't be a whiny lil bitch. That's gross—unless you're sick…then it's kinda cute :) We really do want to take care of you, too. Please let us. We just don't want to be your mommy, FFS.

**Truth Bomb Number 8:** Do not accept chronically petty, domineering or bitchy behavior in your woman—she will never respect you for it and it's not gonna get you laid.

You should never feel like you are walking on eggshells around your woman.

If you did something stupid, make a sincere apology. Be sensitive, but move on. Never cower, make yourself small or be afraid of us. Eww. Show us you're the boss man.

Tip toeing around your woman is about fear. It's unattractive and you deserve to stop being such a pussy. If you are with a woman that has you feeling this way, time to examine the dynamic and when you lost your balls to her or if you ever had them in the first place. Seriously, if you are afraid of her moods, not doing anything right or incurring her wrath at the slightest little thing, then 1) What happened to you? 2) When did you lose your self-respect and self-worth?, and 3) Why are you still putting up with this, bitch? You have permission to man-up or GAFDA!

If your woman has this kind of power over you, you are nothing but her slave. She rules. She has zero respect for you and would cheat on you in a heartbeat. And if not cheat on you, then use you, feel entitled to everything you have, and take you to the cleaners when you try to divorce her—or when she finds a better deal and leaves you.

But she's not worried about you going anywhere because most of you will never even try to leave her. You actually fear this hostile bitch leaving *you*! You act this way because you have zero self-worth, think that she is the best you can do, falsely worship her, and even wonder how she ever chose you in the first place! I'll tell you how—you are a weak man and she is a tyrant. You go together like PB&J.

Men like this are afraid to question their woman about any of her decisions, what she does with all of the money or where she goes every Thursday night. You will bend over backward for this woman for a single crumb of affection or acknowledgment, which she rarely gives you no matter what you do. On those rare occasions that she agrees to have sex with you, she will have you feeling like she did you the biggest favor, even if all she did was lay there. This will never get better. Her scope of control will just get larger as you continue to acquiesce to all her whims in a feeble attempt to please her and make her happy.

The only way to change this dynamic is for you to gain genuine self-worth and to feel that you are deserving and desirous of something more. If you are this man, you have this woman on a very undeserving pedestal and are most likely drowning in a sea of metaphoric self-flagellation. This is exactly where your lil tyrant would have you be—a slave under her thumb. Newsflash: She is the consolation prize for thinking so little of yourSelf.

Open your eyes. This isn't love. For fun, make a list of all the wonderful things you do for her and try to come up with a list even half as long of what she does for you. If all you can come up with is her fabulous presence (which btw, is all she feels she need contribute), she doesn't love you. Stop lying to yourself.

You probably had a very controlling mother if I had to guess. If you had a father, he was most likely completely emasculated by your mom and nothing you did was ever good enough for one or either of them.

This has got to stop. You need help. You may not believe this right now, but you will be so much better off without her. Until you take your power back and learn to love yourself, you can't expect anyone "out there" to do otherwise either. Get out. Take care of you and get a fucking divorce, already.

**Truth Bomb Number 9:** Don't overdo it. Women hate pushovers.

Do not fall all over us, have us feel like you love us way more than we love you, or that you would die without us. Barf.

Yes, we want to feel secure in your love and affection; however, we also want to know that you are a passionate, red-blooded man out in the world that is attractive to the opposite sex—that you too have options. When you act sooo grateful and relieved that a girl like us would be interested in a guy like you, it makes us question our own choice and judgment. Don't make us feel like you are the lucky one and we got the booby prize!

I'm not telling you to try to make us jealous, play on our insecurities or create a fear of losing you. But we do not want to feel like we could treat you like shit, ignore you for eternity, and think you would still be hanging around kissing our ass because this is the best "a guy like you" could ever hope for.

Nor do we want to feel that you are so content and in love with us that you could *never* look at another woman. Yawn. Don't pretend you don't see the obviously beautiful Victoria Secret-like model that just walked by. Pretending not to see her is a lie. Don't start comparing us to her though, that's a jackass move.

As a woman, I want to know that you choose me—and not blindly. That even though there are plenty of other attractive women in the world that might also be attracted to you, I'm still your girl. Keep your woman on her toes, like she'd be wise to do with you, so you don't take each other for granted. I'm not talking about game playing either, just be observant about how the scales are tipping.

Don't withhold your affection, compliments or acknowledgment. Just don't go overboard or allow a major imbalance. Pay attention—if you are always the one giving out compliments and none are coming back, or they are just in response to yours, slow your roll. She's not going to love you more, and she may respect you less.

Make your compliments authentic so they are worth more! I had a sweet husband that would tell me I looked great when I clearly didn't, or that my meal of a basic salad and potatoes was the best meal he'd ever had. C'mon. Though sweet, it's bullshit. Acknowledge the effort, maybe, but don't shovel complimentary shit—keep it real so we trust you. I called him King

Shoveler because he complimented everything, which made nothing special.

Do what you can to maintain the polarity. Make sure she is as into you as you are into her. When that scale is consistently tipped in one direction, respect will be lacking.

Gentlemen, it all boils down to respect—and specifically *your* respect for yourSelf. Women lose interest, cheat or check out because they've lost respect for you. And if they've lost respect for you, chances are it's because you stopped respecting yourSelf. Testosterone is attractive. Lack of self-worth is super-de-duper unattractive.

I'm not saying to start being a dick, but if you'd like her to stay, you should definitely stop being a pushover. Your girl will wonder what got into you and it just may save your relationship. Most of you would do well to just wake up and get a fucking divorce, already.

Warning, some women of lower consciousness really do want a man-slave, so she may leave you if you take your power back. If that happens, it will be the best thing that ever happened to you, though you may be too busy crying about it to realize it. When you wake up and reclaim your manhood and self-worth, you will see all of the ridiculous stories you've had to tell yourSelf to remain in that unhealthy place.

Before you split, manage your shit. You'll need a massive reboot whether you decide to stay or go. You can't allow the masculine polarity to slip through your fingers again unless you want the same results with somebody new. Time to put your big boy pants on, take back the reins, stop being a pussy, and daddy up!!

There is hope on the horizon. Take some time for yourSelf. Get to know who you are without the external need for the validation of a woman. Enjoy the freedom that comes from leaving the cage of slavery, subservience, and being used. Acknowledge yourSelf for your courage to speak up for yourSelf, take your power back and make a positive shift for your own benefit for a change. You are headed in the right direction.

Remember, we teach people how to treat us. Don't be afraid of a woman not wanting you if you put your Self and your mission first—those women are not the droids you are looking for. Just do you for a while, figure out what you value, who you want to be and how you want to show up in the world. Be strong on the inside. That is the result of knowing who you are, not giving a shit about the opinions of others, and just being an authentic human—it's sexy AF.

## Chapter 27

# I Need Your Trust: Is That True?

Though we touched on trust in Truth Bomb Number 6 for the ladies, I decided it deserved a littler expansion for both sexes.

"I *need* to trust you." Is that true?

"I need *you* to trust *me*." Is that true?

Do you really *need* to trust your spouse/partner? Do you *need* them to trust you? What does that even mean?

Ultimately, if I trust mySelf and I trust life, then I don't *need* to trust anyone else. If I didn't have some high level of trust in you to begin with, you wouldn't be in my life. I trust mySelf to choose people that contribute to my life and not suck/drain life energy away from it. I trust mySelf to let go of toxic people, food, environments, and relationships in a timely manner. I trust mySelf to let go of unhealthy and non-nourishing behaviors in favor of their healthy, nourishing counterparts.

My partner can do whatever it is they're going to do, and I will be just fine. I believe that life is always unfolding for my highest good. If you betray that trust, there may be consequences—oh well. If you feel someone betrays you or does you wrong in some way, you have a choice to make. Your partner is going to cheat on you if he wants to, whether you deem him trustworthy or not.

Your kids are going to do whatever they want to do—have sex, drink, smoke weed, whatever—whether you trust them or not. Relax. Life is going to life. You can't control everything and everyone.

As I said before, if you have a *need* to trust, it's probably because you don't already—*you're* suspicious, *you're* worried, *you're* concerned. You believe they're not trustworthy—so that's what you get. Nobody can prove to you beyond all doubt that they are trustworthy, nor do you want them to. A forced pledge of allegiance can never be trusted. People will be trustworthy or they won't.

Your great *need* to trust comes from your own insecurities and lack of self-trust, which results in a desire to control people, situations, and events. You can't just control people into trustworthy behavior. Your best hope is to learn how to trust yourSelf and be in alignment with your own truth. People will reveal themselves in time. If you are trustworthy, you will attract trustworthy people.

If you are a suspicious motherfucker, the kind and benevolent Universe will give you all kinds of reasons, situations, and people to be suspicious of and *not* trust. If I am one of those people, then I will constantly be on the lookout for reasons *not* to trust anyone or anything in my space. And that, my friends, will eat up a shit-ton of my vitality and energy, something I choose not to do. And that's not all—I will inevitably find exactly what I'm looking for!! My booby prize—I get to be RIGHT!!!

Let's define the verb to "trust:" to believe that someone or something is reliable, good, honest, effective, etc.; or, to have confidence in someone or something. So based on that definition, I ask again: "*I need you to trust me.*" Is that true? Nope. I don't need you to think *anything* of me. I will be trustworthy or I won't. No amount of what *you* think of me will make it so or not. Your interpretation or perception of me is just that—YOURS. It is not my business. I don't *need* you to trust me. And I don't give a fuck what you think of me.

Some people will trust you and some won't. So what. What they think of you is not your concern. What YOU think of YOU, is. Can you trust yourSelf? If your answer is "no," don't be pissed if others don't trust you either. If your answer is "yes," good for you! Who gives a shit what somebody else thinks?! You just keep proving yourself trustworthy to YOU! When you do that, and you know the truth of YOU, then it won't matter. If someone can't see your trustworthiness, that is their problem and their own projection.

There are some people I am just going to choose to trust. There are others that feel unsafe for me to extend that courtesy to, so I love them, I bless them, and I release them from my inner circle. I have no expectations of those in my inner circle. I know their character. I don't have to *ask* if they'd have my back. I don't have to trust, hope, and cross my fingers that they will—I just KNOW.

I also know that we all have our moments of feeling out of alignment with our own truth. In those rare moments that someone chooses something that hurts my lil feelings, or makes a choice that I don't like, I get to be OK and just trust that they are doing what is best for them. Then I get to make a choice about what is in *my* best interest—sans drama. I trust myself to be ok with whatever happens in my life—loss, pain or otherwise. I also trust that I will be conscious enough to ask mySelf why I am attracting such people, circumstances, and events into my life and be courageous enough to look within mySelf to acknowledge my own similar shortcomings and self-correct.

I need to trust mySelf—is *that* true? I'm not sure if it is true or if it isn't, but what I do know is that it sure makes life much easier. Choices are more freely made without major deliberation. There is a greater sense of stability and groundedness. Fears of the future dissipate. A certain inner calmness and peace will reside in your being. A feeling of self-respect and unconditional friendliness within one's Self seems to arise. When I trust mySelf, it feels good. It also feels good that I don't *need* to trust you or have you trust me. My happiness is not dependent on that which is outside of mySelf.

Is it good/nice to trust your partner? Sure. And it really doesn't make a big difference. The best way to ensure you attract trustworthy people into your life is to be one. Simple as that.

Being trustworthy to one's Self includes not buying into your own bullshit and lies. It requires being radically honest with yourSelf first and foremost. And then to carry that radical honesty into all areas of your life. You can't be faithful to your romantic partner while concurrently being a lying, cheating business partner, family gossiper or secret sharer and expect your lover to be honest and trustworthy. If you are putting out the energy of dishonesty in *any* area of your life, do not be surprised when it comes back to you from *any* source.

So maybe you are sexually faithful to your husband but you're not really in love with him anymore, but you pretend to be out of a fear of loss, financially or otherwise. You are living a lie. That energy will be felt, no matter how you attempt to hide it. Anything intentionally omitted for your own benefit is an overt attempt at deception. Don't be surprised if your husband cheats or your business partner steals from you. You are not in integrity and will attract the same thing into your life so that you can see exactly that if you care to look.

A few types to be leery of: married people, addicts, and religious folks.

If you consciously choose to enter a relationship with a married person, and you hear them effortlessly lying to their spouse, they will do the same to you and/or in other areas of their life. Hello, you are a cheater, with a cheater. What else could be so? If they have no integrity with their spouse, they will most likely have none with you, unless they have a major state shift.

Addicts are used to lying. Steer clear. Their biggest lie is always to themselves first. They can handle it. (Lie.) One more drink, pill, shot won't hurt. (Lie.) They can choose to quit at any moment. (Lie.) They are in control. (Lie.) It won't effect their (or your) life. (Lie.) They can still be good at their job, roles, and duties. (Lie) Again, I do believe that people who earnestly desire to transform can and do. It is most often hard-won, and comes with radical Self-honesty, humility, and deep Self-inquiry—just like any sincere personal work. I honor those peeps.

And then there's the religious types. I will always choose to align with someone with *personal integrity* as opposed to those who claim religious morality. Here's why religious people are hard to trust. When someone's moral code is attached to something external, be it religion, parents or society, and not their own personal morality, it is easier to break. It's "out there," not an internal code of ethics.

I know, for example, plenty of die-hard Mormons that will argue with you all day that their church is the only true church on the planet. Yet those same Mormons won't think twice about trying to fuck their date, though their church says that premarital sex is next to murder on the you're-going-to-hell scale. Huh? Yuh…dualistic AF, right? Oh, they may feel a little guilt after their one-night stand or their nightly romp with a gf or bf, but if it doesn't get in their way. There appears to be an integrity issue.

Look for people that are honest with and have integrity with themSelves. If they keep their commitments to themSelves, they will to you as well. Look for those that keep their promises to their children, that are on time, that do what they say they are going to do. Observe carefully when you're dating someone, choosing business partners or friends. How we do one thing is often how we do everything.

What I really desire to trust about my partner is that he trusts himSelf. I choose to trust a partner that knows who he is and that is bound by his own truth and heart—not mine, his parents' or his church's. I choose to trust a partner that is solid from within, that knows the voice of his own Soul and is not afraid to speak his truth. I choose to trust a partner that is not swayed to and fro by my every whim and mood. I choose to trust a partner that will put his mission before his relationship with me if I try to get in the way of it.

I choose to create an environment that doesn't have my partner hanging around for years, months or even weeks because he is afraid of hurting my feelings after finding someone else, or "we" are just not working for him anymore. I trust that when there is an issue that we will discuss it and be true to ourSelves and not cave to any dogma or previous arrangement.

Do I need to trust you? No, I don't. I'd love you to be honest with yourSelf though. Do I need you to trust me? Fuck no I don't. I deserve to be honest with mySelf. If I am honest with me, I can't help but be honest with you by sharing my truth. To do otherwise is an act of Self-betrayal.

*Chapter 28*

# Betrayal Trauma: The Ultimate in Victim Mentality

While we are on the topic of betrayal…I recently came across a new term that I was curious about: "Betrayal Trauma." Ever heard of it? It was presented to me as a psychological disorder suffered by women who had been cheated on or who (prepare yourself) had caught their husband watching porn (insert shocked emoji). In my opinion, the manner in which these women were applying the term was a total bastardization from its original meaning—but not surprising, given the new, heightened level of victimhood it allowed them to claim.

Betrayal trauma, in its original conception, refers to young children—young enough to be completely reliant on their caregivers for survival—that are either badly abused or completely abandoned by those expected to care for them. For example, a 3-year-old whose mom takes them to grandma's and says, "Grandma is going to 'babysit' you for a while," and she *never* comes back. That makes sense when applied to young children being betrayed by their own parents, if we are going to make a disorder out of the experience.

But along comes the Victim Industrial Complex, and now the phrase is being co-opted for a much more conniving purpose. I spent some time researching the way women speaking about infidelity were repurposing this term. What I found was a myriad of (mostly female) psychologists and therapists, many of which had themselves been "cheated on" or "betrayed." I couldn't watch for very long. To be honest, I was thoroughly disgusted with the victim mentality surrounding all of it, and the almost 0% accountability that was placed on their side of the equation.[2]

Not only did they label the effects of their husband's infidelity (even if it were simply on a computer screen) betrayal "trauma," but they likened it to actual PTSD in war victims!! Yet nowhere did I see the so-called "victim" take *any* accountability whatsoever for *their* role in the co-creation. Any others daring to do so were touted as "victim shamers," and incurred their wrath. It was all about pointing the finger at the infidel and how their betrayal had *traumatized* them—the "victims."

Can you even imagine a guy claiming he had actual PTSD-level betrayal trauma from his wife's infidelity? He would get laughed right off the golf course.

"Wahhh…your wife was masturbating to porn?!"

"Lucky!"

"Awww your little wifey slept with your boss? You gonna cry about it or should we go kick his ass?"

Or simply, "Time to leave that bitch!"

---

[2] It felt so completely disempowering that I was inspired to create a movement called "She Freedom" to re-empower these women—the victims and the #metoo-ers—to give them back their power through being Self-responsible and re-establishing ownership over their lives. (The way the #metoo movement was repurposed from its original intent also feels completely disempowering to me—but I digress.)

Seriously though, it's not like I don't have any compassion. I'm sure I'd be devastated about *actual* sex my man had with another woman…but porn? I'm sorry, that's just laughable to a Boston girl. Sure, I'd be sad—or pissed about the *real* thing, but *traumatized,* like a veteran returning from the real horror of war? C'mon, man. What world do you live in? You didn't grow up with television? Or ever hear any gossip? Traumatized?!

The way these women were throwing around the term PTSD felt so watered down, it could be applied to practically anything. Make no mistake, PTSD is real—and that's why it shouldn't be diminished and applied to something that just happens to really upset you. That type of repurposing is selfish and self-serving. Watching bombs going off right in front of your face while other humans are blown to bits, or being violently gang raped and beaten, or kidnapped and abused for years, is a far cry from catching your grown-ass husband watching porn or finding out that he'd put his penis in another vagina! For fuck's sake! Get real!! Time to grow a pair ladies. There's a big, bad cruel world out there that awaits you when hubby kicks your whiney ass to the curb! Betrayal trauma…you're gonna wish that's all you had to deal with in the real world.

Anyone can claim to have mild "PTSD" when events in the present contain similar signatures of seemingly traumatic events from our past. It's called being "triggered." It happens often, as the stories we've told ourselves about past events get woven into our subconscious programming. When one of those past emotions are experienced and it reminds us of an undigested and/or unprocessed experience from our past, we get triggered and often react poorly—until we work that shit out, and then we don't.

If you had a father that was absent, abusive or fill in the blank, your story/perception of those behaviors or events from your childhood may manifest as thought forms that become beliefs like: "I'm not lovable," "everybody ignores me," "men can't be trusted," etc. Those are *made-up* stories, and often have no basis in reality.

Those *stories* are what have you feeling shame, grief, anxiety, anger or the like—not necessarily the *actual* thing that happened. Those stories create themes in our programming that continue to repeat themselves throughout our lives. If our story is "men can't be trusted," or "all men want is sex," we will create men in our lives who are untrustworthy or only want sex, until we deal with our own underlying stories and emotions surrounding trust. (See Carl Jung's writings on shadow work, or my upcoming book entitled *Beautiful Darkness,* for a more in-depth treatment of this topic.)

In the majority of these "betrayal trauma" cases, the so-called "victim" has felt similarly victimized in their childhood, whether it be sexual, physical or emotional abuse, or they've had stories of rejection, neglect, abandonment, and/or betrayal. There is inevitably a *signature story* that existed prior, that has undoubtedly reappeared in subsequent and current adult relationships. It doesn't have to be the exact same event each time, it's just the same old "story."

These victimhood peddlers even hijacked *another* term I'd not heard of: "trauma anniversary," or simply "traumaversary." This term actually applies to survivors of disaster and traumatic events, often of a violent or unexpected nature such as a fire, natural disaster, robbery, rape, fatal diagnosis, car accident, etc. My research said it was a response to *unresolved* grief resulting from significant losses and was also known as the Anniversary Effect or Anniversary Reaction, which totally makes sense.

But these opportunistic Victimarketers know a good thing when they see it. Nothing says victimhood like purposely re-living that one fateful day each year that you first caught your man looking at porn. Men, don't forget to buy flowers and obsequiously apologize, year after year.

Or maybe…try resolving your issues! Have some real conversations, rather than just pointing fingers. Ladies, it does you no good to add another day on the calendar to be moody, withholding, self-righteous bitches for years into the future for catching your husband touching himself, or for his repentant revelation that his work trips were often accompanied by happy ending massages. Your unwillingness to let go is not creating the life you desire! Ugh.

Again, can you see a *guy* sitting in a bar with his head in his cocktail, and his buddy says, "Dude, what's wrong?"

"Thanks for asking, Jack….it's my traumaversary of the day my wife told me she'd slept with another woman four years ago. Still can't get over it."

"Aww, buddy…that's rough. Next drink is on me," said no man—ever.

There's such a huge payoff for these adult "victims" to exaggerate their experience and blame their partners when they stray. The victims now have an excuse to indulge their neurosis without being called crazy or being called on the carpet for their own bad behavior. Under the guise of their "PTSD," caused *solely* by their partner (nothing to do with *their* past, of course), they get to be obsessive control freaks and monitor their partners every move—which is what they've wanted all along. They couldn't control their Daddy's behavior, but they sure as hell are going to do their best to control their partner's.

Because of their partner's infidelity, they now feel entitled to tracking their phone, monitoring their call records, reading their texts and emails, and scrutinizing every comment made to or from them on social media. Because of their so-called "trauma," they believe they have a right to keep their partners on a short leash, unable to go anywhere without their every minute accounted for. The "victims" think it's completely acceptable to make their partners jump through endless hoops playing their "I'm not safe" card, while concurrently withdrawing their love, affection, and intimacy. The victim gets *carte blanche* in exhibiting maniacal control over their partners, which they declare is the *only* way they feel they can possibly survive now. Call the Wambulance.

This obsession to control becomes a bottomless pit, one the so-called "perpetrator" can *never* fill. You cannot ass kiss, reassure, coddle or spoil her enough to *ever* make the poor "victim" feel safe. No amount of being faithful, accounting for your every move, deleting all social media, and even changing your phone number will never be enough.

This just feels so icky to me, and anything but empowering. I'd want to slit my wrist if I felt I had to keep track of my partner like that all day. What a buzz kill.

Ladies, do you really want an intimate partner that you have to almost force to be faithful to you? Do you really want to be with anybody that would rather be with someone else? Do you really want to be with someone that you have to heap guilt and shame upon just to stay with you, as you remind him constantly of the commitment he made to you a hundred years ago?

If you answered yes to any of these questions, you have massive self-worth issues. If you were having a conversation in your head that sounded like, "I'm not forcing him…he doesn't really want to be with anybody else. I'm not making him feel guilty…" check yourSelf. Get real. Are you sure? Or just more lies to make yourSelf feel better and ignore your intuition? Are you justifying your controlling behavior? Telling yourself that your dude deserves to be on a leash and should just lay down and take his punishment as payback?

If you're the dude or the unfaithful one, is any of this behavior going to "reform" you? Does being guilted and shamed for your behavior, whether it's the truth or not, leave feelings of love and warmth for your partner welling up in your bosom—or anywhere else for that matter? Does knowing that you're being watched, tracked, and spied upon all day have you feeling amorous when you come home?

Men, if you're going through this, and you don't see an end in sight to your partner's pathetic behavior, how long is this going to work for you? How long do you deserve to pay for your sins if there has been an infidelity? And if you're innocent, how long do you want to keep being falsely accused or made to feel like a total dirtbag for looking at porn on occasion and/or masturbating?

If you are obsessed with porn, that's another story. If you are choosing porn over your willing wife, that too is uncool. You deserve to work out *your* issues and deal with your own shit. However, If your wife is always chilly, uninterested in sex or has had a dramatic shift in her appearance and has no intention of making any changes, she ought to consider herself lucky if your "infidelity" was limited to just a computer screen and your hand. If there are several other things in the relationship that are still not working for you, and you've done your best to fix them to no avail, you may deserve to just get a fucking divorce already.

If you are a woman reading this or a man and the above "betrayal trauma" applies to you, don't you think you'd be happier if you took your power back? This certainly can't be any fun for you either.

If you were able to take your power back, you would have the strength to go; and, if you could own your part in all of this, you may have the courage to change and stay. You would at least feel like you had more options.

Imagine, ladies, instead of being whiny about how much you were hurt and victimized, that you sat your dude down and had some real talk about your relationship. Does he really want to stay? Do you really want him? Maybe some boundaries, such as "if this happens again, you're out." Or if it's just unacceptable, leave already instead of making life hell for both of you and celebrating your traumaversaries each year.

Perhaps instead of using any of your childhood issues as a disorder and, therefore, an excuse to be a victim, you could try a more conscious route. Do your own shadow work, uncover coping mechanisms that you developed in childhood to survive, integrate the painful experiences and reclaim your Highest Self. Consciousness and awareness are the path to releasing you from the prison of the past and will lead you to forgiveness, which is a much more sane, peaceful, and empowering way to thrive.

You are the creator of your life. Re-living the past will create the same future. Learn the tools of truly letting go, so you can create something new. Reliving your traumaversary each year keeps the past world alive and thriving…but I guess for some, that may be exactly what they desire. Somehow you think you'll get to maintain the upper-hand by exercising all of your little control features on someone else's life. Gross—and ineffective.

A great topic for these "victims" to examine that would be much more empowering for them is the term, Post Traumatic Growth. Post Traumatic Growth is a positive psychological change experienced as a result of adversity and other challenges in order to rise to a higher level of functioning. It doesn't deny deep distress, but rather posits that adversity can unintentionally yield changes in understanding oneself, others, and the world. The possibility of cultivating inner-strength through the knowledge that they have overcome some distress feels much better than forever wallowing. If you're going to create a "syndrome," choose Post Traumatic Growth over a traumaversary. Allow the inner payoff of empowerment to be what you seek instead of the outer payoff of sympathy. One expands, the other contracts.

Those who choose to "suffer" from "betrayal trauma" are self-imposed victims of a memory that no longer exists. Transcend the memory and your "story."

Create a new life.

# Part Five
*Illegit Reasons to Stay*

*Chapter 29*

# But I'm Comfortable: Are You Really?

"But I'm comfortable…." Really? Are you *really* comfortable?

Or are you just lazy AF? If I had a nickel for all of the marriages I'm personally aware of that are like this….

A "Comfort Zone Marriage" runs on autopilot, either one or both parties have checked out, and neither is very crazy about the other. It can range from a "friend zone" kind of relationship, to being outwardly hostile. Another term would be a "marriage of convenience," where the couple agrees to stay together because *something* is working, at least for one of them. None of the situations I've shared below need to be a reason for divorce—they're just worth examining.

Marriages like these are very vulnerable to affairs and disruption. If you would like to mitigate this, then you deserve to take a closer look at the relationship and address the situation. See if something can be done to "choose in" to your marriage in a more enthusiastic way.

Clarity is what is needed in any strong relationship. Take a look…see if you fit into any of the following:

1. The "Just Don't Touch Me / Separate Bedrooms" Relationship.

There are those relationships where the disinterest is so great they can't stand to sleep in the same room. (Although, I have to say, that I know great couples that have separate rooms and excellent relationships. It works for some.) However, it's often a sign of "issues." It may start something like this, "I'm just gonna sleep in the guest room tonight…you were snoring too loud," or "I wanted to stay up and watch a show," or "work on…something." And it turns into a nightly thing.

But not all couples have the space to sleep elsewhere. So they share the marital bed, but someone's not happy about it. That bed hasn't seen any action in years, and sometimes decades! Some resort to sleeping on the couch, while others cling to the very edge of their king size bed just so their partner won't "get any ideas" or even think about making an advance.

There are others that are more covert with their disinterest. They will make up all manner of excuses *not* to be intimate, from the classic headache, exhaustion, or "I'm just not in the mood," to actually taking on some type of chronic illness. Some couples sleep in the same room simply to keep up appearances that all is well, believing no one will notice. #dillusional

Do you have anxiety about going to bed at night, hoping you can fall asleep quickly so you don't have to fake another headache? Or what about the inverse: have you noticed your spouse doing this to you? It's likely a sign that they've had it with this relationship.

The wife of a close friend once suggested a weekend away for some "alone time." She was trying to restore a little excitement to a sex life that had withered long ago. Little did she know that the thought of spending a weekend alone with her was literally terrifying to him. He wouldn't have the kids, work or something (anything!) else as an excuse to get out of having sex with her, and he'd lost any interest long ago—not in having sex, but in having sex with *her*.

Maybe you're the one resenting the fact that you are on the floor or the couch, or feeling guilty if you are the one still in the bed while the other sulks in another part of the house. If you are resenting the partner that doesn't want you to touch them, or feeling guilty for not wanting them to touch you, then WTF? If you are wishing there was someone next to you that you actually felt the urge to snuggle with, let alone fuck—then just GTFO. Get a fucking divorce already and go find your person!

2. The "How Will I Manage the Children?" Relationship

Some couples stay together simply for the convenience of a live-in babysitter. (Nice to know you count for something.) These sad folks don't know how they could possibly manage both working and shuttling kids around by themselves. Some may travel a lot for work and the other is there to pick up the slack. Some families with several children have all manner of daily scheduling complexities so dialed in that life can appear impossible without the other.

To that I say, if this is your reason for staying married…yawn. Get a babysitter, and/or chauffeur. Grandparents and teenage neighbors come pretty cheap. Stop using your kids as an excuse to stay married and play small in your life.

3. The "But I'll Miss that Family Vacation!" Relationship

There are those that have settled into decades-long routines and they're just too deep into that rut to contemplate changing anything. They aren't crazy about their partner but, well, some things are working.

They have certain TV shows they binge at night, they enjoy family vacations to certain spots, or particular family celebrations and traditions. They have a set schedule of who cooks dinner on what nights, how the household chores are divided up, who pays the bills, who buys the groceries, who takes care of the cars, and on and on. It's been that way as long as you can remember and you think you'd have no clue how to do any of it alone. Indeed, the thought of an entirely new routine feels debilitating and lonely.

Get a fucking life. Make a new friend. Stay friends with your ex and continue the family vacays and celebrations—together or apart, whatever is more authentic. It's worth examining. Are you actually happy—truly or just "comfortable" in a mindless, habit-driven rut with no real life or vitality to it?

4. The "I Don't Want to Have to Work!" Relationship

There are those that have gotten so used to not *ever* working, who rely so completely on the other for their very existence, that the thought of "working for a living" not only repels them, it terrifies them. They're accustomed to a particular lifestyle that has all been handed to them. They don't feel they could possibly replicate the lifestyle for themselves. To just stay put for these folks feels like the smartest thing they can do—they feel it's necessary for their very survival.

But is it really worth it? All the stuff, and the seeming security, yet you have to sleep next to someone you can barely stand, or are friends with at best. Lying to yourself so you can live with the fact that you'd rather stay with someone you don't love, than worry about how to replace their income. Or the fact that you may actually have to get a job yourself and step into your own power. The horror! Take courage. Have the conversation and ask for support while you get on your feet. FFS.

But hey, maybe true, purpose-fueled, passionate love is just bullshit. And perhaps getting your financial needs met is good enough for you. Just be transparent about it .

5. The "I See Nothing! Ignorance is Bliss" Relationship

There are those that pretend not to know their partner has been having affair after affair right under their nose for years. Why? Because if they "knew" they may be thought the fool for choosing to stay in a marriage like that. If they pretend long enough *not* to see it, maybe it will just go away or end on its own. By not seeing they may get to keep their ego, lifestyle, and maybe even their marriage intact.

I know a man whose wife has been on at least 35 cruises over the years with one particular woman. He has been paying for all of it—while she's gained 100 lbs. and hasn't had sex with him for two decades. I know another man that wanted to believe his wife was really at the gym every evening from 10pm-2am, and that she was actually out "writing in her journal" in her minivan in the middle of the night because she needed to "get out of the house." He made himself believe all manner of craziness because he just didn't want to *see* the writing on the wall.

I've known women that continue to turn a blind eye when seeing makeup on their husband's shirts, smelling different perfume in the Mr.'s car, and putting up with countless nights of hubby saying he has to "work late" again. Just never wanting to put the pieces together because they might have to have a tough conversation and discover something they really don't want to know. Because then they'd be faced with a decision that they really don't want to make.

Do you really want to live like this? Have the courage to address this situation head on. Just know that once you do, somebody may have to *do* something about it. If your partner is unwilling to end the affair, he may use your revelation as his ticket out. Or your partner may decide they want to end the affair and work on your marriage. You now have a choice to make. Forgive and move on or be done. For many it is preferable to just bury their heads in the sand.

#StatusQuoForTheWin

**Psychic Drag**

What you may not realize is that all of these little things take a toll on your soul, and your overall level of happiness. Pretending not to see what is right in front of you, feigning happiness or interest, feeling trapped or not particularly liking the person you live with—it's heavy. My friend calls it "psychic drag." Something in the subconscious is begging for your attention, to take a look, to dig a little deeper.

But if you really allow yourSelf to see what there is to see, that may require you to do something. You'd have to remove your phony blinders. And if you actually saw the truth of the truth, you couldn't *unsee* it. And if you actually saw your *own* truth, you might feel forced to make a decision. And what if it's the decision you've been dreading having to make? What if you felt compelled to just get a fucking divorce already? That could be hard, perhaps costly, and even messy and uncomfortable.

Doing so would free up a lot of your energy and vitality. No more heaviness, no more psychic drag, no more dreading going to sleep at night. If you are on your Path, these choices will be the least of your concerns.

These shifts in lifestyle may be insignificant compared to the shift you may have already experienced in your belief system. What's a little change in your daily routine, or even a huge cut in your income, when you have discovered your life (soul's) purpose?

If you're on your Path, or you want to be, it will never work to be experiencing a mind-blowing new awareness while the rest of your life is humdrum. To be tied to a person you're not excited about, or with whom you no longer resonate, can only last so long—especially if your partner has zero interest in your new passion of Self-discovery.

Alignment is one of the greatest principles of spiritual awakening, and if you are out of alignment in any area you will feel it greater than you ever have before—it's not going to work for you anymore. It's called *awakening* or *enlightening* because we finally take off the blinders and *see* our life for the sham it has become. We see with new eyes all the places that we have been inauthentic, numb, playing the victim, and completely out of alignment with our own Souls.

So, it's probably time for those tough conversations. Either you're going to make a real effort to be happy where you're at, get some therapy or coaching, and make an honest go of aligning all the important aspects of your life with your purpose and your Path…or maybe you'll admit that this marriage really is no longer your truth, and it probably hasn't been for years. Whatever you choose is fine, but if it's the latter, why waste any more time—just get a fucking divorce already!

Yes, change can be challenging. Nobody said it was going to be easy. However, once the dust has settled and there is no more psychic drag—or people under your roof that you really can't stand—then there's a clean canvas on which to create, to paint a new world using all the colors in the box. How awesome is that?

Imagine the liberation, having the bed all to yourself, or someone in it of your own perfect choosing? Imagine going to sleep when you want, eating what you want, creating your own schedule? Whatever will you do with yourself? Though some of those things may sound normal or even ridiculous to the more conscious, autonomous types…the struggle is real for many.

When you finally feel all this new found liberation, you will realize that the "Comfort Zone Marriage" wasn't actually that comfortable after all. There were all manner of restrictions, built up resentments, tongue biting, unnecessary headaches, tummy aches, and illnesses. Just like chronic pain that we choose to ignore and just "live with" because we have no hope of it ever getting better, the "Comfort Zone Marriage" slowly kills us with a thousand cuts. We justify that while it could be worse, you actually have a "nice" life. At least you like your work/home/pet/friends. At least your partner isn't abusive. At least you're not alone. At least you're not out in the dating world.

If you want to transform your life to one of ecstasy over tolerability, you will have to believe that you deserve it, that there is something more for you, and that you are here for a reason. Here's a hint: If you desire an ecstatic life, then one exists for you. But YOU will have to create it. To create something new, the old must die. It does not mean that divorce is inevitable, it just means that it can no longer exist in the "comfort zone."

You've heard that everything you truly desire exists right outside of your comfort zone, yeah? Well, it's true. You will have to leave what you've known and do what you have not done to create something new. Creation is like giving birth—it's rarely very pretty, but it's always worth it.

If the doldrums and humdrum is ok for you both, and you prefer the Muggle Slumber, just stay right where you are. Nothing to see here.

## Chapter 30

# The Timing is Off: When You Know But You Delay…and Delay

Honestly, how long have you known that you've wanted a divorce, or been thinking about it? How long have you known this wasn't going to last? When you project your life into the future, your current mate is never in it, right? You have fantasies of life without the other—or with someone else. You have thoughts like, "When I'm single, that's when I'll change careers, religions, move, find somebody that I'm really into, start painting again, join a band, explore my kinks, etc.…."

You've been dreaming of that day…and yet, you're still here? Hanging on.

Why?

I have heard so many stories of people that knew on or before their wedding day that their intended was not *the one,* and that their marriage was never going to last. A woman recently told me that on her wedding day she was sitting in the bridal room in her church's temple before her "eternal sealing" to her supposed "beloved." Right in front of her over a door was an exit sign—a perfectly *normal* exit sign. Except this particular sign was glowing like the Sun to her. She said she *knew* within herself that it was a clear sign and message to walk out. She didn't. The man she married that day abused their sons over the following 17 years and she is still beating herself up for not taking the exit when it was clearly presented.

I am a firm believer in the idea that everything that occurs in our lives is for our growth and our learning, that nothing is for naught. And I've also learned to pay close attention to the messages, signs, and intuition that are always present, ready to guide us if we'll take a moment to tune in. Whenever I have chosen not to listen, I've been granted a very painful lesson. So…I pay attention much better now. I highly recommend it.

If you're clear that divorce is the best option for you, congratulations! That decision is not always easy to come by no matter what the circumstances. Now what? Whether you've had that clarity for years, or you've just come to it, you are likely still waiting for that elusive "perfect moment" to drop the bomb. Stop the wait! Let's break down some of the things people do and the reasons why they delay the inevitable—and why most of them are bullshit.

1. You schedule a session with a marriage therapist.

Wait…you already know you want out, so why waste the time and money on a therapist? Wouldn't going to a therapist imply you want to work on the marriage, improve it, and live happily ever after? But you know you don't. You know you want out. So…wtf?

You schedule the session, or a whole series of sessions, because you want to look good. So you can say that you tried, that you gave it your best shot but it just wasn't meant to be.

Or, and this is common, you want your therapist to "break the news" to your spouse. Maybe you're praying that your therapist will come to that conclusion herself, that it's never going to work between the two of you, and then tell your spouse. Which means you'll never have to let anyone else know this was *your* intention all along. You get say to say, "See, even the therapist thinks we should divorce." You're home free. Chicken shit, but home free.

That's really why you're paying the therapist, so they'll break the news for you. You want some kind of mediator there just in case there are emotions, tears or rage—you don't want to have to deal with all that. You aren't paying for therapy; you're paying for a trained professional to pick up the pieces and provide you some degree of protection.

Imagine you are the other partner for a minute. If you agreed to go to couple's therapy, in your mind you're thinking, "So you're saying we have a chance!? If I fix everything that isn't working for you, maybe you will want to stay?" Going to therapy typically conveys that you actually care about repairing the relationship, that there is hope.

But if you already know your plan is to exit, it's all a lie. Lies set up to make YOU look good for giving it the ol' college try. Lies that are also about you "care-taking" another's feelings because you judge them to be incapable of handling the actual truth, which is that you want out and no amount of therapy is going to change *anything* for you.

It's a waste of time and money and any emotional capital you may currently have with your soon-to-be ex. Unless you are transparent and decide to get therapy to figure out how to best get through a divorce together and work on some kind of compassionate closure, then don't even bother.

2. You want to get the finances in order.

This could mean all kinds of things depending on what side of the fence you are on—whether you are the family bread winner, or you have no dough at all.

If you're the bread winner, and a decent person, you might do things like consolidating the debt, refinancing the house, encouraging your partner to get a job, pay for some of their training/schooling, etc. If you're a Muggle, you may be trying to hide your money in offshore accounts, hiring the best attorney in town to protect your precious assets or doing any number of nefarious things.

If you are on the other end of that scale, meaning you are mostly or completely dependent on your partner's finances, you may want to be working on finding a job, getting some education or training towards a career, figuring out new and perhaps more affordable living arrangements, etc. Or, if you're a Muggle, you may start spending all of your partner's money that you can preparing yourself to snag your next Daddy—boob jobs, tummy tucks, Botox, lip fillers, and so on. Maybe prepping for your new life looks like getting a new car, stashing cash, opening a secret account to funnel money into or giving it to a friend for safe keeping, or maxing out credit cards unbeknownst to your partner for your future perceived needs.

As you can see, this one can be a lil tricky because…Muggles. It isn't necessarily bad to get things in order, but let's be clear, there may be major repercussions to your honesty. You deserve to fairly protect yourself. I've had multiple clients tell me that within 24 hours of making the announcement, their partner filed a false protective order against them, which removed them from the house immediately.

One friend's wife, with her husband now out of the house, then proceeded to sell all of his antique books, turquoise jewelry his grandfather made, father's art, guns and ammo, liquidated their boat, SUV and the 10k in silver coins from their family safe (which she later pretended had never existed). So, yeah, a little forethought on his part would have been a good idea.

I've also heard of people threatening to pull the plug on financing their partner's education, or threatening to stop helping with their partner's business when they felt threatened with a divorce. That can also be tough. Personally, I've always been a fan of figuring it out myself.

Because of the fear that comes up when threatened with the loss of our basic needs, or even luxuries we've become accustomed to, money issues are often one of the darker reasons that people delay. What on earth will you do without this s.o.b. supporting your ass? How will you make it without this person's income—the person whose feet you can barely stand accidentally touching yours in the night? What if you can't afford to live in your fancy house anymore with all of that disposable income you so enjoy? What if your weekly runs to Nordstrom come to a screeching halt? What if you don't get a big chunk of alimony or child support for the next 20 years? Or what if *you* are the one that will have to pay a huge chunk of your check to alimony and child support? You may have to downsize as well! Horrors!

If you are the conscious one (which is who this book is really for), you will not want to screw anyone over, take what isn't fair and equitable or cut anybody off cold turkey. If your partner is not also on this Path, or you are unsure, don't be too trusting. Hurt people tend to hurt people. Be prepared. Be wise. Get your house in order. Just don't pretend like this is really what's holding you back.

3. You just don't have the balls.

You just can't do it, for any number of reasons, whether it's because you feel guilty for wanting something more, you're having an affair, you don't want to hurt anybody, or you fear what others will think of you. Maybe you are riddled with self-doubt—what if you're making a mistake? Perhaps you think you don't deserve to be happy, maybe you really are just a bad person.

Sometimes when people just don't have the guts to have the big divorce talk, their new plan becomes to be such a dick/ bitch that their *partner* will get fed up with *them* and ask for the divorce first! Then they don't have to look like the "bad guy." Don't act like you never thought of this one.

Whatever it is, you're paralyzed and just can't seem to pull the trigger. #Chickenshit. If you want out and you are crystal clear about it, grow a pair, rip the band aid off, and have the conversation. Let your other know if there is anything at all that would have you change your mind or if there is *nothing* they can do and that your mind is made up. Give them that courtesy—stop dragging it out if you're clear.

Yes, moving forward with a big change can be scary. The perceived negativity you may face and the friendships you may lose are a real possibility. You get to see everyone's true colors in a situation like this, which is never a bad thing. Your freedom to live a life of your choosing, in your highest excitement, will be worth more in the end. The more above board, authentic, and vulnerable you can be, the better your chances of a more positive resolution, no matter what the choice.

4. The Classic: It's Just Bad Timing.

You want to get through the holidays, birthdays, school play, kid's football season, your schooling, etc. Maybe some family member or family pet just got diagnosed with a terminal illness or just died and it is an emotional time. Perhaps you have a big trip or event planned together like a long-awaited vacation, family/class reunion, anniversary party, etc. Maybe you're in school and your partner is paying for and/or watching the kids while you attend and you don't know how you will do it without their assistance. And finally, the granddaddy of reasons for delaying: the kids are still very young and you want to wait til they have all graduated and are out of the house.

Way to waste the best years of your life. When you finally have none of the above happening you'll be dead, or inevitably Mercury will be in retrograde, so for sure you wouldn't want to get a divorce then! Even Muggles know that. So you wait, and wait….and wait.

I'm a big believer in doing unto others as I would like them to do unto me. So I ask myself, would I like to go on some long-planned romantic vacation with a man that is planning to dump me? Or to a family reunion, thinking all is well in my world, just to return to a divorce talk? Would I want to celebrate my birthday (or his) under those false pretenses? No, I would not. I prefer to always have a choice—to be at cause, not effect.

I don't want to be under any illusion that enjoying these special times together means that we are getting closer because we got along so well. If I knew the truth, I could still choose to take the trip or to do the event, but it would be my choice and for my reasons, perhaps to celebrate old times, to inform the family, to take some time together to figure out how best to wrap things up amicably. I would be at choice.

If I find out later that you *knew* you wanted a divorce months or years ago, or that you were in love with someone else, or you are gay, or whatever…I'll be replaying our entire past, wondering what was ever really authentic and what was completely fake and fraudulent on your part. My anger will rise and my respect for you will diminish even if I think you believe you were doing it *for* me.

Ughhh. What I dislike about every one of these reasons, and the many more reasons that exist for your delay, is the utter lack of honesty and transparency, which is probably already a hallmark of your relationship. So same old, same old.

But delaying like this, and the lack of honesty, sucks for soooo many reasons. First, it sucks for you—you're being fake as fuck, all day, every day. Tell me that isn't a heavy weight? Feigning passion—or even interest—when your partner wants to make love, or coming up with a headache or a deadline to avoid it all together because you are so not interested. Pretending to play along with them when they are planning future events, vacations, birthdays, etc., all the while knowing full well those plans are never going to materialize—at least not with you in them. You just smile and reluctantly go along because you're not ready to spill the beans, yet inside you feel like a fraud and the guilt continues to mount. One partner is in business-as-usual mode, while the other is constantly planning their exit strategy.

When you know and you withhold, what you are doing is creating a false sense of security, all the while the other's perceived foundation is crumbling beneath them. To knowingly keep that from me would be to add to the mounting pile of betrayals, which will only complicate our future relationship, co-parenting, and ability to be friends.

## The "Right" Time

The right time to tell them doesn't depend on a single thing that is happening around you, or with your partner. As far as finding the "right" time to tell your spouse, it all has to do with what is happening inside you.

The right time to tell them is when YOU know. When you feel you've done all you could do to change your own mind—you've tried therapy, mind control, talking to your ecclesiastical leader, talking to your mom, talking to God, wishing upon a star, ending your affair—and there still isn't any fire in your belly for this person or this relationship.

When sex becomes repulsive and the thought of another year together feels like you just slit your wrist and you're watching the blood drain out slowly for the next 365. When you feel like there is a noose around your neck and you're headed to slaughter and the thought of staying together has you wracked with doom, apathy, and hopelessness, or anxiety, fear, and trembling.

When those things are happening inside you, what is happening around you becomes irrelevant. Make no mistake, you are never really delaying to protect anybody but yourself—to be seen in a better light, to be liked and not resented, to be thought well of and not disparaged. Ever heard "Honesty is the best policy"? Because most often, it is.

Withholding your clarity does everybody involved a disservice. You hold everybody back from their own progression, from gaining their own clarity, and from their ability to move forward. Nobody is getting any younger. You do not have all the time in the world—our time here is finite. Your partner deserves to start envisioning *their* new life without you in it, like you've been doing for how long now? If you are going to choose to stay together til the kids are a certain age, or get through some trip, event or holiday, you can at least be making that choice *together* in transparency without the wool pulled over one person's eyes.

You got into this relationship together, get out of it together. Love each other enough to be truthful with how you feel about each other. Weigh each other's concerns, listen to each other's hearts and feelings about it. Maybe something will come out of all of this transparency that will finally make a difference and you may just change your mind. Maybe all you needed to hear is how devastated your partner would be if you left.

Newsflash: In your fearful lil brain, there will never be a good time. There will always be some holiday, birthday or anniversary. Someone will always have a championship game, life-altering test, job interview, or play that's just around the corner. I mean…don't be a dick and announce it at her mother's funeral or right before they take the Bar exam. But stop delaying, jackass.

With that new found transparency, all the other external things will fall into place. You can tell them what you are willing to do, and how you are willing to help them move on.

Ask them if they still want to take that trip, get through Christmas before telling the kids and extended fam, or if they prefer to move forward asap. Anything is possible when both parties are finally transparent.

Hiding, denial, betrayal, and fraudulent behavior create zero possibility for resolution. Too much fog and deceit on both sides for anyone to break through. Nobody is clear where they truly stand with each other because, most likely, neither of you are even sure if there is actual attraction, desire or even friendship anymore.

Many of you reading this who are contemplating divorce may have been going through years of this already. Stop being a coward. Do you realize how much just the thought of having this conversation has consumed your life? How much of your life has been on hold or postponed? How much of your creativity has been squelched, uninspired or untapped? How many ideas, purchases, projects or businesses you have put off because it feels impossible to live your dreams with this person?

Your life is waiting. Their life is waiting. Time is slipping through the hour glass. Choose. Speak. Have the conversation and let the chips fall. You keeping your little secret is serving no one—least of all you.

Do the thing, already.

## Chapter 31

# Staying for the Children: The Holy and Noble Grail

I call bullshit. The ol' "staying for the kids" routine is the holy and noble grail for staying in a miserable marriage, while being the biggest lie ever told.

This one is often spoken to friends and family when asked, "Why do you stay with that miserable bitch/s.o.b.?" Rather than give them the real reasons, which you don't even want to look at yourself, you attempt to justify your own stupidity and puff up your "holy-ness" by pulling out the kid card. It's almost akin to saying, "God told me to stay," because most people won't challenge you on it. (Insert eye roll)

It's like you are agreeing that "Yes, I'm married to an idiot," or that "Yes, I know my marriage is a sham," but when you say you're "doing it for the kids," all of a sudden you become some kind of saintly martyr or the dutiful and sacrificing mother or father. Instead of being chastised and shamed—as many are for getting a divorce—people feign approval, roll their eyes behind your back, and say shit like, "I don't know how she does it. Yup—must be some kind of saint." Mission accomplished! You can pretend to feel good about yourself and maintain the façade that *staying* is in your "children's best interest."

You reinforce that belief with every carefully curated blog, podcast, and article you choose to consume that reaffirms what you want to hear and justifies your lie. Because pretending to stay for the children sounds way better than the truth:

1. You're terrified you won't be able to "make it"—a.k.a. afford life on your own. Heaven forbid the kiddos have to change schools, cut back on some music lessons they hate anyway, or that you may no longer have the resources to provide for their (or more importantly *your*) every desire.

2. You're afraid your spouse will take you for everything you've worked a lifetime for—and she/he might. Are all those pretty things making you happy? Maybe you'd get custody of the dog, which I'm sure you'd prefer to your spouse. "Happiness is overrated," you lie to yourself. Sacrificing for your children is much more noble a cause.

3. You're scared you'll never find another soul to put up with your bs and you're terrified of being alone. "At least someone is better than no one," you say. Better to claim it's for the kids than acknowledge your own lack of self-worth.

4. You're afraid your kids will hate you. You know your spouse already does. Let's face it, there's no great love between the two of you. What if your kids get angry that you are the one that choose to break up their comfy lil façade of a life and they want to leave you, too?

Just get real—at least with yourself. Stop using your kids as some moral high ground for staying in a shitty marriage. You're not doing them any favors. If you would not choose your husband/wife if you met them on the street today, or if you'd get the fuck out if you had $5 million in your bank account, you are *not* staying for your kids. Cut the self-righteous bullshit and just call a spade a spade.

Is wasting the best years of your life with someone you can hardly stomach, or at best have become semi-tolerant roommates with, modeling the kind of marriage you'd wish upon your kids? Do you want to teach your children to stay in their marriage at all costs because they "made a commitment" to someone (probably when they were in their 20's)? Would you want *them* to see it through for time and all eternity if they felt the same way about their marriage as you do about yours?

If you're going to stay, just do everyone a favor and tell it like it is.

"I don't know how I'd support myself and the kids."

"I don't want to start over with nothing."

"I just don't want to be alone."

"My kids will hate me if I leave him."

But "staying for the kids"? It's a lie. And everybody knows it.

## Chapter 32

# But Marriage is Sacred, Right?

Let's talk about the *real* sanctity of marriage for a minute, shall we? Do you have it in your relationship or don't you? Have you ever, will you ever, and does it matter? What does that even mean to you?

I'd like to propose that the sanctity of most marriages has devolved to encompass things like duty, dogma, and obligation. When one wakes up to the truth of this, it's like finding yourself in a prison, programmed by the collective that you willingly bought into while you were asleep. Yup, you've have been programmed for slavery—marriage is just one of the aspects of your life where this tends to be the case. It's old school and frankly, the Muggle way to do marriage.

I believe the highest form of love is not commitment, duty or service—but DEVOTION. On the path of enlightenment, devotion is essential. In this space, your heart is your compass. Devotion is your only truth. Your true north.

We've become so attached to our "duty" that we can't even feel our hearts anymore. We've confused that which deserves to be *most* important for a static book of law. We've been brainwashed to think the dark is the Light and that the Light is the dark. What we think are all the *right* reasons to stay married, are really just about our programming, and may actually be all of the wrong reasons! It's time to separate and distinguish duty and dogma from devotion and the truth of your own heart.

We need to break down what the sanctity of marriage really means vs. what's become the norm in Muggle Land. I believe our old view of marriage—heavy on the "duty" side—will no longer be sustainable once you wake up. It doesn't mean your marriage has to end. However, you will need to transform it in order for it to remain viable. Staying married because you're "supposed to" will no longer cut it.

For clarity, let's start by defining a few words. What exactly does "sanctity" mean? We always hear it in reference to marriage. Sanctity means the state or quality of being holy, sacred or saintly, of ultimate importance and inviolability. Sacred means you regard something with great reverence and respect.

Newsflash: Just because you got married in a church, by the justice of the peace, or married at all, does not make your relationship holy. It's a nice, outward symbol and declaration of your love at a particular point in time, but a legal certificate of sorts does not a "holy contract" make. And if a "holy union" was your initial intention, yet you're treating your partner or relationship in any of the archetypal ways mentioned in the previous chapters, or with any disrespect and dishonor—there goes your "sanctity."

What truly makes your relationship holy is the *ongoing state of your heart*.

Let's examine this other infrequently used word in the definition of sanctity: inviolability. Inviolable means never to be broken, infringed or dishonored. Infringed is a verb that means to actively break the terms of a law, agreement, etc., or to act as to limit, undermine or encroach upon something or someone.

So whenever you are undermining your partner's person, ideas or dreams, or encroaching upon who they are—pushing who you'd *rather* they be with your disappointment, disapproval or evil eye-rolls—you are completely "infringing" upon the sanctity of your marriage. That marriage is made up of the two of you. What you inflict/infringe upon each other, by definition, you ultimately inflict upon your marriage. Capiche?

So then marriage, being a holy, sacred, and important contract, only remains so as long as it is never broken, infringed upon or dishonored. And though I have a hard time with the word never, how I perceive it in this definition is that when you do infringe, encroach, defile, etc., you simply destroy the sanctity. Make sense?

What you end up with is a mere static contract or commitment of duty and obligation. Like a contract you enter to buy new windows—you pay, they deliver, and that's the end of it. The "sanctity of marriage" doesn't persist just by calling it so.

How I envision the sanctity of a partnership is more like a living, breathing, evolving third entity created consciously and nurtured by the couple. One in which the couple can grow together, change their minds about certain things, re-evaluate, and re-structure. If some of the things you've agreed upon get broken, it can be repaired and entered back into if both agree—thus maintaining and *renewing* the "sanctity."

In a more conscious marriage, practices would be put in place to uphold, maintain, grow, and repair that sanctity, if need be. In a traditional marriage, the sanctity/soul of the relationship has been waylaid, with the only "proof" left of that sanctity being your obedience and adherence to dogma. It's assumed to be sacred just by merely existing—even if it has gone cold.

If a marriage is being held together solely by obedience and adherence to dogma, or some fear of loss, is it really sacred to you? Just because you can check the boxes—providing for: check; not cheating: check; doing your duties: check—that doesn't mean you have a sacred union, or one worth keeping intact.

Let's define duty, shall we? Duty is an obligation, a responsibility or a requirement done from a sense of moral obligation rather than pleasure, desire or enthusiasm. For example: It is your "marital duty" to x, y, z. Being the "dutiful wife" has come to mean being subservient, placing his dreams above your own, being accommodating to your husband's sexual desires, feeding said husband, and cleaning his castle. Being the "dutiful husband" has come to mean being the protector and the provider of money, sex, food, etc.—in essence being the caretaker of all the physical needs.

The "dutiful spouse," whether male or female, has also come to mean acquiescing our needs for that of the other. Once again confusing the dark for the Light, i.e., *sacrificing* our own autonomy for doing our *sacred* duty and fulfilling the "marital expectation." It is not sacred to sacrifice the truth of ourSelves for the needs and desires of the other. It's an abomination and the worst betrayal—that of the Self. Once one betrays one's Self, it will not be long before the one is betraying the other. Or the other is showing up in a way to betray you.

We have been taught to believe that it's honorable to do your *marital duties* and that we are behaving poorly/dishonorably when we don't. There is a "letter of the law" vibe to it that, frankly, I detest when in the absence of devotion and whole-hearted service.

Here is the truth of the truth about what is *dishonorable*: doing your *marital duties* when your heart is not in it. Doing your marital duty because it is your responsibility, obligation, and because you "should." When *performing* (pun intended) your marital duties, whatever you believe them to be, if not done from a place of authenticity, pure devotion, and/or enthusiasm, you are 100% out of the realm of the sacred. It's total Self-betrayal and there is a cost to your soul.

If duty is your come from, your marriage will feel heavy and hard. Have fun *enduring to the end* or for time and all eternity. How does that feel to the heart? A lil heavy? But gee, you sure did follow the rules. Bonus points, anyone?

Imagine your spouse making love to you because it is their "marital duty." Sink into that one. How does that *feel* to you... on either side? Your partner having sex with you because she knows she's *supposed* to. She pretends to be into it, but you totally know that she isn't, and you go along with her lie so you can get off and go to sleep. Gross.

How does it *feel* to pretend you're into it? If you just close your eyes, make a few moans, maybe he'll get it over with quickly. Feeling pretty righteous though, right? Like you just did your "duty," collecting tokens for your pass through the pearly gates? Eww.

Apparently some women believe this is the utmost display of the "dutiful wife." I've heard of women in couple's therapy, in an attempt to prove the depth of their *sacrifice*, say things like, "I never denied him sex," or "I always made myself available to him for sex," which implies, of course, that she didn't really want anything to do with it. Barf. Maybe you should get an Academy Award nomination—but not Wife of the Year, sweetheart.

And how does it feel to fuck someone that just isn't that into you? Or to just take what you want anyway because you feel like you deserve it? Hmmm, also a lil self-righteous? Because, well...she's your wife, god damnit! And fuck, you provide everything for her, it's the least she can do, right? This is what I'm talking about people. Let's not pretend that you've never been here. It's gross.

~ ~ ~

The realm of duty and dogma does not reside in the realm of the sacred. The realm of the sacred is the realm of devotion and the path of joy.

Do you think Rumi wrote all the beautiful shit he did to his God and his Beloved because he felt *obligated*? Are you fucking kidding me? Those kinds of words of devotion, ecstasy, and joy only come from a true devotee. A devotee thinks nothing of duty. A devotee thinks nothing of payback, my turn or "getting mine." A devotee does so with zero expectation of any return. A true devotee does so out of the abundance of love spilling over from their heart.

If you have allowed that overflowing love to permeate your being, it's because you also love yourSelf with devotion. When you find it for yourSelf, it's easy to have for the Other. One cannot solicit authentic devotion *from* another if you do not rapturously hold it for yourself. Nor would you treat another in an inauthentic manor or feign interest, were it not genuinely there. Period. The end.

If this is not the case, you may want to ask yourSelf where you've fallen short in loving yourSelf, such that you've willingly handed over your sovereignty and put your faith in another's dogma and duty? "Doing your duty" appears to be more about being lazy and blindly following the rules handed to you, than figuring out your *own* truth and moral code and living into that truth with joy and enthusiasm. When someone says, "I've done my duty," it rarely means they went above and beyond. It means, "I've met the bare minimum requirement, and I'm washing my hands of it." #Muggle101

When you abdicate your own authority and power by not gaining clarity about who you are, your own personal morality, and what lights your soul on fire…you've allowed yourself to be lulled to sleep by the voice of everything and everyone, *except you*—family, friends, church, government, collective conscious. It's a soul-sucking place, and it will no longer do for the conscious direction you're headed.

~ ~ ~

On the path, you learn that *you* are sovereign, that your heart has a voice, and that is where your truth resides. On the path you let go of all "in order to's," "should's," and "ought to's." You re-evaluate all dogma that you took on as truth through the lens of a higher power—You. You get clarity about all the voices in your head that don't originate with you and relegate them to their proper place. You learn to connect your ego and personality with your heart and allow your intuition to guide you.

In this new world of relating, there will be a variety of relationships. There is no one guaranteed nirvana—Muggles will always exist in every type of relationship. There will be new dogma's put in place. People will lie and cheat like we've done for millennia. What I'm talking about here is the *sacred* marriage or partnership—doesn't matter the configuration, whether it's people of the same sex, different sex, different races, etc. What matters on this conscious path of relating is transparency, personal responsibility, and a dedication to personal evolution. Instead of a static contract sealed in one moment of time, never to be altered, this entity is alive and ever evolving like the couple themselves.

In the sacred marriage on this conscious path, I see devotion replacing duty, the sacred replacing dogma, transparency replacing manipulation, and authenticity replacing the fake. I see previously defined roles of breadwinner and caretaker becoming much more fluid according to the needs, skills, and circumstances of the moment. I see both partners contributing financially, as well as with child care and household management. This is all possible with a higher level of consciousness, where each member is 100% accountable for themselves and their own happiness. Where each has a heartfelt desire and devotion to their collective merger. It requires unparalleled honesty and a depth of intimacy not common among most.

In this new paradigm of relating, devotion is a much higher law than commitment, duty or service. In my opinion, duty is a four-letter word and here's why:

Duty and obligation come from a place of "I have to," (e.g., cook, clean, sex) while devotion comes from a place of "I get to," (e.g., the same). Which would you prefer to live with? One feels heavy, like force; the other feels light, like liberation and joy. I would NEVER want my partner to stay with me because he "made a commitment" or it was his "duty." See how heavy that feels? I want him to freely choose into us every day because there is no place else he'd rather be, because he enthusiastically delights in me, my intellect, my heart, and my presence in his life.

How often have you told yourself, over and over, "This is my job, my duty, I'm supposed to want this. Something must be wrong with me if I don't. I made a commitment before God. I must be a bad husband/wife." No. You've just been programmed to be a slave to your dogma and somebody else's rules for your life. Your sense of duty has blinded you to the truth of the only thing that matters—the deep knowing in your heart.

Do not mistake what I'm saying for some kind of hippie-dippie, free-love, go-with-the-flow kinda vibe. Do not mistake your vain, egoic, lustful desires of the flesh for the true desire of your higher heart. This is not a free pass for your ego. I'm not talking about being bored with your spouse due to *your* lack of effort or investment, either.

I'm talking about a love that transcends duty and obligation. I'm talking about devotion, the hallmark of an enlightened relationship. The place we go to experience God and true oneness.

Allow me to define it again. Devotion: love, loyalty or enthusiasm for a person, activity or cause; akin to religious worship. Yup. *Akin to religious worship*. Put that in your sacrilegious pipe. Think Rumi, Hafiz, and the Rig Veda. At the risk of repeating mySelf, we've mistaken the Light for the dark and the dark for the Light.

So ask yourSelf, what percentage of your life feels heavy with duty and obligation? What percentage of your life feels overflowing with vitality, devotion, and optimism for creating an amazing future? What if "doing your duty" was not your ticket into heaven, after all? What if "doing your duty" in the end only meant that you willingly gave up your sovereignty for another's dogma and fell short of the real goal of Self-discovery and giving your heart the first vote? What if following your bliss and the most sacred desires of your heart was the only path worth your time, devotion, and resources?

I can't know for sure, but I'd be willing to bet that upon your life's review, you will be more pleased because you were a rebel that followed your heart to the ends of the earth, than one who played it safe with the sheep, ignoring every prompting of your Soul for that of some dusty, old book of law. But hey…that's just me.

## Chapter 33

# If It Isn't a "Hell Yes," it's a "Fuck No!"

Let's discuss why it's so important to just get a fucking divorce already once you've tried all else, revealed your truth, and your partner wants nothing to do with your new direction.

Your relationship affects every aspect of your entire life. Who you share your sacred sexuality with, or who you are just lying next to at night sans any sex at all, has a major impact on your life and well-being. It is a massive co-mingling of energies. If any part of it is not harmonic, or is inauthentic, it will color your world in a negative way.

This is more than being in a job you can barely stomach, or living in a city that you can't wait to get out of. The person with whom you share your daily life and who you are energetically tied to via sex, marriage license, contractual religious ceremony, etc., can be anything from the air that ignites your fire, passion, and mission, to the noose around your neck that keeps you from everything you desire in life. So it may be time to ask yourself, "Is this still your person?"

Most people in this situation wear protective blinders, stick their fingers in their ears, and guard carefully against any authentic words about their lackluster marriage dropping from their lips and into the light of day or their own consciousness. For to see this clearly, is to realize one's own unhappiness, discontent, and painful reality. The truth of which is often more devastating than the illusion in which they are living. The truth can be extremely unsettling.

These truth-avoidant folks have a tape they've put on repeat to keep them safe (or so they think) from ever really hearing the answer to that question: "Is this still my person?" Different folks have different tapes according to their programming and dogma.

This repetitive tape may sound something like this:

"It's not *that* bad." "It could be way worse." "I deserve this for all the shit I've done in the past."

Maybe it's, "Suck it up." "Stop complaining." "You made your bed."

Or "You are doing the right thing." "You made a commitment." "You have a mortgage and children." "You don't get to leave." "You're following the commandments." "It's the only way to heaven." "You'll be rewarded in the next life."

Perhaps it's "A divorce will look *really* bad to my family, church, community." "'They' may not like me anymore." "I may get passed over for a promotion." "It'll ruin my chances at election." "I'll never be eligible for that church position."

Still others, "My life is pretty good right now, if I get divorced, I may not be able to afford x." "I may have to move out of this house I've worked so hard for." "I may have to start working." "I won't be able to do x."

It just keeps going, "Maybe the life I'm dreaming of is just some stupid made-up fantasy." "Maybe it won't last with the person I'm really in love with." "Maybe this new life will be worse than the one I'm in." "Maybe I don't deserve to be that happy." "Maybe my kids will hate me forever."

And on and on the old programming goes to keep you paralyzed from ever breaking free of the matrix.

When you are in a place like this with the most prominent relationship in your life, it will taint *everything* else that is good in your life. The things you used to love will no longer generate the same enthusiasm. If you loved your career, it will dampen that enjoyment. If you loved your home and where you live, you will want to be there less, or you'll wish there was somebody else under your roof with whom you could really enjoy it. Your hobbies will be an excuse to leave the house. Your ambition, an unfulfilled embarrassment.

If you loved your fitness routine, spiritual practice or time with your friends etc., you won't even want to share them, or you'll do them less or give them up entirely. Something your soul celebrates will be hard to do in the space of this energy because it just doesn't resonate. Pretending to live in a place of "Happy happy, joy joy," when your relationship feels like a life draining energy suck isn't compatible or sustainable!

When your relationship is inauthentic, you will inevitably make additional choices that lack integrity to compensate for your misery in this marital nucleus. You may work late at a job you can't stand just to get away, or stay in a job you don't even like because you don't want to disappoint anyone with a change in income or status. You may choose not to start the business of your dreams because your partner doesn't approve, you don't want them to taint your dreams, or it just doesn't sound like any fun to do with them in your life. You know that if they disapprove, there will be no encouragement and they will only be waiting for you to fail so they can say, "I told ya so." Fun times.

All of this is sucking your life force, your chi, and your vitality.

Doing what you don't want to do, with someone you don't want to be doing it with, is draining to say the least. Because of the miserably counterfeit life you've been living and heavy emotions you've been repressing, you may be susceptible to even more shitty choices to mask the unconscious pain you've been unwilling to face—including, but not limited to drinking more often, binging Netflix, spending more hours at work, comfort eating, gambling, doing recreational drugs, having emotional affairs, and plain old actual affairs, to mention a few!

The real reason we feel the need to "get away from people" is because we can't be ourSelves around them. To constantly be putting on a show, wearing a mask, and pretending to be someone you are not exhausting. If you regularly find yourself needing to "get away" from certain people, especially your spouse, take note. It's always hard to breathe when you're living a fake life.

You may have stopped working out, meditating, praying, spending time in nature, and eating healthy. You may still be going along with old activities you used to like with this person, but really haven't enjoyed for years—hunting, watching sports, golfing, antiquing, going to movies... whatever. It's not your jam anymore, yet you keep doing it—because it's just what you've always done in this relationship. Heavy.

People, if this is you, when would be a good time to GTFO? Your life is waiting. It's no longer biz as usual. We are living in different times. You have a purpose and a mission here, and it isn't to follow all the rules so you can return safely to the fold. It's to step out of the matrix and figure out your role. Hint: it will not be life draining and it deserves to be meaningful. Consider this:

> *I am here to seduce you into a love of life; to help you to become a little more poetic; to help you die to the mundane and to the ordinary so that the extra ordinary explodes in your life.* ~Bhagwan Shree Rajneesh

Follow your curiosity and excitement. Your purpose and mission should enliven your soul, it should bring joy to your heart, it should stretch you and make you grow. So should the person you choose to share your sacred life and livelihood with.

Can you see how moving forward with your greatest excitement, with anyone you're not crazy about, would hinder and dampen the experience and joy? When you think of your dreams or the thing you would be the most excited to do, do you see the person you are now with by your side? Does the thought of inserting your current partner into your vision, make it less possible, less exciting, or less accessible for any reason? If you've never even dared to imagine what a life of meaning and purpose would look like, check into your heart right now and conjure it up. Would the first person you'd want to share that dream with be your current partner? You deserve to become consciously aware of your answer. What does your heart say?

If it's not an enthusiastic "Hell yes!" it's probably a "Fuck no!" (Remember this is *after* you've done all the work.)

If it's a "Fuck no!" for you, chances are it won't be a "Hell yes!" for your partner, either. It's nearly impossible for one partner to be so authentically pro the relationship and the other to be a solid "Fuck no!" It's common for one to *think* they are a "yes" due to the programming or fear of loss. It's also common for one to *feign* interest when they fear loss, as well. When one is faking some part of the relationship, guaranteed the other is as well—it can be no other way. And if you are whole-heartedly into a relationship and the other is not, or simply pretending to be, if you are honest with yourself, you've known it. Maybe for years, but hope springs eternal, and we often only see and feel what we *want* to see and feel—which is most often a false reality.

So if you can't envision your partner ever being part of your dream, or your highest ideal and vision for your life, no matter what changes, then, wtf?!?! GAFDA. Your dreams are waiting—and so are theirs! If it's not a clear, "Hell yes," dude…it's a "Fuck No!"

# Part Six
*Kids Are People, Too*

## Chapter 34

# Consciously Consider the Children In Your Choice

Let's talk about the children. If you have them, they deserve to be part of your heart-centered decision. Not in a way that holds you back from the choice you feel the need to make, but in a way that makes you aware of the potential effects your decision will have on them. Being a conscientious role model for the kiddos will go a long way towards their well-being and the quality of your relationship with them long into the future.

Before I had my first child in 1991, I was blessed to read *The Prophet* by Kahlil Gibran. I was so moved by the chapter "On Children" that it became the gold standard of my parenting. It continues to influence and inspire the way I view and treat children and how I see our roles as parents, bonus-parents, and grandparents. Here it is:

*And a woman who held a babe against her bosom said, Speak to us of Children.*

*And he said:*

*Your children are not your children.*

*They are the sons and daughters of Life's longing for itself. They come through you but not from you,*

*And though they are with you yet they belong not to you.*

*You may give them your love but not your thoughts,*

*For they have their own thoughts.*

*You may house their bodies but not their souls,*

*For their souls dwell in the house of tomorrow, which you cannot visit, not even in your dreams.*

*You may strive to be like them, but seek not to make them like you.*

*For life goes not backward nor tarries with yesterday.*

*You are the bows from which your children as living arrows are sent forth.*

*The archer sees the mark upon the path of the infinite, and He bends you with His might that His arrows may go swift and far.*

*Let your bending in the archer's hand be for gladness;*

*For even as He loves the arrow that flies, so He loves also the bow that is stable.*

~ *The Prophet* (Knopf, 1923)

Several things stood out to me as I pondered these words:

1. Do not attempt to mold your children into mini me's!

2. Regardless of what you think, just because you birthed them doesn't mean they're your property, nor do they belong to you. At best, you've been given the honor of being their steward for a time. (Don't fuck it up!)

3. Being little has nothing to do with the depth of their souls. Just because they're young, doesn't mean they aren't wise. You ought not attempt to program them with your every thought, belief, and tradition. Better to simply present what you will as you would a variety of foods to a foreign guest, with no attachment to how it is received. Honor their preferences and what resonates with their Being without inflicting shame or disappointment if it happens to be different from your own.

Ultimately, they are here to choose for themSelves, not to please and obey you by taking on all of your rules, dogma, and societal or religious beliefs. Gay, straight or in-between, Catholic, Jew, Muslim, vegan, carnivore, plant-based…all *their* choice—not yours.

To do otherwise (to force feed) is clearly not your role. You are the bow from which they as arrows will go forth. Your job is to be a safe and stable launching pad by providing for their physical and emotional well-being—respecting and acknowledging their thoughts, ideas, and dreams. Trust that they too have a mission and a reason for being here, just like you do.

The best thing we can do is to assist them in learning how to tune into the voice of their own hearts and empower them to trust themselves and their inner-knowing. Teaching little people to look within themselves for answers and not outside of themselves will create an amazing generation of humans. If we teach our children this skill, they will never need *our* book of law or any another Holy Writ to figure out what is right or wrong for them.

Children are people, too. They are eternal, wise beings of Light. Treat them with respect. I honored my children by listening to them and allowing them age-appropriate nourishing choices. I did my best not to push my beliefs on them but to present them with multiple possibilities. Meditation, prayer or both? Organic broccoli or organic squash? This outfit or that? Gymnastics, ballet or acting? I did my best to foster any interest and talent that I saw organically occurring in them, not those that were *my* preferences if it weren't also theirs. "Strive to be like them, but seek not to *make them* like you." Just know they are capable, creative, strong, intuitive, and brave.

So what does this have to do with divorce? Only everything. If you have children, they too are part of this journey. You deserve to give this decision some conscious forethought. It will make a huge difference in the life and future of your children if you are able to consciously uncouple and become conscious co-parents—not only with your current partner, but any future partners you may bring into their lives.

Know that the manner in which you go forward, even if you are only considering divorce, matters immensely. These little people are always watching you. The programming you instill now will follow them their whole lives. Will it be liberating or enslaving? Kind and generous or mean and vengeful? Life affirming or life draining?

How you choose to handle your break up, whether you are the one leaving or the one being left, will show you and your children a lot about who YOU are. There are lessons for them to learn on both sides of that coin. Indeed, you will learn more about your partner than you thought you knew in your 20 years together. There is no greater petri dish for someone's true colors to ooze out than in a divorce situation. And if you think you're learning about your partner through this process, think about how much those incredibly observant little kiddos are learning about both of you!

The following is meant to curtail the toxic slime from burying your kiddos in the shit storm of a typical Muggle divorce.

First, let's be clear, we don't do our kids any favors when we deny and suffocate our own truth. You may think you're protecting them by avoiding divorce, even if that means denying yourself, but you are doing just the opposite. All you are teaching them is to do the same. If we choose to stay in an unhappy, lifeless partnership where there is little to no passion or affection, that is the life your children will mimic.

When you stay with someone that is verbally, emotionally or physically abusive, or even if they're dismissive, disrespectful or contentious, you are modeling to your children that duty, obligation, and tradition are more important than well-being, respect, passion, devotion, and affinity. They learn it's preferable to remain in the traditions of their forefathers and endure til the end than to follow their hearts. Is that the experience you want for your bright, shiny littles—to put up with a marriage like that regardless of the suck factor?

And just because you think you and your partner have mastered being civil to each other in front of them, make no mistake, kids are clear if you're really into each other or not. Your energy doesn't lie, though your words and actions may try to. They're smarter than us. They read/feel our energy much more than what we say and do.

I can assure you, your children will be much better served by your joy and vitality than by witnessing your lifeless duty, compromise, and sacrifice that you pretend is on their behalf. What might be possible if you felt more liberated, joyful, creative, and alive? Hmmmm….do you think you could generate more income? Let's be honest…more money means more opportunities in the form of better schools, neighborhoods, travel, lessons, life experiences, etc.

What if following your heart didn't equate to more money and you faced downsizing as a result? What if your kids had to go to public schools or live in a smaller home, but their mommy/daddy was genuinely happy—perhaps pursuing their long-stifled dreams or being with a partner that makes them smile? What would that kind of energy feel like in their home? What's possible for everyone in that kind of nourishing environment?

Carl Jung said, "Nothing has a stronger influence psychologically on their environment and especially on their children than the unlived life of the parent."

Time to get real with yourSelf and ask your heart, "what is your marriage teaching your children"? Would you wish for them to have the same kind of marriage you are experiencing? Would you be thrilled for them to be treated the way you have been treated? Would you wish for them to endure all that you have endured for as long as you have? If they were miserable, for any reason, would you counsel them to stay married—for decades, til death they were parted?

And if you would not choose a marriage like your own for your precious children, why do you accept it for yourSelf? Do you not love yourSelf as much as you do your own offspring? Don't *you* deserve for you what you would wish for them? Why is it *not* ok for you to be happy? Why does it feel selfish for you, yet preferable for them? What's that all about?

Check your self-love, self-respect, and self-honesty—get some clarity for yourSelf around this. Let go of the delusions, what's societally acceptable, and what your programming says you "should" do and what you "should" desire.

When you are on a conscious path, you start to see everything through a different lens. You've heard of taking the 10,000-foot view? What I'm describing here is more like the cosmic view—exponentially more than 10k feet, but more real to the soul. Try on the possibility that there is more to life than our programming and traditions of the past—like "life can be joyful," and that it was actually *meant* to be—for all of us.

Like most normal young people that have children, if you were anything like me, you couldn't even imagine (pre-kid) ever loving anything the way you do these little humans the moment they pop out, right? To illustrate a small fraction of this love, the way I feel it, I'm going to include this note I wrote to my oldest daughter just before her 29th birthday, as it was the inspiration for this chapter:

*Sooo grateful for the love I learned by having you. I never loved anything or anyone more in my whole life until I had your sibs. I was seriously afraid I wouldn't be able to love them as much as I did you.*

*Just thinking of you and your birthday coming up, this may sound like a weird thing to say, but you'll understand when you have a child: I am soooo in love with you (and both of your sibs) since the day you were all born. In love! I adore you! All that you are, have been, and will be. All your strengths, challenges, and choices. You will only always get love and total acceptance from me.*

*My hope and intention is that you (all) will learn to love yourselves even more than I love you...with all the awe, joy, and inspiration I experience. Just the thought of you or the random pics I see on Insta brings up sooo much love and emotion. Makes my heart smile sooo big knowing I got the honor of bringing YOU into this beautiful planet. You make this Earth life such a miraculous place for me to exist. Thank you...for being one of my top three miracles here. I love you forever, Sarah.*

I believe the love we have for our children is one of the strongest and most unconditional that we experience as humans. *That* love is what I'm going to appeal to as we discuss how you go about divorcing—because it matters to those little people. Keep ever present in your mind that you are writing the story that your children will either be cursed with or blessed by. The pen is in your hands. Will your story be a tragedy with casualties of war, devastation, and total financial ruin, or an example of life just life-ing in which you have the opportunity to teach them how to handle a difficult situation with love, grace, and in the spirit of friendship?

You have the power to make this situation a positive experience. Or it can be one they will eventually hate you for while they spend years on the therapist couch trying to get over their self-loathing and unnecessary trauma YOU inflicted. Do not underestimate the power *your behavior* will have on these little people, or abdicate your own responsibility just because you may not have been the one to initiate the divorce. Please hear that.

Proceed with the end in mind. Just because you think you were the righteous one for staying in your marriage, that does not give you a free pass to now be an unconscionable asshole because you are the one being left. And if you are the one leaving, be gentle and kind. Treat the other the way you would want to be treated.

## Chapter 35

# Best Way to Help Your Kiddos? Don't Be an Asshole

Once the decision to divorce has been made, work out a game plan and discuss how best to break the news to your children, considering each of them individually. It will be best if you sit your kids down for the "divorce talk" with both of you together and united—not one of you off sharing separately without the other parent. That immediately sets up an "us and them" mentality or "you vs. the other parent."

It's important to come together on this. This doesn't have to be a horrible, dreaded event. Your energy and attitude will make a huge difference for your kids. If you remain positive about it, trusting that it will be best for everyone in the end, they will too. However, if you are super negative, casting blame, and being dramatic, you will create the same experience for them. Don't.

Your objective is to make your kiddos feel safe. Safe that they will not be losing anybody's love, and that they will not have to choose between their Mommy or their Daddy. Safe that whatever big changes may be coming their way as a result, that you will *both* be supporting them in their transition. Let them know that you still love each other but that sometimes love shifts to a different kind of love and that you will always be a family no matter what.

However, If one of the parties insists on remaining in Muggle Land and being an unconscious fuck, be prepared for them to say shit like, "Your Daddy doesn't love me anymore and he's leaving us!"; or "Your mother has a boyfriend, and wants to take you away from me and give you a new Daddy!"; or "Your dad fucked a prostitute and gave me herpes!"; or "Your mother got a new job and wants to take you across the country and away from me." This kind of talk in front of your children is reprehensible, and is not their burden to carry.

Unfortunately it happens and you deserve to have a plan B to remove the shrapnel and help the kiddos pick up the pieces of their devastated little souls. This is where you start to see who you were *really* married to and, unfortunately, it's just the beginning if this is how it went down with the kids.

To the Muggles:

Try to remember your precious children are not 100% you or yours…they share their DNA with a person you used to love, or at least said you did. When you start talking shit and do everything in your power to destroy and decimate your former "beloved," you do the same to your children.

When you choose to spend tens of thousands of dollars on attorney's fees—money that you may or may not have and that you have to borrow, go into debt for or expect the other parent to pay—you are *stealing* from your children. Not only from their future, but their current well-being and quality of life! Keep in mind, *your* hate and desire for revenge may cost your kids their home and your ability to provide for them.

When you attempt everything possible to discredit, damage, and destroy your former partner's reputation by spreading lies, half-truths, unflattering rumors, and disseminating sensitive personal information about them, just know that this monster persona your venom is creating is who your kids call their mommy or daddy. You (the person your children look to for truth) are creating that horrific image about someone *they* love every bit as much as they do you. If you don't think this is soul crushing for them, think again.

Do not come at me with a single "but…" or with tales of how horrible your ex is. Truth is, if you are the one creating all of the drama—YOU ARE THE MONSTER. Period, the end. It's not a crime to want a divorce. It's called evolution. People change, fall out of love, get fed up, and call it quits every day. It's a reality.

If you are the one that is being left, for any reason, suck it up. If you now want to claim how horrible your partner was, how bad of a parent, drug addict, porn addict, or pathetic human they were—or whatever other "stories" you want to come up with from their past—then why the flying fuck didn't *you* leave *them* years ago? (There's a lot of shadow material to unpack with that question. None of which will make you out to be Mother Theresa.)

Newsflash: If somebody's leaving you, there's a reason. It's never a one-sided deal. All the bullshit you come up with about them now will only be a projection of your own perceived inadequacies.

> *Projections change the world into the replica of one's own unknown face.*
> *~Carl Jung*

My experience with Muggles (a.k.a. unconscious humans) is that when they realize their partner is serious about uncoupling, they immediately begin a comprehensive smear campaign—completely and negligently unconscious of the kiddos in their orbit. Nobody is excluded. Anyone with a heartbeat, email address, social media account, or stranger in line at the parent teacher conference is fair game for their assault on you. They start by amassing an army of shit talkers and ne'er-do-wells onto their side of the playing field. Their recruiting efforts know no bounds, from neighbors and mutual friends to people they haven't spoken to in years.

I know of a man whose ex would go to events put on by members of *his* family, it appeared, simply for the opportunity to spread lies about him. It didn't matter who she was sharing with—they could be (and often were) total strangers who had the bad fortune of striking up a conversation with her. ("Oh, you went to elementary school with Betsy? That's so cool! Did you know that I married Betsy's cousin but then he cheated on me and left me and my children destitute and won't give me the house and cars and alimony for life! What a total douche bag!") Pathetic.

These Muggles exhibit no shame, and may even have the nerve to enlist members of the church you attended together, along with your very own family, siblings, business associates, and friends! Your former tribe is bombarded with bombastic stories of why they should now hate the very sight of you and never speak to you again. All the whilst, the disgruntled partner is regaling her new minions with stories of her own sainthood and perfect parenting. Soon these Muggles start believing the very lies they've been incessantly repeating to anyone who would listen.

Anyone relate? I'm sure this has never happened to anyone you know (insert eye roll). My wish is that this kind of behavior becomes an anomaly someday. Unfortunately, for now, it appears to be the norm on Planet Muggle Land.

Whether all of your stories get back to your children or not, don't kid yourself that your negative energy toward their other parent isn't felt. If you're the one behaving this way, and your partner is doing their best to take the high road and not participate in destructive bs, years from now, when the kiddos can choose for themselves where to go for the holidays, it won't be your place. You are doing irreparable damage. Karma is a bitch—but only when you are.

So stop. Acknowledge that all you can see right now is yourself, *your* rage, *your* future, *your* damaged pride, *your* well-being, *your* sense of entitlement, *your* greed, *your* injustice, *your* quality of life, *your* fear, *your* SHIT. Take a breath. Reel your vomit in. Cut your Jerry Springer shit, for fuck's sake. I know it sucks. I get that you're hurting. You will be ok. You're a grown-ass adult. Try to remember that. Your kids however….

Think of what you are teaching your children with this behavior. Would you ever want your son or daughter to be treated the way you are treating their other parent? Do you not understand that your children are listening, and more importantly feeling all of your venom and vitriol? This is a very impressionable time for them. They are watching everything the two of you do. Is this how you want them to remember you? Please consider them.

If you truly loved or cared about the person that is requesting to dissolve their contract with you, you would *never* act this way. In fact, your vicious behavior will only be proof to your partner that they should've gotten out sooner. Your vile and unconscionable actions are evidence that you've been harboring contempt and resentment for a long time. Your actions reveal *you (not them)* and nobody else is to blame for *your* behavior.

There is zero to gain by this kind of conduct, and everything is at stake. If you succeed by limiting the other's parent time, you are damaging your children. If you succeed in financially ruining your spouse, you have robbed your children. If you win these selfish battles you've sunk your teeth into, you will always lose the war. The wounded and bloodied on the battle field of your hate will be your children, not your ex. He/ She will be happy to be as far away from you as possible—at any cost.

Those on a true, spiritual path, that want to transition out of their marriage, often go through a lot of soul searching, personal accountability, and genuine concern for the well-being of those they are leaving. It is not an easy choice to make for them. I understand this isn't universal, just a generality from my 50 years here, my personal experience, and the countless I've coached.

When you do your inner work, a funny thing happens: you get more honest with yourSelf. You begin to know the voice of your own spirit. The more you get in touch with that, the more aware you become to that which insults your very soul. You begin to shift bad habits and take better care of yourself. You leave jobs you hate, cut ties with friends and even family that provide nothing but negativity, and eventually face the reality that you are in a toxic relationship that is robbing you of your very vitality.

Thus, if you are a remotely conscious human, no matter what side of the equation you are on, you will want to limit the negative impact on your littles. Divorce can be an unsettling, challenging time for everyone, even for the one requesting it. You are capable of softening the blow for your youngsters by putting your wounded ego aside and dropping your sword, if only for them.

You can make a difference in their overall well-being and avoid potential trauma by your effort to make this as smooth a transition as possible. Take your negative emotions for your ex out of the equation and replace it with the love of your children and go forth with that being center stage.

Muggles, cut the fantasy bs about your partner being a horrible parent, which is now your self-righteous reason for fighting them tooth and nail. "I have to do this for the kids," you wail. "He/she is unfit," you cry. Really? Funny, they weren't unfit to watch them while you were working 60-plus hours a week, or you while you've been on your chronic fatigue death-bed for the last decade, unable to lift a finger towards their care. They weren't unfit while you were out of the country on business trips, or when you went on all your girl's weekend retreats.

Digging up things they may have done years ago, a job they were fired from in 1997, cheating on a board game when they were 10 or having their mother admit they were a ruthless child, does not a bad parent make decades later! I don't care if they used to smoke weed every day in college, cheated on you years ago (or yesterday), raised their voice that one time or if they're unliked by a bunch of disgruntled, jealous siblings. IT DOESN'T MAKE THEM A BAD PARENT. Guaranteed if the other party were as petty as you, they could come up with similar or worse things about you. It's all stupid shit. And…can you say "projection"?

Helloooo…..your children are waiting to move on with their lives and return to some kind of normalcy. When are *you* going to be ready to move on? All you're doing is creating a lot of negative energy by dragging this out, and wasting time and money. Let it go. None of the bs above is about you "protecting" anything more than your precious reputation and feeding your narcissism and grandiosity.

That behavior *is not* advised by child experts to be modeled by you in the creation of awesome adults. It's small, a waste of resources, and is 100% self-serving. I can promise you, everyone in your orbit is sick of hearing it already—even the judge. The *only* benefactors in a war like this are the attorneys.

All this behavior is total bullshit, and you know it. And so do your kids.

## Chapter 36

# Why Divorce Really Hurts Kids: YOU!

No…divorce, intrinsically, is not "damaging" to children. That is all about your stories. Children will respond in the way you tell them to respond. They will mirror your emotions and take on the "stories" you choose to tell them about it. If you present your divorce as merely a simple change, let them know what's going to happen, and assure them they will not be losing anything or anyone, it will be readily and easily accepted by these adjustable lil creatures.

Share that you will always be their family but you will now be living in separate households. Create a plan with your soon-to-be ex and explain how the logistics are going to look for the kiddos. Let them know that they will get to spend time with both of you, and they will be taken care of. And then proceed to be considerate, conscious, decent humans to each other—and your kids will be just fine.

Evidence suggests that it's *parental conflict* that has the most damaging effect on kids. Kids themselves say that they would rather their parents divorce than stay in an unhappy marriage. Gee, kids are sooo fucking smart. It's real simple for them. Are you happy together or not? Do you like each other or not? And don't think that just because you may not fight in front of them that they don't know exactly how you feel about each other. Kids are experts in authenticity and reading energy.

Before my first divorce could be finalized, we were required to take the "divorce class." Unfortunately, this did not apply to in-laws or the soon-to-be step-parents. The one piece of advice I got in that class that stuck was worth its weight in gold, and I paraphrase: Whenever you say something shitty about your ex (like: "your father is a liar," "your mother is a whore," "your father is a greedy bastard," "all your mother cares about is money,") your beautiful, innocent child, who knows he is made of half you and half your partner, thinks, "Well…if I'm half them, then I must be all of those horrible things, too."

O.M.G. Pause. Consider the venom with which you speak these things and imagine your child feeling that you are talking about them. Let that sink in. I did. It cured me, right from the beginning. Do you really want your babies feeling that way about themselves? I certainly hope not!

Is your need to be right or to be the favorite parent so great that you would attempt to poison your own children with such slander and mudslinging? Is your rage and narcissism so out of control, that you care nothing for your child's well-being? Are you able to take a breath and think of the repercussions of your behavior? You deserve to. Step out of your it's-all-about-me bubble.

This nasty, pathetic behavior that goes on between two "adults" when they get a divorce is what is difficult for children. The negative, self-serving, soul crushing actions of formerly stable grown-ass adults turned demon spawn is what hurts the littles—no matter how old they are. When one or both of the parties are constantly putting down the other, name calling their other parent, using the children as pawns, and forcing them to choose sides—that's what's fucking miserable for kids.

When you feel it's necessary to tell your children about every last sordid detail as to why you left their other parent, or why you think they left you, that's YOU being selfish, narcissistic, and just plain petty—and it's damaging. There is no reason your kids deserve to know about your or your partner's infidelity, annoying/bad habits, visits to prostitutes, dishonesty, lies, porn/gambling/drug addiction or that they were bad in bed, etc. The only reason you would share these things is for *you* to feel superior, to justify yourself and any of your *own* bad behavior. Those personal things are between the two of you and are none of your children's business. No but's!

None of your character defamations affect the love your spouse has for their children. By sharing those things, you are intentionally attempting to drive a wedge between the kids and the other parent and push them to take sides. It's gross. You're gross. Don't do it.

A few last things to mention regarding unconscious parents and what really hurts your kiddos:

**The Disney Parent**

Buying your kids love, and your shameful failure in not disciplining them for anything, hurts your kids. Don't be the Disneyland parent so they will love you more. At your house they have no chores, you give them everything they want, allow them to stay up past their bedtime, feed them shitty fast food, allow them unlimited hours of video games and internet surfing, and never seem to get to their homework. Really? Do you think that is helping your children? Meanwhile, the legit good parent is trying to teach them to like healthy food, be accountable for themselves by doing chores and homework, and is limiting their screen time.

It's easy to fall into this trap, especially for dads because they tend to get less time with their kids. I had a good male friend that said, "If my time is limited with the kids, then I'm going to make sure we spend that time bonding and having fun!" The practical outcome was that although he really was an excellent dad, they fell into some bad habits.

He'd do the bare minimum homework with them so they could rush off to the park or the movies. He bought them shitty kid food (fast food, pizza, chicken nuggets, no veggies in sight) because he didn't want to "waste time cooking," instead of using that time to *teach them* about healthy food and how to cook with him. He watched movies with them and then did the dishes himself after the kids went to bed, instead of teaching *them* to pitch in. He did all the things he would never have allowed when he was full-time Dad. Sure, the kids wanted to be at his house—and he started to suck as a parent.

When you behave this way, not only are you *not* doing your kids any favors in their development as amazing, healthy humans, but you're being selfish AF. Yuh, it's easier (you think) to pick up McDonalds, sit them in front of the Xbox and leave the homework for the ex. Wake-up, Dad (or Mom). You're also being a super shitty co-parent. Cut the Disney shit. Find some balance.

Now, you parents with most of the custodial time are now feeling justified by that paragraph and are pointing your fingers and saying, "Yuh!! That's exactly what he does!" Well, if you weren't such a selfish lil bitch and had just agreed to share your kiddos 50/50, this would not be such a problem. The other parent wouldn't feel robbed, diminished, and completely shortchanged and, therefore, a little collaboration would be much easier to navigate.

And another thing…don't use your kids as the go-between.

"Tell your mother I'm not going to pay her alimony unless she lets you come on this trip with me."

"Tell your father I'm not going to let you go to his house if his new girlfriend is there."

"Tell your mom she's the reason you are failing that class—because *she* isn't helping you."

"Tell your dad to stop feeding you candy before bed because you won't be able to sleep"

"Tell your dad about your school play."

"Tell your mom she needs to pay half of your orthodontist bill."

Put on your big girl/boy pants and pick up the damn phone. Do NOT do this to your children. Do you think it will have more of an impact with your ex if you have your kids tell them? (Self-serving!) Are you really hoping they forget to tell the other about their school activities so they will miss the event and you can absolve yourself of any wrong doing? (Shitty!) Have you put yourself in your kid's position—having to tell the other parent something that feels yucky for them to say? "Dad said he's not going to pay for that because you sold his boat without permission." Eww. Inappropriate. Selfish. Gross.

They are not little pawns for you to use to get back at your ex for doing x, y or z. Work out your issues out of their little earshot. Do not have these conversations in front of them either. No yelling at the other on the phone or in person in front of them. Stop.

Get out of your own way and, if only momentarily, consider that though you may hate your ex with every fiber of your being, that same person is someone your children love and deserve to have a good relationship with for the rest of their lives. So, if you really love your kids: Cut. The. Shit.

## Chapter 37

# Conscious Co-Parenting with a New Partner

If you are a parent, you and your kiddos are a package deal. Period. The end. (Unless you plan to abandon the littles completely, which again, this would not be the book for you). If and when you find somebody else to marry or choose as a life partner, you get to carefully consider with that future partner if they are up to the task of conscious co-parenting with you.

Is your intended ready and willing to step into that role? I'd like to strongly suggest that it matters whether they are or not. Your choice deserves to be made with this consideration front and center.

I prefer to use the term "conscious co-parent" instead of step-parent. The etymology of "step," comes from the Old English *steop* which connotes "loss" as in "to bereave or to deprive of parents" and was associated with becoming a parent to an orphaned child. This is no longer an accurate depiction, nor does it speak to the type of parenting I would like to address that is more in alignment in this new age of consciousness.

In this light, the child will not be *losing* anything, but gaining another adult that can model new ways of being, learning, and living—that can share friendship, love, and affection. Conscious co-parenting makes more sense, feels better, and carries more responsibility.

If you are the one choosing to marry someone with children, ponder mindfully if you are ready to be a conscious co-parent to another's kids. Are you willing to put in the time and effort as if they were your own? Are you willing to play the role of chef, chauffeur, teacher, and referee, and offer emotional support to someone else's child?

Don't fall into the trap of unconsciously assuming that your new family life will somehow just "all work itself out," like some old re-run of the Brady Bunch. Or worse, choose to completely bury your head in the sand acting as if none of those responsibilities will ever fall to you. Your blended family deserves some real forethought, discussion, and a unified plan as to how you *intend to blend*.

This issue is paramount and definitely nothing worth leaving to chance, or avoiding altogether. We only do that when we are afraid of hearing the truth out loud or committing to any kind of responsibility, while preferring to live in our fantasy land.

In regards to co-parenting another's kids, your fantasy land may look something like this:

"They have a real dad/mom, I don't need to take on that role."

"I'll just head out on a fishing trip/girl's weekend when they're around."

"They'll be at school all day; I'll hardly see them."

"I'll be at work all day; we'll rarely interact."

"They're not my responsibility."

"I can tolerate a little inconvenience every other weekend."

"I'm marrying my partner, not their kids."

"I can put up with them for 3 years til the last one turns 18."

That "putting up with" and "tolerating" attitude is exactly what may be the cause of your *next* divorce. If your new partner can't fully embrace your littles, or you hers, take a breather and re-think your union! Would you really want to be with anyone that can't also love your children? Is that a battle worth taking on?

Does your partner even want the role of conscious co-parent or is she/he just into *you*? Don't assume. Have that conversation. Many try to avoid this conversation because if you had the hard facts—that they wanted nothing to do with your lil brats—you would know that your next move would be to call it off. Some women may only be thinking of the perks you provide—the money, security, travel, sex, etc.; whereas some men may think that you're just such a hottie, he doesn't care if you have kids or not. It deserves crystal clarity.

Obviously, due to the huge divorce rate and people re-marrying or simply co-habitating, there is a proportional increase in blended families being created. And when you *both* have children, you add all of that extra complexity to the mix. Along with merged families come contrary beliefs, practices, daily habits, new dwellings, relationships, and expectations. As a result, emotions can run high; understandably, there may be feelings of displacement, resentment, confusion, anger, jealousy, and fear. No doubt there may concurrently be positive feelings of excitement, adventure, and new affections. You can handle that part.

One of the main reasons second marriages don't work out—even when both parents are invested in co-parenting—is because couples fail to discuss, plan, and take seriously their role as a conscious co-parent. It's a tough conversation that is often neglected.

What typically happens is the unrealistic fantasy doesn't play out, the lack of forethought can no longer be brushed aside, and reality sets in. Jealousy can occur on all sides—kids jealous of their parent's affection directed at a new partner, one partner jealous of the new spouse's affection consumed by kids, etc. Power plays may result forcing kids, parents or partners to choose their loyalties. Contempt can set in, and this is where co-parents become step-monsters and get a bad name, and previously good partnerships fall apart. A little vetting beforehand, and transparency of expectations, may just save you from another divorce.

My first husband remarried a woman with 7 children of her own. My two daughters had only spent *one week* with their new step-siblings prior to the wedding. Difficult circumstances emerged immediately after, which became a real problem in the future for one of my daughters. Had they waited a few weeks or months more and allowed the kids to get to know each other, these issues may have presented themselves earlier and the wedding may have been put on hold or the issues may have been nipped in the bud. In the end, everybody got the painful lessons they apparently needed to get for their own soul's growth. It was not without a heavy cost.

What we are focusing on in this book is a more conscious approach to *all* of it. If you plan to remarry or re-couple be sure your eyes are open, that your partner can accept and embrace the new souls in their life, and that you feel you are choosing someone that is not only a good fit for you but for your kids as well.

If you are the one remarrying someone with children, go into it with the possibility that you may end up with these kids full-time. It's possible…what if something happened to their other parent, and you ended up with them not only half the time, but full-time? Would you be OK with that? Could you honestly embrace these little people and treat them like your own? If you can't honestly affirm that, reconsider.

As mentioned in some of my initial tenets, not only is the world speeding up but so is our evolution. We are co-creators of all that enters our orbit. If you believe that we are eternal, may I suggest that we also have a plan before we enter each life—we are not running about all willy-nilly here. If part of that plan involved choosing our own parents, would it not stand to reason that we also had a general plan for the rest of our lives as well? Would we just have chosen something as important as our parents, then left the next 100 years up to chance? Follow the logic through. You may believe/feel it was destiny to meet your new partner, would it not also be your children's "destiny" or their co-creation to partake of that new energy/partner as well?

Just as we may not be able to get everything we need for our soul's growth from being with just one partner our whole lives, our souls may also be a request for additional parental figures. It only stands to reason. Your littles are on a journey of their own, just as you are. And though it looks like you are making all of the decisions and they are at affect, make no mistake: they signed up for this and the particular lessons that choosing *you* as a parent would bring their way.

If you are on the conscious path, this will be something to deeply consider as you are making massive changes and transformations in your life. So be gentle and mindful of these beautiful souls under your stewardship, and stay as conscious as possible as you assist your children through their own process that your divorce may trigger.

So to be clear, although I am a huge advocate of following your heart, I am also a fan of integration of the mind, heart, and soul. I believe in massive self-responsibility. As such, I do my best to be conscious of how my choices are going to affect others in my orbit. If a man does not want to embrace my children, or I his, I will not be moving forward with that person.

I have no doubt that my daughters were a request for both of the mothers that they received—though it was not apparent initially. When I divorced their father, he remarried within 6 months to a woman who was very much my opposite. Though they were challenged by the shift at first, I believe their step-mother served my daughters in countless ways.

On the surface here is how it looked: she was a religious woman, while I was a spiritual woman. She was very structured and somewhat of a task master, I was more laissez-faire and free flowing. She was organized with job charts and color-coded folders for each child, while I might let dishes sit in the sink for a couple days in favor of more spontaneity.

I was warmer, affectionate, and friendly, while she was more of a disciplinarian and maternal. She was more judgmental and restrictive, while I was more accepting and allowing. I encouraged more freedom of expression and individuality, while she demanded children be seen and not heard. In her defense, she had a household of 10 children to manage while I only had three. I have no doubt I would have had to be more organized and disciplinarian-like as a result of having that many children.

I'm also not saying that one way is any better than the other. Between the two extremes, my daughters were presented with differing ways of being that each has integrated in various ways, from how they organize their kitchens, to the flexible work schedules they've created doing work they love.

They also gained a step-father soon after and both adored him from the beginning, and continue a relationship with him, as I do a friendship, 15 years after my second divorce. He and their dad are also very different men, and both made a significant impact. I believe that it really does take a village and that children can never have enough good people in their lives that love them.

Let me repeat that once again, *children can never have enough good people in their lives that love them.*

What about when kids get shitty bonus-parents? Why that too, is for their growth, as is the case with shitty bio-parents. There are themes and lessons that we signed up for and came to the Earth School to experience for our soul's evolution. As parents we would love to shelter our lil cuties from ever shedding a tear, or experiencing heartbreak. Deep down we understand that any experience can be for their good and growth, can provide a better understanding of humanity, and is often necessary in the development of compassionate, well-rounded humans.

This should go without saying, but at the risk of being repetitive I'm going to state it here again. Although I believe *all* experiences are for our growth and evolution, abuse of any kind is not to be tolerated. Not to you and *especially* not to your children. Remember we are always teaching people how to treat us and what is acceptable behavior and what is not. Your children will model this. If you wouldn't put up with it for them, don't for yourself either. This too is conscious co-parenting.

Choose wisely. Have the conversations you're afraid of having—especially those! Allow everyone the space to get to know each other. Don't force things. Be gentle. Approach this with love and excitement, not fear and trembling.

I see the ability to love another's children as another way to love *all* aspects of my Beloved. And vice versa. What my Beloved cannot love in my child, he will not love in me. We are extensions of each other. We are here to expand.

## Chapter 38

# Custody: Beyond Money and Misery

While we're on the kid topic...

In my very humble opinion, unless one parent is a hardcore drug addict, alcoholic or has been physically, sexually or emotionally abusive (like for real), your starting point should be shared/joint physical custody. From that point, if one party wants to *grant* the other sole custody because of living arrangements, because one person travels for their work, because of health issues or it just happens to be your preference, then do so—always with an agreement of willingly revisiting the arrangement if anything changes. If you think there's going to be a fight about it, just fucking SHARE 50/50 and save yourselves tens of thousands of dollars and your kids a living hell for years to come.

Clearly there are enough studies (not to mention common sense) that show that kids do best with two loving parents. So why do couples fight to the death and detriment of all involved for more than their fair share of time with the kiddos? If both are willing and desirous to share the responsibility equally, why not start with shared custody?

I'll tell you why. Because one or both of you is a Muggle that wants to leverage an innocent child for your own selfish desires. Muggles aren't fighting for more time than the other parent with the kiddos because they love them any more…if they truly did, they would never want to deny or limit them access to their other parent. FFS—duh.

They do it for two simple reasons: money or misery—and sometimes both!

Let's start with the money. Everybody knows the more time you have your kids, the more child support you qualify for, or the less you have to pay. Wanting your precious littles for either of those (less than noble) reasons typically results in neglected kids playing video games all day with no adult in sight—but at least you got an extra couple hundred bucks, or you didn't have to fork over that same amount! You really won that one—but the kids sure didn't! Asshole!!

Now misery, "…what's that all about," you ask, feigning innocence. Some of you Muggles are just so butt hurt that your ass got left (see what I did there?) you will do *anything* in your power to see that your ex suffers! Best way to do that—take their children! You worthless pieces of shit! It's all about the pain and punishment for you, and somehow you feel completely justified. All of a sudden you are coming up with all kinds of outrageous, ridiculous exaggerations and outright lies about your ex's fitness as a parent that never (ever!) surfaced prior. The children are just the tools you use to hurt your partner; but for you, the end justifies the means.

FYI: Using your kids for monetary gain or to get back at your ex is not only juvenile, it's fucking deplorable. The more you can take your petty emotions and money-grubbing ways out of this equation, the better it will turn out for everyone involved. Got it?

~ ~ ~

I have a very simple rule for you when it comes to custody: Don't be dicks. There's probably nothing worse for kids (and parents) than having to go through a custody battle and/or full-blown custody evaluation. Having to prove to a total stranger that you are a decent parent can be stressful. Especially if you know your ex is in war mode and not beneath lying about you to get what they want.

To have to fight for something that should never be fought over *in a normal situation* is total crap. It's completely uncalled for if both of you are remotely decent humans that love your children. It takes years, sometimes decades, before it's *ever* wrapped up. Not to mention that the exorbitant cost may far exceed the pricey divorce that left you both penniless. And, after you've all been through an emotional meat grinder, you most likely will end up where you should have started in the first place: with 50/50.

It doesn't matter who's been the primary caretaker. Whoever that happened to be, most likely the breadwinner parent was working their ass off so you could stay home. Their love and efforts provided that benefit *to you* and saved your kids from being raised by strangers in a filthy daycare.

Breadwinner parents should *not* be punished for that. Their work was as valiant as yours. More than likely you won't be able to just stay home taking care of the kids full-time anymore if you want to maintain your quality of life—so perhaps some gratitude might be in order.

To state the obvious, it costs more to maintain two separate households. The reality is that entering the work force after a long absence may require additional schooling for you and putting in your time to get where you'd like to be. You will be grateful to have the person who loves your kids the most spending at least 50% of the time with them so you can do all that. Parents are always the preferred option to daycare, nannies or leaving them to fend for themselves.

If you've been doing both, bringing home the bacon *and* doing the majority of the child care, I'm sorry. That's a lot to shoulder. Whether it's been due to some chronic illness (feigned or real), laziness or selfishness on your spouse's part, you've likely been carrying the load for years. Yes, you totally deserve the majority of the kid time, or even sole custody. That would be the fairest, and probably the easiest for you to pull off since nothing would change, you'll just continue to do it all. Same shit, different day. However, if you feel your kids are not in danger (actual danger—not just made-up bullshit), I still recommend you attempting the 50/50 thing.

It will give your ex the opportunity to step it up after years of you being the workhorse. They can finally get a dose of what you've been doing for years and perhaps have an ounce of appreciation. (Don't hold your breath.) If you get reports that your older kids are picking up the slack where you left off with the childcare and household chores, being chronically late for school or being at the neighbors all the time, you may want to have a little chat with the ex. Clearly, your former partner *still* can't cut it. It may not be egregious or grounds for Child Protective Services to step in, but before you decide it's time for that full-blown custody evaluation, it's definitely worth a grown-up conversation. Perhaps now this sub-par parent would be more than *willing* to give you additional time with the kids—that is, as long as you keep making those payments.

If you're the one making all the dough, share what is fair. Maybe you could support you ex financially by furthering their education and skill set, knowing it will benefit everyone involved in the end. If you're not the one contributing financially, be grateful you've been able to be home with the littles as long as you have, and then put on your adulting hat. It's time to get a career and take care of yourself. Do not resist this. You will be a better person for it. You will be more empowered, feel better about yourSelf, and you will not fall prey to the first guy/gal that comes along offering to take care of you! I can assure you, that will most likely not be your best choice.

An imbalance in power is never good in any relationship. If you are 100% reliant on your partner for your survival, it keeps you in the relationship for all the wrong reasons. You are a slave to somebody else's resources. Time to create some of your own—and with it, your independence. I highly recommend it, whether you're merely contemplating divorce or you're happily married. Get going on the new business, education or skill set to start bringing in some dough. If you do decide to go through with the break up, you won't feel so helpless or like you have to resort to deceptive behavior to win all the toys.

**For You Religious Muggles:**

You self-righteous assholes deserve special recognition. Let's look at some of the *made-up* reasons you think you should have sole custody and your baby daddy/momma should eat shit. I find in these situations that at least one of the parents (usually the most Muggle of the two) is trying to make themselves out to be the Mother Theresa and their ex as Jack the Ripper. Why would anybody do this? Again, it's simple…money or misery.

Newsflash for you holier-than-thou types of Muggles: if your ex leaves your religion of choice, sleeps with someone before they're re-married, has a drink or two of wine at dinner, goes to a strip club on occasion (or is an actual fucking stripper)—that does not make them an unfit parent! These are not legit reasons for you to be handed sole custody. "Whaaaaaat?!!" Shocking, I know. Nor does it mean your kids are "unsafe" in your "fallen" partner's presence. Put that in your sacrilegious pipe.

Outside of your very narrow, pious bubble, nobody cares about any of that. What is more damaging to children is the venom with which you vilify and attack your child's other parent while justifying your own shitty behavior due to some self-declared religious piety. You sanctimonious types are typically the ones that exhibit no compassion and disown your offspring that come out as gay, are caught smoking weed or choose to have an abortion.

Those of you that feel your ex is the devil because their boyfriend moved in, are the same people your kids will never be able to talk to about their first kiss, let alone birth control, when they need it. Your kids will hide their truth from you, sneak out at night, and rebel against you. Most often these are also the parents that commit incest or do weird sex shit—or turn a blind eye when it happens in their own home. They are the ones shaming and guilting the kids into their desired behavior, punishing and shaming them for masturbation, and forcing them to attend their church of choice. Barf.

What this really is—listen closely—is simply *a difference of opinion* as to how your children should be raised. Just because your ex drank the Kool-Aid and was on board with this religious, archaic bullshit for years along with you, doesn't mean she/he can't change their mind. That change of heart does not make them unfit. You may not see eye to eye anymore. Tough. Deal with it.

Remember the poem by Gibran, "You may give them your love but not your thoughts, For they have their own thoughts." It goes for your beliefs, as well. Your actions and your energy will always speak louder than your words. Diversity is good for kids. Present what you will, and allow them their choice.

**Do What Works**

Just try being conscious adults, focusing on what is best for the kids, nobody trying to screw over or hurt the other. I have faith you will come up with beautiful and creative solutions. To be flexible with the children, sans attorneys and court involvement, is the best for everyone. It's a lot easier to make a phone call and ask if you can trade weekends because something important has come up, as opposed to getting a court order or leaving the kids with a babysitter.

Your ability to give and take will go far. You and your baby daddy/momma will always come up with a better solution for your precious littles than paid strangers who, incidentally, make more money the more you disagree. Fueling the fire between the two of you keeps attorneys in business.

Be open to non-traditional arrangements, like continuing to live in the same house or having a cheap shared apartment the other goes to when it's not their week with the kids so the kids get to stay in the same house. It's not something that typically works forever, but it can be a good initial transition, while the dust settles and you figure out how to manage two households. Just be open to what it gets to look like.

Don't be rigid and set in your ways. Seeing the two of you work things out as conscious and considerate adults will be invaluable for the kiddos. Be flexible, have compassion, treat your partner the way you'd want *your child* to be treated if he/she found themselves in the same situation.

My second husband and I did this with our son. We never involved attorneys or the court system. There were years where our son mainly lived with his dad and years he lived with me according to our circumstances and what was best for our son. Neither of us paid the other anything, but both contributed when our son needed things or when the other parent wasn't able. We still share holidays and birthdays together and it has been mostly harmonious because we've both behaved like grown-ass adults who just love our son and respect each other.

Our son never felt like he had to choose between the two of us and our divorce was not a traumatic event for him. He is 22 now, enjoys a healthy relationship with both of us, and would not say our divorce had any negative effect on him.

It's possible people. Studies confirm my son's experience, that when conflict between parents was low after divorce, children reported that they were better off or unaffected by divorce. It doesn't have to be hell for you, and you should never *make it* hell for your kiddos.

~ ~ ~

Just be nice. Exercise the Golden Rule. Treat your ex the way you'd like to be treated. Forget about the circumstances of your divorce, who did what, who left who and why—and don't use your kids to get back at each other. Your kids deserve to have both of you in their lives equally.

Be considerate of each other's schedules, be accommodating whenever possible. Don't put your ex in the position of answering the question, "Why can't we see you more, Mommy/Daddy?" on the one evening a week they've been allotted to be with the kids. You don't want the answer to be "because Mommy lied in court," or "Daddy had better attorneys," or "the judge thinks being at your Mom's is better for you."

And to state the obvious, even if some stupid court or custody evaluator has declared a particular outcome, that does *not* mean the two of you can't just say, "Fuck it, we want to do something else." Only begrudging morons, seeking misery or cashola, feel the need to stick to any of the draconian measures established by some court. I'll say this again: no custody evaluator or judge knows what's better for your kids than the two of you do.

Be easy about it. Start at 50/50 and go from there. You can do it! Don't be dicks!

# Part Seven
*Your Heart-Felt Decision*

## Chapter 39

# When Hope Arises from the Ashes

*When you let go, you create space for better things to enter your life.*
*~Buddhist Proverb*

We've covered a lot here. Hopefully along the way you've made some great new revelations about yourself, and perhaps have even managed to repair your marriage and have found a new path forward together. If that's the case, congratulations are in order!

If, however, after doing a thorough examination of your own projections, Self-correcting, and doing all that you can to clean up your own side of the street…

If after doing a deep dive into your own heart and coming to a clear "inner"-standing that your spouse is just not your person…that no matter what they do, nothing is going to change your feelings for them…

If you've had decades of misery, and just needed someone to let you know that more is available to you and give you permission to GTFO….

If you've actually met someone that you're crazy about, that you can't imagine life without…someone that makes your authentic heart sing, and that inspires your mission and vision…

And you're ready to just get a fucking divorce already….

Then congratulations to you as well. The decision to divorce should never be made lightly. Nor should you stay in a relationship that has long since expired.

I honor all your authentic, heartfelt choices.

Sometimes difficult things happen—heartbreaking things like a break-up, losing a job, being robbed, your house burns down or you get a divorce. And almost simultaneously, while you are in the midst of the heartbreak, there is an energy of hope and possibility arising within the devastation. We can hold both sadness and grief right alongside of the excitement of a new beginning and hope seeing the light at the end of the tunnel. It can be confusing. Allow yourself all the feels.

For example, without the weight of the job you just lost, new opportunities are now endless. Maybe it happened sooner than you planned or expected, but on some level a part of you was probably done with it long ago. And while you were waiting for "the right timing" to exit…the Universe had other plans for you and sped things up. And somehow, against all odds, you are feeling a sense of hope. Something within you feels like Spring.

Years ago, my computer was stolen, along with the hard drive I'd finally purchased to back up my years of writing. For about 20 minutes, I was devastated. Until I realized how heavy the thought had been of going through all of my work to sort my writings for various books. I realized the Universe was taking that burden away from me and it was time for a fresh start. There was something very liberating about that.

I had a client that became a very good friend. His son had been a heroin addict for a long time. His son went to jail. Shortly after being released, he was found dead in a hotel bathroom due to a tragic overdose. Through the devastation of losing his beloved son, he was also dealing with some guilt because, concurrently, he also felt an unsettling sense of relief. He would no longer wake up in the middle of the night worrying where his beautiful son was sleeping, or if he had a place to sleep at all. He would no longer wonder if his son were cold, if he'd had anything to eat that day, or if he were safe. There was an unsettling peace that arose with his troubled son's untimely death.

A completely devastating example, I know. But divorce too can feel as devastating as death—and indeed it *is* a death of sorts. For some it may feel like their whole world is crumbling, like they can't go on. For those that have been coupled for a long time, they may feel their entire identity has been wrapped up in being Mr. and Mrs. So-and-So. They no longer know who they are without that title. And even for those that have wanted a divorce for decades, or who've been abused, belittled, and/or neglected, they too may experience a loss or a void in their lives. Though the separation may have been welcomed, there may still be a sadness and a sense of loss.

Even in a horrible relationship, there is a steadiness in the everyday-ness of it. A warm body in the bed, someone to talk to, perhaps a sense of safety in different ways. Maybe your guy was an s.o.b., but he was *your* s.o.b. Maybe there hasn't been any intimacy for years, but they still make your coffee the way you like it in the morning. It's something.

This is often where the romanticizing of a bad relationship comes in. After people have parted, when they think about the marriage they only remember the good parts—the first 6 months or the honey moon phase. Don't fall into this trap. My mother was once involved in a very toxic, yet passionate relationship—one she returned to over and over, "chasing" those first six amazing months. Kind of like an addict who continues to chase their first high with a particular substance and never quite arriving. More often than not, the good you're romanticizing just doesn't come back, not nearly in proportion to how horrible it has become. The more the relationship (or addiction) has devolved, the less chance of something healthy arising.

Move on. You're attempts at resuscitation have long passed their expiration date.

> *Nothing in his life became him like the leaving it. ~Shakespeare, from Macbeth*

As great (or not so great) as your relationship may have been, if it's over, there may be new things that are now possible that weren't possible before. Maybe your partner liked to sleep in and you've always been a morning person and had to tip toe around each morning for decades. Now that she's gone, you will be able to get up as early as you want, meditate, exercise, and play your music loud at 6am!

Maybe you loved chick flicks but have been relegated to superhero movies. Maybe you've wanted to travel but your partner hates to fly. Now you are free to explore the world. Maybe you've wanted to start that new business but your partner was always against it—now you are the boss of you. And so on and so on.

Nothing to hold you back any longer. Yet your heart may still ache, while other parts of you are coming to life. There is a sacred pause between, when "life as you know it" ends and your new life begins. It's a space where all potential lies. Don't miss it. Take a breath. Before you jump right into the "next thing," pause, evaluate, think, feel. Don't bypass your feelings or the deep evaluation of your past relationship.

The problem with bypassing and jumping straight into the next thing or relationship is that without some Self-examination, we are doomed to recreate the same situation. This is one of the best times to hire a life coach—one of my favorite times to work with people to assist them in creating a life they've only dreamed of before now. Your Higher Self has an understanding, even an appreciation (however deep that may be), that this Earth School has lessons for your soul that cannot be bypassed. There is an inner-knowing that life is always happening for us and forging our souls with every heartbreak and joy.

All good things leave a mark—like blueberries and turmeric. Don't be so quick to wash, erase, forget or delete them from your life and memories. Leaving a mark can be a beautiful thing. It means you were touched in a deeply significant way that forged your soul on some level. Never regret those things. Just like the butterfly or a baby chick needs to make its way out of its chrysalis or shell on its own, so too do our challenges forge us through the refiner's fire so we can emerge as the next greatest version of ourSelves.

Allow yourself a little stillness…a little quiet. Stop talking about the divorce with every single person you encounter. Stop vilifying your ex. Stop drinking, drugging, one-night-standing, and checking out in all the ways. Put your phone down. Turn off the TV. *Be* with yourSelf. Allow yourSelf to actually *feel*. What are you feeling under all the upset, blaming, shaming, rage, and pointed fingers? Breathe. Let go of the fake ego bullshit. Tune into your heart, anger is always a secondary emotion for something deeper. How is your heart really *feeling*?

Allow yourSelf to sit with any emotions that come up. Treat yourSelf like you would a best friend. No negative Self-talk allowed. Have compassion for your Self. Let it all out. Have a good cry. Punch a pillow. Write in your journal. Write about what you'll miss. Write out all the good things about your former partner that you can think of. Even if it's just that they were a good parent. Have gratitude for the good times and the not-so-good—all are for your learning and growth. See it *all* as fertilizer for the new you that you will be birthing.

Gregg Braden talks about this very thing—the power of the "in between" in his book *Secrets of the Lost Mode of Prayer: The Hidden Power of Beauty, Blessings, and Wisdom*. He states:

*There's a power that lives in the space 'between,' that subtle instant when something ends, and what follows next hasn't yet begun. From the birth and death of galaxies to the beginning and ending of careers and relationships, and even the simplicity of breathing in and out, creation is the story of beginnings and endings: cycles that start and stop, expand and contract, live and die.*

*Regardless of scale, between the 'beginning' and the 'end,' there is a moment in time when neither one has fully happened. That moment is where magic and miracles come from!*

*In the instant of between, all possibilities exist, and none have been chosen. From this place, we're given the power to heal our bodies, change our lives, and bring peace to the world. All events originate from this powerful, magical moment.*

Don't miss the show. This twilight time, where the sun has just set on your old life, and your new life has yet to begin, is so filled with possibility. Allow yourSelf to feel a sense of excitement and life just beneath the surface.

All things are possible from this place. What will you do differently to create a more satisfying and meaningful future? What have you learned is most important to you in a relationship? How will you shift your own behavior to attract exactly what you desire? What will you do to better maintain a sense of Self in your next relationship? Can you learn to *be* the partner you'd like to *have*? All things to ponder in this beautiful "space between."

~ ~ ~

Welcome to your beautiful life! You are exactly where you are meant to be. Life as you knew it is now over. In this space between, all things are now possible.

# Epilogue

Dear Human,

When will you understand that your feelings matter? When will you stop ignoring your beautiful heart? When will you get that you deserve to be happy? When will it be clear that you were not sent here once again to sacrifice this precious incarnation, but to claim your joy and dharma? When will you get that other's feelings and happiness are not more important than your own? When will you see that to give up on your dream for another's, or for their perceived safety and security, is a betrayal to yourSelf?

You have lived countless lifetimes in sacrifice, martyrdom, and victimhood. You've been hung, beheaded, burnt at the stake, executed point blank, gassed, and experienced all manner of horrific endings for your beliefs, for those you love, for your politics, for your religion, and your race. You've been through war after war, holocaust, genocides, and famines. You've been enslaved, forced to do things you never wanted to do, raped, used, and abused. You've been put on trial for your magic, your use of plants, your healing capabilities, your spot-on intuition, and your beliefs. You've been shamed for your sensuality, sexuality, loving someone of the same sex, or someone that belonged to another. Your precious heart has been made wrong for everything that it has ever loved or desired.

NEWSFLASH: This ain't that life!! This is the life that you let all of that go. That's right. This is the life you deal with all of your past wounds, attend to your own healing, and forgive ALL for EVERYTHING. For, make no mistake, you were both abuser and abused, perpetrator and victim, slaveholder and slave, tyrant and lamb, accuser and accused.

This is not that day. And it *never* will be again. This is a new era that YOU, my Beloveds, are here to usher in. We must all do our part to bring peace, to accept and allow each their space to breathe, to live, and to love. We must first offer that gift to ourSelves before we can authentically offer it to another. Now is the time to learn the voice of your own heart and soul. To allow yourSelf to love what you love and be who you are. To follow your passion, your excitement, and your dream.

Today it is required of you to live your highest truth, to speak from your heart without fear, to live the life of your greatest authenticity with no apologies. If you are in a job, career, relationship, home, religion or spiritual practice that drains your vitality or brings chronic negativity to your soul and spirit, it is time to reevaluate and either figure out how to truly heal it or get the fuck out. True healing requires more than a metaphoric band-aid. If you can't love what you do, who you share your sacred energy with, where you live, or whom you worship… or if it's only lukewarm, it's no longer acceptable. "Just ok" will not cut it in this new paradigm.

It's time for all to become accountable for the mediocre lives they've been living. To stop complaining and blaming and recognize that you are a conscious co-creator with the Universe. And that you, yes YOU, have the power, to create amazing. If your life isn't AWE-mazing, you are the *only* one to blame. When you create a life that you love, of your own choosing, sans your programming and toxic emotions of guilt, shame, grief, apathy, and anger, what will be available to you is a tremendous amount of vitality, energy, health, peace, and well-being like you have never known. What do you think will be possible for you when that is the case?

A new surge of creativity, brilliance, inventiveness, and inspiration will be free to grace your Be-ing. And the world will know new hope because YOU will know new hope. All will be available to you. Your joy will create the fertile field for transformation. Peace will be possible. Love will reign. Souls will return to their sovereignty.

When we return to *our* true nature, we will connect with nature. We will care about our waters, air, energy, and environment. We will have the vitality to be a contribution!

When our lives are in harmony with our souls, love overflows and we have more than enough to be of joyful service in the areas that set our souls on fire.

When we put our lives in another's hands, deny the whisperings of our own heart, believe that someone else knows better for us than we do, and live a life of another's choosing, that will always be heavy. It will *always* feel like a burden. Your energy will be depleted. Your health will invariably be compromised. And you will lack the vitality to barely make it through your day.

Do not take this as some trite "love and light," follow your bliss bs. Your life of duty, obligation, and commitment is killing you—*literally*. It's making you sick, tired, and it's sucking your soul. If you don't see those duties and obligations as a sacred honor, if you are no longer or never were passionate about the service to which you have committed yourself—service that is no longer authentic—it's time to wake up from your duty-bound, blue-pill slumber. Time to take the red pill, peeps!

Your time of living an inauthentic life to please the masses is coming to a violent end. It will be much easier if you wake up on your own and start being honest with yourSelf and those around you first. You serve NO ONE by living a life that you no longer want to live. Your employer is not served, nor is your spouse or children—and you are modeling slave behavior to your littles.

Time to be the change already and start living a life you love—the one you were born to live. Stop resisting your own flowering and be the You that you were created capable of being. You may not even know what that looks like right now, just your pull to know is enough. The journey of Self-discovery is the journey we are here to take. In the words of the Alchemist, "To realize one's destiny is a person's only obligation."

Many Blessings on Your Most Sacred of Journeys,

Laurie Frazier,

Maven of Moksha

# Appendix A

## Map of Consciousness by David Hawkins

| God-View | Life-view | LEVEL | | Log | Emotion | Process |
|---|---|---|---|---|---|---|
| Self | Is | ENLIGHTENMENT | ◄► | 700-1000 | Ineffable | Pure Consciousness |
| All-Being | Perfect | PEACE | ◄► | 600 | Bliss | Illumination |
| One | Complete | JOY | ◄► | 540 | Serenity | Transfiguration |
| Loving | Benign | LOVE | ◄► | 500 | Reverence | Revelation |
| Wise | Meaningful | REASON | ◄► | 400 | Understanding | Abstraction |
| Merciful | Harmonious | ACCEPTANCE | ◄► | 350 | Forgiveness | Transcendence |
| Inspiring | Hopeful | WILLINGNESS | ◄► | 310 | Optimism | Intention |
| Enabling | Satisfactory | NEUTRALITY | ◄► | 250 | Trust | Release |
| Permitting | Feasible | COURAGE | ◄► | 200 | Affirmation | Empowerment |
| Indifferent | Demanding | PRIDE | ► | 175 | Scorn | Inflation |
| Vengeful | Antagonistic | ANGER | ► | 150 | Hate | Aggression |
| Denying | Disappointing | DESIRE | ► | 125 | Craving | Enslavement |
| Punitive | Frightening | FEAR | ► | 100 | Anxiety | Withdrawal |
| Disdainful | Tragic | GRIEF | ► | 75 | Regret | Despondency |
| Condemning | Hopeless | APATHY | ► | 50 | Despair | Abdication |
| Vindictive | Evil | GUILT | ► | 30 | Blame | Destruction |
| Despising | Miserable | SHAME | ► | 20 | Humiliation | Elimination |

# Acknowledgments

This book is dedicated to the strong and independent women that raised me—my mother, grandmother, and all my Aunties. You *Frazier Girls* are and were the powerful force I built my own foundation upon. Thank you, thank you, thank you for your mighty example. I am strong because of you.

To Lord Mercury—my person, love, and editor. Thank you for your inspiration without which this book may not have been written. So much gratitude to you for assisting me in getting (all) the messages I want to share out of my computer and into the world! I adore you!

To my best friend, Merrill Chandler, for being my before, during, and after. Thank you for paving the way to all the details of self-publishing and how to be a bad ass. I love you to the moon and back!

To my sister Tracey for always believing in me, and encouraging me to publish *this* book first. Your encouragement and "reprimanding" has always been welcomed and just the push I needed. Thank you for being the "funny one" all of our lives—it's finally started to rub off on me!

To my brilliant, beautiful, and creative children: Sarah, my shining Star and mini-me; Hannah, my lil Sunshine; and Nic, my unique Blue Moon. Thank you for being my eternal Source of joy and inspiration and for always believing in me. I love you three soooo big!!

To my best girlfriends for being such brilliant and insightful sounding boards. I am forever grateful for your love, support, and friendship that goes beyond this physical plane.

To the clients and students of my work: Thank you for your trust in allowing me to help guide you back to your Selves and to the truth of your hearts. It is always such an honor.

And finally, to all the cute little Muggles still remaining in their lower consciousness and victimhood. Thank you for giving me such great material to work with. My wish for you is that this book will make you angry as hell. Angry enough to pull yourselves up, own your bullshit, and take charge of your lives. May you learn to be accountable for your circumstances and consciously create something miraculous. Because you can.

# About The Author

Hi. I'm Laurie. I have been a spiritual teacher for over 40 fucking years. It's what I've done all day, every day, since I was 15 years old. In high school, I started reading the Bible for myself because my own religion wasn't giving me credible answers to my questions. I joined a group called Fellowship of Christian Athletes to learn more and help others. This was in the early 80's, loooong before Goggle was the oracle of choice.

I taught Bible Study classes in high school and college while I searched for a church I could align with. In my quest for truth, I even majored and graduated in Theology & World Religions at Boston College.

From my early teens, I had an unceasing interest in astrology, numerology, and all things metaphysical…that interest continued even though many of the churches I attended said it was "of the devil." How ridiculous I thought…the stars are clearly the language of the gods. I was always the rebel, questioning authority when it made no sense to my young sensibilities.

By my early 20's I'd "graduated" from 2 more major Christian religions and started reading Deepak Chopra, Gary Zukav, and Elkhart Tolle. I became interested in and immersed myself in Eastern Religions, meditation, yoga, and more sacred and meaningful ways of life. I became a Chopra (as in Deepak) Certified Instructor and an Ayurvedic Wellness Counselor.

When my kids were young, I divorced and had more time on my hands. In 2011, I created a spiritual community that is now simply called The House of Moksha (on FB).

Because we met on every new and full moon for nearly 7 years until I moved away for a time, it was affectionately dubbed "The Moon Show." From that group, a youth group was born called the Moksha Millennials. Both were a place to discuss topics of consciousness, meditation, spirituality, various religious "holy days," and alignment with the cycles of nature, the elements, planets, and stars.

What's "Moksha" you ask? Perhaps you've found me on the socials as @MavenofMoksha (a title given to me in the corporate world—a story for another time). Moksha is a Sanskrit sutra (a mantra with meaning) that means freedom, liberation, nirvana. It just so happens to encapsulate my mission here, why I wrote this particular book, and anything and everything that I have ever (or will ever) teach. I want every contribution I make to this beautiful planet to be something that liberates and frees humanity in one way or another. Whether it's from their past, from heavy and low vibe emotions like shame, guilt, fear, and anger, or from toxic relationships and environments.

It is our birthright to be free, to speak our truth, and to follow our hearts to the ends of this Earth and beyond. In doing so, we will find joy beyond measure—living lives we are truly in love with and with people that truly excite us.

It has been my relentless dedication to seek and expose truth, whether that be within various religious or spiritual communities, from purveyors of health and wellness, or from politicians and big pharma. I've developed a well-honed bullshit meter and can easily spot the truth (or lack thereof) of my client's heart and words.

If you'd like to work with me and are ready to stop being a victim and take 100% ownership and accountability for your life…

If you're ready to see all the areas that you have surrendered your power, consciously and unconsciously…

If you're ready to see all that is too small for the grand Being that you are—and let it all go…

If you are ready to be the designer, architect, and builder of your one, wild and precious life…and reclaim your Sovereignty…then contact me at shefreedom@protonmail.com.

Possible side effects include liberation, an empowered life, and true happiness. Enter at your own risk. It's not for the faint of heart. Time to put your big boy/girl pants on. I believe in you.

In the words of Ram Das, "We are all just walking each other home." There is another way. You are your own Truth, and the Truth shall set you free.

Many Blessings on Your Sacred Journey,

*Laurie Frazier*

*Maven of Moksha*

# Resources

**Additional Resources & Bonus Material**

To keep up to date on Laurie's future books, courses, and retreats, visit her website: www.lauriefrazier.com.

Follow Laurie on all the Socials: @MavenofMoksha

(MOKSHA=Emotional Freedom, Liberation, Nirvana)

For Relationship & Divorce Support, Advice & Humor

Join our Facebook Group: Get A F*cking Divorce Already

https://www.facebook.com/groups/getafckingdivorcealready (just leave out the U)

And Like our Page:

https://www.facebook.com/getafckingdivorcealready (again, just leave out the U)

Follow us on Insta @getafuckingdivorcealready

Please, if you have found this book helpful on your journey, I would LOVE IT if you left me a review on Amazon.

If you know anyone that just deserves to "Get A Fucking Divorce Already" please buy them a copy or send them to our website or Amazon to get their own. Sharing is caring!

If you want to work with Laurie one-on-one or with your partner…

If you'd like to have Laurie speak on your podcast, your social media channel, or to your group…

If you'd like to connect with her in anyway…

Please contact her at: shefreedom@protonmail.com

www.ingramcontent.com/pod-product-compliance
Lightning Source LLC
Chambersburg PA
CBHW071806080526
44589CB00012B/710